D0057820

THE BASEBALL FAN'S BUCKET LIST

162 THINGS YOU MUST SEE, DO, GET, AND EXPERIENCE BEFORE YOU DIE

ROBERT SANTELLI and JENNA SANTELLI

RUNNING PRESS
PHILADELPHIA · LONDON

© 2010 by Robert Santelli and Jenna Santelli

All rights reserved under the Pan-American and
International Copyright Conventions

Printed in the United States

*This book may not be reproduced in whole or in part, in any form or by any means,
electronic or mechanical, including photocopying, recording, or by any information storage and retrieval system now known or hereafter invented, without written permission
from the publisher.*

9   8   7   6   5   4   3   2   1
Digit on the right indicates the number of this printing

Library of Congress Control Number: 2009938624

ISBN 978-0-7624-3855-6

Cover and Interior Design by Joshua McDonnell
Edited by Greg Jones

Cover Illustration by David Reidbold

Photo Credits:
Jenna Santelli: pp 37, 46, 52, 86, 88, 90, 107, 116, 119, 121, 129, 147, 151,
155, 195, 213, 215, 232, 234, 260, 266
Joshua McDonnell: pp 17, 19, 31, 77, 176
iStockphoto, TriggerPhoto: p 28
Scorecard (p 40) courtesy of Shannon P. Hatch
Bill Chapman: p 56
Courtesty of Baltimore Orioles: p 72
Dan Mendlik/Cleveland Indians: p 100
Courtesty of Cindy De La Hoz: p 103
Courtesty of the Babe Ruth Museum: p 159
Eric Stock: p 287

Running Press Book Publishers
2300 Chestnut Street
Philadelphia, PA 19103-4371

Visit us on the web!
www.runningpress.com

CONTENTS

INTRODUCTION

Baseball fans—and there are many millions of us in America, and beyond—love lists. Lists are like line-ups. They can bring order to the game and can provide clarity to what unfolds on the baseball diamond. They can also provide plenty of ammunition for baseball talk and playful arguments in the bar, at the Sunday barbecue, and, of course, at the ballpark. It's an irresistible part of baseball culture to rank the top hitters of all time, the most dominating pitchers, the finest films, the best ballparks, the biggest heroes, the worst flops, and so on.

You can probably think of a lot of different baseball lists. One of the most important and certainly most personal is the baseball bucket list. That's the list of all the things we want—or, for some of us, absolutely need—to do, to see, to read, to watch, to own, and to experience, baseball-wise, before we "kick the bucket." Both the term and the concept grew popular in 2008 after the Jack Nicholson and Morgan Freeman film, *The Bucket List*, hit movie theaters across the country. In the film, Nicholson and Freeman play a couple of aging men who are trying to finish the things on their bucket lists before it's too late. It's a good film—funny and touching and wise. It made a lot of people think about completing the items on their own bucket list, or if they didn't have such a list, to start making one.

I had one, which had to do with baseball, and I convinced my second daughter, Jenna, who is almost as big a fan of the game as I am, to create a baseball fan bucket list of her own. There was no need to wait until you were older to start one, I assured her. Put one together now and let it grow as your love of the game grows. Jenna took my advice; she jotted down the baseball things she wanted to do in her life and the ballparks she wanted to visit. I helped her with the baseball books I thought she should read. She already knew the films and the museums she wanted to see. When it was done, Jenna and I realized that what she had drawn up was a road map to a life-long pursuit of baseball joy.

When Jenna was a student at Oregon State University, the Beavers went to the NCAA College World Series three times, winning the national championship in 2006 and 2007. It was a remarkable feat for any school to win two NCAA baseball titles in a row, but it was especially sweet for OSU, a university that had won only one other NCAA championship—in cross country—during its entire history of collegiate athletic competition.

When the Beaver baseball team went to the College World Series in '07, Jenna and I decided to go, too. Since attending the College World Series at some point was on both of our baseball fan bucket lists, why not, we thought, go when OSU would be defending its title? Jenna got the tickets, and we had a great time together, father and daughter sharing a common baseball love and cheering on the Beavers to victory in one of the great College World Series of all time. We both felt a wonderful sense of satisfaction when together, we checked off that we had been to the College World Series, the premier event in college baseball, and that our team had won.

While in Omaha, perennial home of the College World Series, Jenna and I met other people who were on a similar baseball mission. I don't recall exactly when it hit us to create a universal baseball fan bucket list and to blend our own personal lists with the things we believed that all baseball fans should have on theirs. But I'm glad it happened. Visiting Wrigley Field, finally reading Roger Kahn's *The Boys of Summer*, seeing a game in every major league ballpark and completing dozens of the other items on my bucket list have been some of the most rewarding things I've done as a baseball fan. The idea behind *The Baseball Fan's Bucket List* was to share such fun and enjoyment with fellow baseball fans as well as the knowledge Jenna and I have accumulated during our baseball journeys.

I'll be honest: I haven't completed all the items included in *The Baseball Fan's Bucket List*, and certainly Jenna, with much of her baseball life in front of her, has a long way to go before she's done them all. But I've gotten through many, actually most of them, thanks to this book, and it's my goal that before I round the bases for the final time, my baseball fan bucket list is finished, too.

Why create and complete a baseball fan bucket list? Mostly because it keeps you connected to the game, along with its history and traditions and how and why it came to be the national pastime. Baseball is a special game to Americans. Most of us are introduced to it at an early age and, if we're lucky, it stays with us until we kick the bucket. As a fan, I follow other sports, but baseball is in my heart and soul. It commands a lot of my leisure time, and it's a reflection of who I am. I still play, though my legs aren't what they used to be and my bat speed gets worse by the year. But, perhaps like you, I can't imagine living without baseball.

People ask me what team I root for when they learn of my baseball passion. Fact is, I grew up a Yankees fan, having been born and raised in New Jersey during the golden age of baseball in the 1950s and early 60s. Mickey Mantle was the player I worshipped the most, hence my love of chasing down fly balls in center field as a young ballplayer. But in my travels I became partial to small market teams, especially the Cleveland Indians. I moved with my family from New Jersey to Cleveland in 1995 to be the first Director of Education at the brand new Rock and Roll Hall of Fame and Museum. The Cleveland Indians clincher for me was living in the city during the Tribe's mid-90s glory years and experiencing my first couple of World Series and my first All-Star game.

Some of my fondest baseball memories are of sitting at then-Jacobs Field (now Progressive Field) with my wife, Cindy, and our three kids cheering on

Jim Thome, Omar Vizquel, Manny Ramirez, Orel Hershiser and the other Indians in their quest to win a world championship for the city that hadn't enjoyed one since 1948. Unfortunately, it wasn't meant to be, and it broke every Cleveland Indians fan's heart to see the team come up short in 1995, and then again in 1997. But my baseball memories from those years are rich and enduring, and it was in Cleveland that I put together my original baseball fan bucket list. I've been checking off items on it ever since.

I know a lot of baseball fans. Many of us are incurable romantics. We're myth lovers, traditionalists, preservationists, nostalgia nuts, and self-professed keepers of baseball's eternal flame. We make pilgrimages to hallowed ballparks like Fenway Park in Boston and Wrigley Field in Chicago as if they were sacred places of worship, and to most baseball fans, they are. We go on road trips, crisscrossing the country to watch ballgames in Seattle, Detroit, Oakland, and Kansas City to soak up the local baseball excitement and to say we've been to this ballpark and to that one. In March, we head to Florida or Arizona for the annual ritual of spring training, where every fan's faith in his or her favorite team is restored, and we leave thinking that maybe, just maybe, this will be the year they win it all.

There's a lot more that goes with being a true baseball fan. Over 300,000 of us visit the National Baseball Hall of Fame and Museum in out-of-the-way Cooperstown, New York each year. Opening Day is practically an American holiday for baseball fans, and we turn out for it in droves to Major League Baseball parks. We coach Little League baseball and watch our sons play high school baseball. We read the latest baseball books and see the latest baseball movies. Despite the recent steroids scandal, the obscene salaries, and the soaring ticket prices, attendance at major league and minor league games is greater than ever because baseball is more popular than ever.

For most of us, our love of baseball begins with playing the game as a kid and then, over time, hanging up the glove and cleats and becoming a full-time fan. The older we get, the more memories of the game we store inside ourselves and the more precious they become. For men especially, baseball is the last remnant of our youth. It keeps us comfortably nestled between innocence and responsibility. It's what makes adults seek autographs from players half our age, collect baseball cards with the same vigor we did as kids, and wear the cap of our favorite team with unabashed pride.

So, is *The Baseball Fan's Bucket List* your bucket list? It could be. You could follow it as a travel guide to the national pastime exactly as it appears on the following pages. Or you could re-order it or change it with deletions and additions of your own. Because despite all our research and conversations with hundreds of other fans, historians, museum curators, and journalists, Jenna and

I created *The Baseball Fan's Bucket List* not as the last word in the things you should do as a true baseball fan, but more as a starting point for other baseball fans to create their own bucket lists. If nothing else, use the list and the essays connected to them to help broaden your knowledge of the game and further your passion for it.

Admittedly, the entries in *The Baseball Fan's Bucket List* and especially their ranking are subjective. You could easily argue that a visit to Fenway Park should occur before one to Wrigley Field, or that you should see *The Natural* before *Bull Durham*. A book like this is meant to provoke dialogue and contemplation. But in the end, *The Baseball Fan's Bucket List* exists mostly as a personal baseball diary, a companion book to living the baseball life. Enjoy your baseball journey through life. I know I am.

—Robert Santelli, Summer 2009

My love of baseball began in 1995 when my family moved to Cleveland from New Jersey. I didn't play organized baseball growing up, though I did play summer league softball. Instead, I was a swimmer, which took much of the time I had for sports. But not all of my time. Whatever was left I saved for baseball. Not only did I like the game, but I also liked that baseball created a bond between me and my father. While living in Shaker Heights, just outside of Cleveland, we used to go to Tribe games all summer long. A lot of times, it was just the two of us, and we used that time to connect on a level that became very special to me.

We weren't just fans; we were part of something bigger those years in Cleveland. I remember how in 1995 nearly everyone I met that fall was wearing Indians' gear, and they were so excited to see the team in its first World Series since 1954. My dad and I, despite being newcomers to the Indians, jumped right in. Somehow, he got tickets to the World Series. I remember crying when the Indians lost to the Atlanta Braves. I knew then that I had become a real fan of the Cleveland Indians—and of baseball, and that the game would forever be a part of me.

For me, baseball is more than a game. It's a lifestyle. Baseball got me going in a career in journalism and sports information. I went to Oregon State University and swam on the women's team there. But after swim season was over, I found myself totally engaged in baseball. I wanted to be a part of the game, so I interned with the OSU Sports Information Department. In addition to covering sporting events for my college newspaper, *The Daily Barometer*, I also wrote a weekly column. My favorite topic to write about? Oregon State Baseball.

Being a student at Oregon State during the Beavers' three trips to the College World Series gave me some of my fondest moments as a college baseball fan, and, with my father's prodding, I started my baseball fan bucket list. At first, the list mostly had to do with the Cleveland Indians, the Beavers' baseball team, and Pac-10 baseball. But the list eventually turned into more than that. Now my personal list is the book you have in your hand.

Writing *The Baseball Fan's Bucket List* with my dad has been fun and educational. However, my goal in doing it wasn't just to share more baseball time with him, but also to encourage more young women to become baseball fans. I hope they do, and that many go on to use this book to help create and fulfill their own baseball bucket lists.

—Jenna Santelli, Summer 2009

TAKE A BASEBALL ROAD TRIP ✦✦✦

It's the lure of the road and the start of a baseball adventure. It's the chance to do baseball things that you've dreamed of doing for a long time. It is baseball talk, baseball games, baseball food and baseball friends. It's a baseball road trip: the ultimate way to experience the baseball life.

Taking a baseball road trip is the first entry of *The Baseball Fan's Bucket List* because so many of the other entries in the book can only be accomplished by getting out on the road and traveling to baseball landmarks, games and ballparks. If you're a die-hard baseball fan, it's practically impossible *not* to have taken a baseball road trip at some point in your life. So, checking off this entry should be a cinch for most. If you're new to the baseball life, then sit down with a map and start planning a trip.

These days, a road trip doesn't always mean traveling to a baseball destination by car, though that's usually the best way to get there. It's the traditional definition of a baseball road trip, and most likely, the most satisfying and memorable one to undertake. But flying or taking a train counts, too. The point is to travel to a baseball place, preferably one on *The Baseball Fan's Bucket List*.

The baseball road trip can take many forms. It could be a dash from one major league city to another to squeeze in as many games as a week or two will allow. It might mean a trip to Cooperstown to see the National Baseball Hall of Fame and Museum. Or a journey to the Negro Leagues Baseball Museum in Kansas City. You might want to go play catch on the *Field of Dreams* movie site in Iowa or visit Babe Ruth's birthplace in Baltimore. All of these are worthwhile destinations, and they're all *Baseball Fan's Bucket List* entries, as you'll see in the pages that follow.

However, before you get too excited about going on a baseball road trip, be aware of the less romantic aspects of it. For most of us, a traditional baseball road trip means lots of miles by car, too many fast food meals, and sleeping in cheap motels. Getting gritty in the name of baseball is admirable. But if you can travel first class, stay in the best hotels and eat at five-star restaurants on your baseball road trip, then by all means have at it. You don't get bonus points on the road trip by denying yourself the good things in life. What counts is that you head out on a baseball mission, and that you accomplish it.

There are a few important things to consider when planning your trip. Number one is your partner or partners, assuming you have them. Going on a baseball road trip solo is only for a special breed of baseball fan, namely one who needs to communicate with the game directly, without interference or distraction. These baseball fans are hardcore. To them, baseball is a business: the business of life itself. But for most of us, baseball road trips are social experiences. The key is to choose your fellow trippers wisely. Think endurance, persistence, and an unwavering commitment to complete the baseball road trip, no matter what the obstacles. One of the worst things that can happen is a member of the road trip team quitting before the baseball goals are met. So choose a dedicated partner, because *Baseball Fan's Bucket List* items need to be taken seriously.

Fine-tune your road trip goals before leaving. What is it, exactly, you want to accomplish, and is everyone who is going on the trip in line with those goals? The baseball road trip that fails is the one that lacks true definable goals. Driving from Seattle to Alaska to attend the Midnight Sun Baseball Classic—a game that happens just once a year and in only one place—rates a worthy road trip objective. Just make sure everyone with you believes that as much as you do. You don't want to turn around halfway through Canada.

The final thing to consider is pacing. Driving from one ballpark to the next can be a tedious experience; driving to Alaska from anywhere is definitely a tedious experience. Unless your mission is to see seven games in seven days, don't rush through the trip. The baseball road trip is meant to be fun. It's meant to be memorable for all the right reasons.

There are some fine books available to help you map out your baseball road trip. *Ballpark Vacations* by Bruce Adams and Margaret Engel (Fodor's, 1997) is a family guide to minor and major league ballparks. *Roadside Baseball* by Chris Epting (Santa Monica Press, 2009) lists nearly every classic and obscure baseball landmark in America. *The Ultimate Minor League Baseball Road Trip* by Josh Pahigian (Lyons Press, 2007) is indispensable for minor league trips. Pahigian's other book, *101 Baseball Places To See Before You Strike Out* (Lyons Press, 2008), is also essential reading. Use these books as references, but in the end, it's much more satisfying to customize your own baseball road trip itinerary.

You can order *Roadside Baseball*, *The Ultimate Minor League Baseball Road Trip* and *101 Baseball Places To See Before You Strike Out* from most bookstores and online booksellers. *Ballpark Vacations* is available from many used bookstores and online used booksellers.

2 VISIT THE NATIONAL BASEBALL HALL OF FAME AND MUSEUM

Located in Cooperstown, New York, the National Baseball Hall of Fame and Museum serves as the hub of all things baseball and the place that every baseball fan must visit. It is the grand storehouse of baseball tradition, the keeper of the game's history and the place where baseball is celebrated every day of the year. You can't truly understand the role that the game has played in American history and culture without spending a day at the National Baseball Hall of Fame and Museum.

As sports museums go, the National Baseball Hall of Fame and Museum ranks as the best in America. The exhibits are engaging and the scholarship impeccable. Each exhibit enlightens and entertains as it unfolds a particular piece of baseball history. Museum exhibits are not meant to be definitive historical statements; instead, they should present refreshing points of view and inspire further exploration. The exhibits at the National Baseball Hall of Fame and Museum do just that.

The National Baseball Hall of Fame and Museum opened in June of 1939 in Cooperstown, where one hundred years earlier Abner Doubleday is said to have modified the rules of the game known as "town ball" into what ultimately became "base ball." That story came from the Mills Commission, appointed in 1905 at the urging of baseball promoter Albert G. Spalding to determine the origins of the game. Today, of course, we know that wasn't the case. But in 1934, the discovery of a mid-19th century baseball in a home just outside Cooperstown further solidified the Mills Commission's claim and ignited interest in creating a permanent baseball museum in Cooperstown. Five years later, the National Baseball Hall of Fame and Museum opened its doors to the public.

Instead of just housing artifacts from the sport's earliest days, the museum also included a home for the Hall of Fame to honor baseball's greatest figures. In 1936, the Hall of Fame inducted its first class, which consisted of former playing greats Ty Cobb, Babe Ruth, Honus Wagner, Christy Mathewson, and Walter Johnson. By the time the National Baseball Hall of Fame and Museum opened three years later, there were 25 inductees, 11 of whom journeyed to Cooperstown for the grand opening.

Nearly 300 baseball legends had been inducted into the Hall of Fame through 2009. Each inductee is honored with a bronze plaque that summarizes his career and achievements in the marble and oak Hall of Fame Gallery on the museum's first floor. Plan to spend a chunk of your museum visit here. The first floor of the museum also contains a baseball art gallery, along with a tribute to baseball journalists and announcers, and an overview of baseball movies and the role that Hollywood has played in popularizing the national pastime.

With two more floors and over 36,000 artifacts, plus more than 130,000 baseball cards in its permanent collection, the National Baseball Hall of Fame and Museum tells the full story of baseball. Its "Taking the Field: the 19th Century" exhibit details the earliest days of the game and the origins of professional baseball. Artifacts are often rotated for conservation purposes, so it's difficult to say what might be on display at the time of your visit. But for a compelling interpretation of baseball's early years, you'll find no better presentation.

Other highlights include the Babe Ruth Gallery, which pays tribute to the game's most important and popular player. You'll see his famous #3 Yankee jersey hanging in his Yankee Stadium locker, at least one of his fielding gloves, photographs, posters, and other Ruth memorabilia. "Pride and Passion" deals with the important roles African-Americans played in making baseball America's pastime, while "Diamond Dreams" does the same for women. One exhibit celebrates every no-hitter thrown over the years, while another displays the most famous, rare, and expensive baseball card of all time: the 1909 T206 Honus Wagner tobacco card. An exhibit on contemporary baseball features the museum's most recent artifacts and a re-creation of a major league locker room in which each locker represents one of the 30 Major League Baseball teams.

The National Baseball Hall of Fame's 3rd floor *Sacred Ground* area.

On the third floor, you'll find "Sacred Ground," an exhibit that honors baseball's greatest ballparks, past and present. Brooklyn Dodger fans can recall the glory of Ebbets Field, while artifacts such as a turnstile from the Polo Grounds, home of the New York Giants, and a ticket booth from the original Yankee Stadium make certain that no New York fan goes away disappointed. You'll find plenty to attract your attention in the Records Room, where statistical leaders of every baseball category are displayed. "Autumn Glory" is all about the World Series. It recalls the classic plays and most memorable moments of post-season play and features trophies, programs, the glove Willie Mays used in 1954 against the Cleveland Indians to make "The Catch," and plenty of World Series jewelry, including the coveted World Champion ring in all its various forms.

How much time you spend at the National Baseball Hall of Fame and Museum depends on the depth of your interest in baseball history. Two hours is the minimum, though you could just as easily spend two days. Plan your trip accordingly.

For information about cost of admission, hours, special events and public programs, and how to become a member of the National Baseball Hall of Fame and Museum, go to its website at www.baseballhall.org or call (888) HALL-

---

3 GO TO OPENING DAY

Opening Day is the grandest day of the Major League Baseball season. Hope fills the air. Everyone at the ballpark feels it—from the food vendors and ticket takers, to the fans who sit in the last row of the bleachers to the players warming up on the field. No matter where your team is projected to finish the season, no matter how dismal a spring training your team's pitching staff suffered through, or how unlikely a trip to the World Series might seem, on Opening Day every Major League Baseball club has the same record. They are all in first place.

On Opening Day, the high price of a cold beer doesn't matter. The peanuts and hot dogs never taste better, the national anthem never sounds better. You feel the anticipation as it flows through the crowd when the starting line-ups are announced and the umpires take the field. And when you hear the words you waited for all winter ("Play ball!"), admit it, a chill runs down your spine. It's time, once again, for baseball, the American pastime. On Opening Day, life is good.

The best place to enjoy Opening Day is in Cincinnati. For many years, Major League Baseball opened its season there as a way of paying tribute to the city that gave birth to professional baseball all the way back in 1876. That doesn't happen anymore, but Cincinnati's long baseball tradition is, nonetheless, still recalled with an Opening Day parade and other baseball festivities. You might not be a fan of the Reds, but you have to admire the way Cincinnati celebrates the start of the baseball season.

Two long-standing traditions have evolved from Opening Day. The first has to the do with the pitching match-ups. Being named a starting pitcher on Opening Day is an honor; it unofficially proclaims that you are the ace of the staff. Of course, a team also starts its best pitcher on Opening Day because it wants to win the first game of the season. Then it can count on the giddy optimism its fans entered the park with to still be with them when they exit—and at least for a few days longer.

The second tradition also takes place on the pitcher's mound—but it occurs just before the game begins. Someone famous can be counted on to "throw out the first pitch." On occasion, that special person has been the President of the United States. The first President to kick off the baseball season was William Howard Taft in 1910. Since then, virtually every other U.S. President has done the honors during his stay in the White House. And if it's not the President trying to throw the ceremonial first pitch, it's someone else of consequence—another politician, a movie star, a singer, a baseball legend. Baseball is full of traditions and throwing out the first pitch on Opening Day

2008 Opening Day at Citizens Bank Park, Philadelphia.

ranks as one of the most prestigious.

For most major league teams, Opening Day occurs during the work week—usually on Monday. Don't let that stop you from attending. On Opening Day, you need to get the day off from work. Take a vacation day or call in sick. Your boss may or may not understand. It doesn't matter.

Every baseball fan must attend Opening Day at least once. Dedicated fans need to be there every year. And therein lies the problem. Not everyone who wants to go to Opening Day will be able to get a ticket. Opening Day is almost always a sell-out. There are 162 games in a major league season, and everybody, it seems, wants to be at that first one. No other sport generates such enthusiasm or excitement for the first game of the season. Whether it's because baseball is so rich in tradition or because the beginning of baseball almost always means the onset of spring and the feeling of rebirth, Opening Day is one tough ticket to come by.

It doesn't help that more and more major league teams are including Opening Day tickets in multi-game ticket packages as an incentive to purchase them, thus making single-game Opening Day tickets that much harder to secure. And most of the new ballparks have fewer seats than the ones they replaced, which means fewer Opening Day tickets.

What's a dedicated baseball fan to do? Buy Opening Day tickets the first day they go on sale. Find out when your team plans to sell single-game tickets and be one of the first on the box office line, or online. At many ballparks, Opening Day tickets—the few made available to the single-game ticket buyer—will be gone in a matter of minutes. Your position on line and the fickle sway of the baseball gods will determine if you are one of the lucky few to say, "I know where I'll be on Opening Day."

And if you don't manage to get a ticket, you can say what many baseball fans will be mumbling by May, once the optimism of Opening Day has faded from memory and reality has sunk in: "Wait 'til next year."

To get the Opening Day schedule and information on how to buy tickets, go to Major League Baseball's website *www.mlb.com*. Then click on "Team Sites" and find the link to the club whose Opening Day you want to attend. If your favorite team is scheduled to play its Opening Day game away from home, well, check out the #1 *Bucket List* item: Take a Baseball Road Trip.

4 ATTEND A WORLD SERIES GAME

Even if your favorite team never makes the World Series, attending a Fall Classic game remains a *Bucket List* must. It's about experiencing the majesty of the more than century-old World Series tradition and witnessing the latest chapter of baseball history. People who don't even call themselves baseball fans become fans during the World Series. Red, white and blue bunting gets hung around the ballpark celebrating baseball as the nation's pastime. Celebrities and politicians, even Presidents, turn out for a game. For a short stretch every year, nearly everyone in the country reconnects with baseball as the best-of-seven series unfolds in the autumn air.

The first World Series was played in 1903 between the Boston Pilgrims (also known as the Americans and after 1907 known as the Red Sox) of the American League and the Pittsburgh Pirates of the National League. Boston won, taking five games while the Pirates only won three in the best-of-nine series. The seven-game series format wasn't established until two years later. But the World Series tradition was set: the best team from the National League would play the best team from the American League every year to determine a world champion.

The World Series grew in popularity and stature, establishing itself as the nation's premier sporting event until the calamity of 1919, when a group of Chicago White Sox players conspired with gamblers to throw the Series (see *Bucket List* item #32). The "Black Sox" scandal, as it became known, severely tarnished the game's integrity and threatened its survival. However, thanks to the appointment of Judge Kenesaw Mountain Landis as baseball's first commissioner and his swift, unwavering decision—to ban eight White Sox players, including the great "Shoeless" Joe Jackson, from ever again playing professional baseball—the game and the Series were saved.

The World Series endured the Great Depression, World War II, and dramatic cultural changes in the game and the country. Pro football, a growing rival to Major League Baseball, created the Super Bowl in 1967. As the years passed, the Super Bowl ultimately became the biggest single sporting event in the U.S. But the World Series carried on too, growing larger and more prestigious as it continued to serve as the baseball season's grand finale.

World Series history provides baseball fans, writers, and historians with plenty of great moments to remember and savor. Which moment was the greatest? Was it the final pitch of Yankee pitcher Don Larsen's perfect game in 1956 against the rival Brooklyn Dodgers? How about when Yankee slugger Babe Ruth "called" his home run against the Chicago Cubs in 1932? Certainly Bill Mazeroski's home run against the Yankees in the bottom of the ninth inning in the final game of the 1960 World Series, making the Pirates world champions, deserves serious consideration, as does Carlton Fisk's shot in Game 6 of the 1975 Series that gave the Red Sox life against the Cincinnati Reds. What about Dodger Kirk Gibson's pinch-hit blast to win the first game of the 1988 Series against the Oakland A's? And can anyone who watched it ever forget Red Sox first baseman Bill Buckner's tenth-inning error that allowed the New York Mets to take Game 6 in the 1986 World Series? And these are only a few of the classic World Series memories to cherish and recall.

Unfortunately, tickets to any World Series game are quite difficult to come by. When big market teams like the Yankees or Dodgers or Mets make it to the Series, tickets are next to impossible to get. The truth is there are no easy ways to secure World Series tickets for face value. Fans who are not season ticket holders of a team playing in the World Series, or who don't work for a corporation that has purchased blocks of tickets, most likely will have to resort to *StubHub* or the other ticket agencies where tickets with grossly inflated prices might be available.

It is a pity that the World Series, like the Super Bowl and other high-profile sporting events in America, has become largely inaccessible to the ordinary fan because of the high cost of tickets. But for a baseball fan, just being at a World Series game will make it more than worth the cost.

> To get details on how to purchase World Series tickets, go to the Major League Baseball website www.mlb.com, then check the links to the sites for the teams participating in the Series. It's a good idea to check the websites or call teams' ticket offices during the latter parts of the regular season when World Series favorites are emerging.

5 | SEE THE CUBS PLAY AT WRIGLEY FIELD

Completing the full *Baseball Fan's Bucket List* requires visits to all 30 Major League Baseball ballparks. It's a tough task, and it usually takes years to complete. But it's a feat well worth accomplishing.

So, where do you start? Admittedly, a lot of subjectivity went into the ranking process, and you might not agree with a few of the placements, which is understandable. But it is difficult to deny the rankings of the two most important major league ballparks to visit: Fenway Park in Boston, home of the Red Sox, and Wrigley Field, the grand dame of American baseball parks and the longtime home of the Chicago Cubs.

Visit Wrigley Field first. It is an undeniable classic, a Chicago landmark and a baseball treasure. Its beauty belies its age. Having opened in 1914, it ranks second to Fenway as the oldest major league ballpark still in existence. Yet despite the thousands of games played there and the annual frustration suffered by Cubs fans, as year after year their team finds a way to let them down, Wrigley Field is never a disappointment. With its ivy-covered outfield walls, its intimate seating, and a postcard-perfect location in the heart of Chicago, Wrigley Field is an American baseball gem.

It's not necessary to take a tour of every major league ballpark—most all of them offer tours these days, usually when the team is playing away, and during the offseason. But you must tour Wrigley. If you do, you'll get to see the clubhouse, check out the dugout, and most importantly, walk along the outfield warning track (not on the grass!) where the Wrigley ivy grows on its brick wall ever so beautifully (see *Bucket List* item #79 to find the surprise identity of the man responsible for Wrigley's ivy). You can look at it and take a picture of it, but you can't touch it.

Another thing you need to do is travel to Wrigley Field by the 'L'—as in elevated train, Chicago's equally classic mass transportation system. Arriving at Wrigley any other way doesn't cut it. There's something truly special about being jammed into a train packed with Cubs fans, even if you're not a Cubs fan, and stepping out of the car at the Addison stop, and there she is, wonderful Wrigley Field. It's as if you've just stepped into baseball history.

The train stop is just a half-block away from the park, but before you enter, spend some time touring Wrigleyville, the area around the park where Cubs mania blooms all spring and summer long. Grab a beer at Murphy's at the corner of Waveland and Sheffield Streets, one of the best sports bars in America. After the game, get another cold one at Harry Caray's Tavern near the corner of Addison and Sheffield. (Caray, of course, was the Cubs' legendary announcer; a statue of him with his famous smile and horn-rimmed glasses stands just across the street at the entrance to Wrigley.) For Wrigley Field memorabilia, check out any one of the stores on Addison that sell everything from Wrigley t-shirts and hoodies, to hats and pajamas, jackets and neckties. Walk around the outside of Wrigley, passing the Ernie Banks ("Mr. Cub") statue in front of the ticket windows on Clark Street, where you'll also find the home-plate entrance to the park and the famous red sign that proclaims: *"Wrigley Field Home of Chicago Cubs."*

The entrance to Wrigley Field.

As you pass the outfield walls on Waveland and Sheffield, you'll pass the regular inhabitants of Wrigleyville, namely those lucky Cub fans whose apartment house just across the street from the ballpark has bleachers built for viewing the games from the comfort of their roof. Cubs' officials clearly don't like them and have, over the years, tried to prevent their presence or block their views, but for every game, they're still filled with fans.

Inside Wrigley, the bleachers offer the ideal place to watch the game. Bleacher seats are hard to come by and aren't the cheap seats in Wrigley as they are in other parks. But this is where the Cubs' famous "bleacher bums" reside, and if you're bent on experiencing the best of Wrigley Field baseball culture, the bleachers are the place to be. If bleacher seats aren't available, don't fret. There isn't a bad seat in Wrigley and just being there is reward enough. Admire Wrigley's intimacy; take in her classic lines, beautiful brick, and traditional scoreboard and, of course, its outfield ivy. Walk inside and underneath the grandstand, where the concession stands are, and you'll swear you've gone back in baseball time.

The Wrigley Field experience is so

For more information about tours and game tickets at Wrigley, check the Chicago Cubs website *www.cubs.com.* Wrigley Field tours fill up fast; it's best to purchase a tour ticket well in advance of your visit. The same is true of Cubs games. Your best bet is to take in a day game in the middle of the week before the All-Star break.

rich that staying connected to the game on the field is difficult. If you've ever wondered why Cubs' fans seem to be such a happy lot despite so many losing seasons, well, in part it's because of Wrigley. It casts a spell over you that lightens the load of losing and allows you to leave the ballpark—win or lose—with a feeling that you've just experienced some of the best of what baseball has to offer.

6 WATCH THE KEN BURNS DOCUMENTARY, *BASEBALL*

In 1994, Ken Burns, the acclaimed New Hampshire-based documentary filmmaker, brought the history of baseball into the living rooms of America. Like he had done a few years earlier with his widely praised public television series, *The Civil War,* and would later do with many other topics, Burns took a topic that was woven into the cultural and historical fabric of the nation and told its distinctly American story.

Before Burns, the documentary film was often a dull, dry way to deal with important historical issues. Hollywood movies always seemed to make history more interesting, even if most directors and scriptwriters emphasized melodrama over the truth. But Burns found a way to give old film clips new life and old stories new meaning. He recast events with new points of view and re-introduced us to, in the case of *Baseball*, players we already knew about—Ty Cobb, Babe Ruth, Jackie Robinson, Ted Williams, Joe DiMaggio, and others—so that we knew them just a little bit better. He also introduced us to players most didn't know about, but should have, like Buck O'Neil of the Negro Leagues.

Baseball premiered on public television. Over nine episodes—just like the nine-inning baseball game—Burns recounted the history of America's pastime. Histories had been written about baseball, of course, and filmmakers prior to Burns had tackled the complex story of baseball and what it had meant to America since the game's inception in the 19th century. But no one had told the story so thoroughly, personally, and passionately. That was Burns' secret for success: humanize the game—show its triumphs and failures and how and why both affected the nation. Tell the story of the legend and the fan. Show how baseball was far more than just a game. Reveal how baseball was really *our* story.

One reviewer wrote that "*Baseball* contemplates the game as a profound and evolving metaphor for the American experience." Burns must have been pleased with the assessment, since that had been his goal from day one on the project.

In *Baseball*, Burns used rare—and in some cases, never-before-seen—photographs and film clips from baseball archives across America. His research team mined compelling bits of historical data that had previously been overlooked by baseball historians. In each episode, he presented engaging interviews with the best and brightest baseball minds, along with good writing and music, making baseball history come alive.

Over the nine episodes (there is a tenth "extra inning" disc in the *Baseball* set that details the making of the series), you might say that Burns built four pillars upon which to rest the baseball story. The first had to do with our romantic notions of the origins of baseball—that it began in the green pastures of pastoral America. Burns gave baseball fans the truth—the game was born in cities like Brooklyn and Hoboken. He paid respect to the pastoral myth of the national pastime's genesis at the same time as he deconstructed it.

Baseball's second pillar, according to Burns, was that it began as a gentleman's game, but broadened into a professional one that crooks and cheats nearly ruined. The shame of the "Black Sox" Scandal in 1919, when members of the Chicago White Sox threw the World Series, was the low point of baseball history. But the game survived and grew stronger.

For pillar number three—the strongest and most persistent of them all in *Baseball*—Burns reminded us that for too long baseball, like America, carried the ugly stain of racism, lightened with the Major League Baseball debut of Jackie Robinson in 1947. Burns was at his best when presenting the case that, despite its earlier sins, baseball was one of the first American institutions to take on racial segregation, and with Jackie Robinson forging the way, eventually beat it. For Burns, Robinson rates as baseball's greatest figure and most heroic player.

Burns' and *Baseball's* final pillar was that the game is remarkably resilient. When World War II threatened professional baseball, President Franklin Roosevelt insisted that it somehow carry on to brighten the nation's darkest moments. It did so with a professional women's league and an odd assortment of gimmicks and players,

Ken Burns' *Baseball* still airs on PBS affiliates and the MLB Network. Check your local listings for dates and times, especially in the month before the start of the baseball season or post-season. Many public libraries own copies that you can check out for viewing. You can purchase the DVD version from most video stores and online movie retailers. VHS versions of the series are available from many used video merchants.

like 15-year-old pitcher Joe Nuxhall.

You can watch *Baseball* during the off-season to keep connected to the game. You can watch it during spring training to get ready for the new season. Or you can watch it during the baseball season as a complement to the pennant races or as a way to give the game more meaning and history. Watch it whenever, and for whatever reason, but watch it. No book and certainly no other film have done for baseball what Ken Burns has done for the national pastime. *Baseball* is a grand slam and mandatory viewing for all fans of the game.

7 | SEE THE RED SOX PLAY 8-4-92 AT FENWAY PARK ✰✰✰✰

Fenway Park is to the American League what Wrigley Field is to the National League—a grand old ballpark that has aged ever so gracefully and defies the notion that being old means it's time to be replaced. Opening in 1912 as home of the Boston Red Sox, Fenway is the oldest of all the major league ballparks. Like Wrigley, Fenway Park is beloved by its team's fans and city. For so many years, Fenway has escaped the wrecking ball that took down so many other older stadiums across America because of Boston's love for Fenway and because the Red Sox simply wouldn't be the team they are—or have the fans they do—without it.

A short walk from Boston's Kenmore Square, Fenway sits in a blue collar neighborhood, not far from the Kenmore subway station (Green Line) that brings Red Sox fans to the ballpark each summer. (Going to Fenway by car is usually a nightmare; avoid driving and take mass transit.) Your visit to Fenway Park begins on Yawkey Way, in many ways an extension of the park. Here you'll find plenty of Red Sox souvenir stores, concession stands, and Sox fans milling about as the smell of great food and beer fill the air. As baseball streets go, Yawkey Way is tops. Get to it early enough before the ballgame so that you can treat yourself to the best ballpark food in the majors. The sausage sandwiches, smothered with peppers and onions, are unrivaled, while the hot dogs, thick and cooked just right, are impossible to ignore.

Before you enter Fenway, take a walk around the outside of it. Word has it that when Roger Clemens first showed up in Boston and was taken to Fenway, he thought the driver had made a mistake and dropped him off at a factory warehouse. If you appreciate working class architecture and a ballpark that beautifully blends into the neighborhood, you'll appreciate Fenway's setting. It's nothing spectacular, mind you. What you get, however, is the affirmation that over the years, a whole lot of baseball has been played in this ballpark, all of it an integral part of summer in Boston.

Once you're inside Fenway, you'll notice how small it is. Fenway holds 39,000 (only three other major league ballparks are smaller, as of the end of the 2009 season). But it seems even more quaint, thanks to its quirky field dimensions. Nooks and crannies in right-center field can ricochet a well-hit baseball in unexpected directions and create havoc for the outfielder trying to retrieve it. The fans in the low end of the right-field bleachers seem to *sit* in right field; that's how close they are to the action.

One of the most imposing Fenway landmarks, the Green Monster, is also one of baseball's most famous. Making up Fenway's left-field wall, the Green Monster is little more than 300 feet from home plate, but it stands 37 feet high. Knowing how to play a ball blasted against the Green Monster rates as one of an American League left fielder's most important skills. The Green Monster also features a hand-operated scoreboard, one of the few left in the major leagues. For traditionalists, it is a joy to watch the green or red light (ball or strike) brighten with each pitch thrown.

Another Fenway landmark is the lone red seat in the right-field bleachers

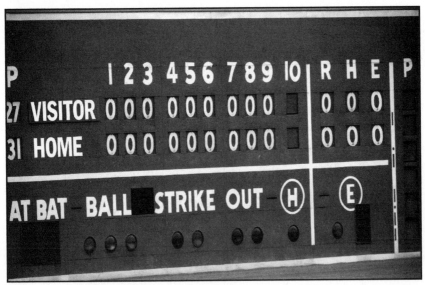

The hand-operated scoreboard at Fenway Park.

(Section 42, Row 37, Seat 21) that commemorates the landing spot of the longest measurable home run ever hit at Fenway; in 1946, Ted Williams, Boston's greatest hitter, smacked a ball 502 feet into that seat during a game against the Detroit Tigers. Also, be sure to check out Pesky's Pole, the right-field foul line pole named after former Red Sox infielder Johnny Pesky. Not exactly an intimidating power hitter, Pesky hit only 17 home runs his entire career. But he curled one of them around that pole on Opening Day in 1946 to win the game and gain the honor.

In 1999, the Red Sox, taken by all the new ballparks going up around the major leagues, announced plans for a new Fenway Park. The Red Sox Nation revolted and the plans were halted. Instead of building a new ballpark, the Red Sox found ways to add seats in Fenway. They found the most space atop the Green Monster, and those seats quickly became some of the most coveted in Fenway. For the foreseeable future, Fenway, with all its tradition and glory, will remain the home of the Red Sox and the pride of Boston baseball. The team, the fans, and the city plan a big celebration for Fenway's centennial in 2012.

Fenway has a wonderful history; read up on the ballpark before you go. There seems to have been more books written about Fenway than any other ballpark. Among the most worthwhile are *One Day at Fenway* by Steve Kettmann; *Fenway: A Biography in Words and Pictures* by Dan Shaughnessy, with a foreword by Ted Williams and photos by Stan Grossfeld; and *Our House: A Tribute to Fenway Park* by Curt Smith.

For information about Fenway Park tours and Red Sox tickets, visit the team's website at *www.redsox.com*. Securing tickets for a game at Fenway isn't easy. Sell-outs are the rule. A ticket agency might be your best bet, though if you arrive early enough to the ballpark, scalpers are almost always at work.

EXPERIENCE A HALL OF FAME INDUCTION WEEKEND IN COOPERSTOWN

8

The annual National Baseball Hall of Fame's Induction Ceremony caps one of the most memorable weekends on the baseball calendar. Held each July in Cooperstown, the induction of the game's greats into the Hall of Fame is not only a celebration of personal baseball achievement, it's also a tribute to the national pastime and a gathering of some of its legendary figures. During the Hall of Fame Weekend, fans and media converge on the village of Cooperstown. The National Baseball Hall of Fame and Museum features special events and programs. Baseball memorabilia shops along Main Street sponsor autograph signings with former Hall of Famers. Everywhere you go in Cooperstown, baseball is in the air, making Induction Weekend a one-of-a-kind event.

The National Baseball Hall of Fame began in 1936 with a class consisting Ty Cobb, Honus Wagner, Babe Ruth, Christy Mathewson and Walter Johnson. But it took three years for the museum and Hall of Fame to be built, so the first actual induction ceremony in Cooperstown occurred in 1939.

A Great Day in Cooperstown: The Improbable Birth of Baseball's Hall of Fame (Da Capo, 2006) by Jim Reisler is a good read if you care to know about how the Hall of Fame and museum came to be.

In order to accommodate the increasingly large crowds, the Hall of Fame induction ceremony now takes place just outside the village of Cooperstown in a large field. Although the event is free, the induction ceremony features a ticketed section of reserved seating for museum members. The event can be enjoyed without a ticket by claiming a spot on the hillside beyond the fenced ticketed area. But it can get hot and steamy sitting in the midday summer sun during the Hall of Fame afternoon, so bring water, sunscreen, and a hat and dress coolly. Lawn chairs and a blanket are also a good idea. Arrive early and you'll get a good position on the grassy hill that looks down to the tented area where the inductees and special guests sit.

It makes the weekend even more meaningful if you attend an induction ceremony when a favorite player is honored. You can check the National Baseball

Hall of Fame weekend in Cooperstown, N.Y.

Hall of Fame's website for a list of potential Hall of Fame inductees and make your plans accordingly. Whenever a legend from either the Boston Red Sox or New York Yankees is inducted, you can expect big crowds in Cooperstown. Not only do these two teams own huge fan bases, but their relatively close proximity to Cooperstown makes the trip easy and affordable for most of their fans. Certain players whose popularity extends beyond that of their teams' core fan bases also attract large crowds. When, for instance, Cal Ripken, Jr. was inducted in 2007, more than 75,000 fans showed up in Cooperstown.

The actual Hall of Fame is in the National Baseball Hall of Fame and Museum on Main Street in Cooperstown. But the institution does not decide who gets inducted each year. That responsibility lies with the Baseball Writers' Association of America. To be considered for induction, a ballplayer must have played at least ten years, been retired at least five years and not be on Major League Baseball's ineligible list. It is rare, but on occasion the Baseball Writers' Association has made exceptions to these rules. In 1939 Lou Gehrig gained induction after he was diagnosed with amyotrophic lateral sclerosis, later known as Lou Gehrig's Disease, and forced to quit baseball earlier that year. Also, when the great Latin player Roberto Clemente was killed in a plane crash in 1972 while delivering supplies to Nicaraguan earthquake victims, he was voted in the following year.

In order to get into the Hall, a ballplayer must receive 75% of the annual vote. This is difficult to do, as evidenced by the relatively few players honored each year. For every 100 players who log time in the majors, only one makes it into the Hall of Fame. Players aren't the only ones who are eligible for induction. Managers, umpires, and executives are eligible, as are players from the 19th century and from the Negro Leagues. If a player doesn't get voted in, he could make the Hall by virtue of the Baseball Hall of Fame Committee on Baseball Veterans, which has the power to select players who came up short with the Baseball Writers' Association. The Committee on Baseball Veterans makes its choices "based on changing historical perspectives."

Baseball writers and broadcasters are also honored during Hall of Fame Weekend, filling out the festivities. Technically, they aren't Hall of Famers; rather, they're called "honorees." Writers so honored are awarded the J.G. Taylor Spink Award, while broadcasters win the Ford C. Frick Award. They have their own exhibit and tribute area in the museum.

In all, there are 289 members in the National Baseball Hall of Fame as of 2009. You can see their bronze plaques that summarize their careers and baseball accomplishments in the museum's Hall of Fame gallery. Not surprisingly, the gallery is jammed during Hall of Fame Induction Weekend. Get there early because you'll find yourself immersed in the baseball lives of these legends and want to spend enough time to review all the Hall of Fame classes.

> Go to www.baseballhall.org for a full list of Hall of Fame inductees, further information on the Hall of Fame balloting process, and details about the Hall of Fame Induction Weekend. You can also get more information by calling 1-888-HALL-OF-FAME.

9 PLAY FANTASY BASEBALL IN A ROTISSERIE LEAGUE

Be careful with this *Bucket List* entry: it is habit-forming, time-consuming, and costly. It could cause marital problems. It may even drive you to drink. Playing fantasy baseball is risky business. Then why play, you ask? Aside from the fact that it is fun and that it will stir every competitive bone in your body, just one season of fantasy baseball instills you with an incredible amount of knowledge about baseball, especially about the job of a general manager. And if you keep your urge to win under control and enjoy the day-to-day process of playing fantasy baseball for what it is—a game—then you won't be robbed of your life and your loved ones in the process.

A suggestion before you commit to fantasy baseball: read the book *Fantasyland* (2006) by Sam Walker, an insightful and often hilarious account of one sportswriter's quest to play in Tout Wars, one of the toughest, most competitive fantasy baseball leagues ever put together. Not only is it a remarkably good read, but it will also give you an idea of what might be awaiting you should you take the fantasy baseball plunge and dive deep. Another must read is the classic baseball novel, *The Universal Baseball Association, Inc., J. Henry Waugh, Prop.* (see *Bucket List* item #151). Written by Robert Coover and published in 1968, it preceded the rise of fantasy baseball by more than a decade but is still considered one of the best novels ever written about the culture of baseball and the obsessive behaviors it can inspire.

Millions of baseball fans—men and women, young and old—play fantasy baseball each season. Websites are dedicated to the game and baseball newspapers and magazines regularly report on players and issues that might affect fantasy league choices. There is specialty software for fantasy baseball players and prize money for league winners. If you're truly obsessed, you could hire a fantasy baseball consultant as Walker did. *USA Today* has estimated that fantasy sports, which includes baseball, pro football and other sports, is a $1.5 billion dollar industry.

That explains why in 2008 Major League Baseball sought to have the United States Supreme Court overturn lower court rulings that allowed fantasy league companies to operate without compensating the sports leagues they focused on. Baseball officials claimed that companies specializing in fantasy baseball were using the names and statistics of major league players without permission. The Supreme Court refused to issue an opinion on the lower courts' rulings, which were based on first amendment rights, and fantasy baseball fans everywhere let out a loud cheer.

What, exactly, is fantasy baseball? In order to play, you must live in a fantasy world, at least when engaged in the game. Fantasy baseball is a place where you are the general manager of a major league team, except that the team you manage doesn't really exist. You don't, for instance, run the New York Yankees or the Los Angeles Dodgers. Rather, you create your own "fantasy" team of players from a variety of major league teams taken in a pre-season draft. You select them based on your hunch on how they'll perform that season. The odd thing about fantasy baseball is that it is not about winning games. It's about your players posting the highest number of home runs, stolen bases, batting averages, runs batted in, wins, saves and something called WHIP that measures the number of batters a pitcher allows to reach base per inning.

Fantasy baseball is made up of Rotisserie Leagues. The name comes from the New York restaurant *La Rotisserie Francaise*, where Daniel Okrent and a few other sports journalists created the basic rules of fantasy baseball in 1980. Games based on baseball statistics had been around before 1980; Strat-O-Matic (see *Bucket List* item #125) and APBA (see *Bucket List* item #117) began using the statistics of real major league players years before, but the allure of these games was mostly limited to baseball stat geeks and hardcore fans.

Fantasy baseball is now an undeniable part of baseball culture, and fantasy sports leagues are a permanent part of American pop culture. Millions of fantasy baseball league participants wake up every morning and—before they brush their teeth or take a sip of their coffee—check box scores online or in the newspaper to chart how their players did the previous night. They'll watch *Baseball Tonight* on ESPN with the same concentration and concern for detail as they would put into reading a mortgage contract. In the end, it's all about fun and enjoying the game of baseball in a way that provides the kind of insight into it that you can't experience any other way.

> To find out more information about fantasy baseball or to join a Rotisserie League, check websites such as *www.espn.com*, *www.sports.yahoo.com*, and *www.mlb.com/fantasy*. Ask folks at the local ballpark or sports bar about any fantasy leagues operating in your town. Or you can form your own Rotisserie League using instructions you can find from numerous books, magazines and websites.

10 GO TO A MAJOR LEAGUE BASEBALL ALL-STAR GAME

Unlike the World Series, which celebrates two pennant-winning teams and their quest for a world championship, the annual Major League Baseball All-Star Game honors the game's current best—and most popular—individual players. Amidst the pageantry and tradition, a select group of major league ballplayers from both the American and National leagues come together just after the Fourth of July each season to showcase their talents. It wasn't always this way, but winning the contest is now important, since home field advantage during the World Series a few months later is at stake. But even so, it's still the individual All-Star player, rather than the team, that commands the most attention.

The All-Star Game is the only Major League Baseball game that the fans wield significant control over. We are the ones who make players All-Stars by voting for them. When we come to the ballpark for games beginning in mid-May, we're handed All-Star Game ballots by stadium ushers. There are no rules that prevent us from voting more than once; let's be honest, many of us do. There are no pre-conditions either. A five-year-old fan who can barely read has a vote as does his 45-year-old father. In a way, the All-Star Game is Major League Baseball's tip of the hat to democracy and the American way. Everyone can vote, everyone can exercise an opinion about what players belong on the field. Are we fans always right in our selections? No. All-Star Game voting is a popularity contest, more than an accurate assessment of baseball skill and production. But no one in baseball seems to mind too much.

For a few days each summer, the pennant race tension subsides while the All-Star Game, held in a different major league city each season, takes center stage. Over the years, the game has transformed into a mid-summer fan fest, with all kinds of things going on around it that celebrate baseball. There are autograph sessions with former baseball greats, interactive game simulations where fans can measure the speed of their pitches and take batting practice. There is a home-run hitting contest involving MLB players that attracts nearly as much attention as the game itself. A "Futures" game pits minor league players from the U.S. against players born overseas. There's even a celebrity softball game.

Players are more relaxed and accessible to the media and fans during All-Star festivities. It all adds up to a much-needed break in the middle of the baseball season. Those players not voted to the All-Star team, or not selected by the All-Star manager as substitutes, go fishing or go home. They know to get whatever rest they can, because after the All-Star Game, pennant races take on added intensity and the July 31 trade deadline looms.

The first All-Star Game was held in 1933 at Chicago's Comiskey Park, home of the American League White Sox, and featured the likes of Babe Ruth, Lou Gehrig, Lefty Grove and Jimmie Foxx. The American League won, 4-2. The game was meant to coincide with the city's "Century of Progress Exposition," a sort of World's Fair that reminded

For more information about the dates and location of the next annual Major League Baseball All-Star Game, check the website of Major League Baseball, *www.mlb.com*. Getting tickets to the All-Star Game is not easy; find out when tickets go on sale and be ready with your credit card. Advance hotel reservations are also a must, so plan ahead. Also be sure to find out how you can take part in all the other events leading up to the All-Star Game by getting in touch with the team hosting the game that year.

Americans dealing with the Great Depression that there were still good things happening in the country. Fans loved the idea of seeing so many baseball greats on one field at the same time, so Major League Baseball decided to make the game an annual celebration. The next year, the game was played in New York at the Polo Grounds, home of the National League Giants, and the tradition was set to alternate the site of the All-Star Game between American and National League cities each season.

The Mid-Summer Classic, as it's now affectionately known, has been going on ever since. The only time it wasn't played was in 1945, when it was scheduled for Fenway Park, but cancelled due to World War II. By the next summer, the war was over, Fenway got the chance to host the game, and the All-Star Game tradition resumed. There is no formula as to how Major League Baseball selects the host city for the All-Star Game. Lobbying by owners for the privilege of hosting the game certainly counts. However, since the early 1990s, Major League Baseball has used the game to show off its slew of shiny new ballparks around both leagues—along with many of its brightest stars.

11 VISIT THE NEGRO LEAGUES BASEBALL MUSEUM

The Negro Leagues Baseball Museum, located in Kansas City, Missouri, tells the story of the black ballplayer in professional baseball. Most of the exhibits deal with the pre-Jackie Robinson era, before Major League Baseball, when blacks played their own brand of the game, had their own stars, and contributed to the national pastime in a way that was both entertaining and courageous. As baseball museums go, only the National Baseball Hall of Fame and Museum in Cooperstown outranks it because it is bigger, better financed, and deals with the ongoing story of baseball. But the Negro Leagues Baseball Museum tells its own incredible story of baseball—and of America.

The Negro Leagues Baseball Museum sits in the cultural district known as Eighteenth and Vine, a historic area where, during the years before World War II, jumping jazz joints, stores, shops, and restaurants made this segregated part of Kansas City one of the most exciting black sections of any American city. Located at 1616 East 18th Street, the museum shares its space, appropriately, with the American Jazz Museum, which also celebrates a component of black American culture that flourished in Kansas City in the first half of the 20th century.

The museum stands around the corner from the Paseo YMCA, the building where league founder Andrew "Rube" Foster met with several other team owners to formalize the start of the Negro Leagues in 1920. The new Negro League allowed black players to play professionally, despite the racism that shut them out of Major League Baseball. The establishment of black professional baseball also offered black baseball fans the opportunity to cheer for black teams and watch black baseball legends such as Satchel Paige, Josh Gibson, and Cool Papa Bell play the American game.

While it tells the story of the Negro Leagues and celebrates its greatest players, the museum also details the challenges black players and clubs faced in pre-civil rights America. It is a sad, often disturbing story, but it is ultimately a triumphant one. Because despite the overt racism and oppression black players faced as they traveled around the country, the quality of their baseball often matched that played by their white counterparts.

The museum opened in 1991 in a single room with limited artifacts and small displays. Six years later, thanks to the leadership of John "Buck" O'Neil, a Negro Leagues legend who dedicated himself to getting the museum a proper space, the Negro Leagues Baseball Museum moved into its current location.

The Coors Field of Legends serves as the facility's centerpiece. A replica of

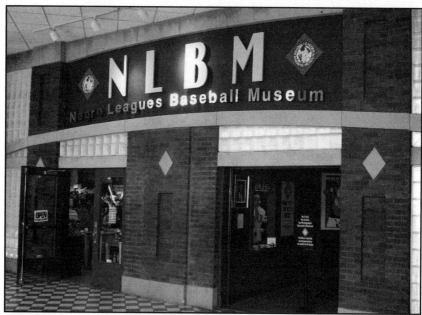

Welcome to the Negro Leagues Baseball Museum in Kansas City, Mo.

an old Negro Leagues ballpark, it presents bronze statues of a team of legends, including Paige, Gibson and Bell. As you walk amongst these legends, you come to appreciate their accomplishments and learn why most of them are also members of the National Baseball Hall of Fame in Cooperstown.

Adjacent to the Coors Field of Legends stands the Grandstand Theater, where a 15-minute film, *They Were All Stars*, narrated by James Earl Jones, gives visitors a tidy history of the Negro Leagues and its top players. It also recounts the racism that prevented many black ballplayers from playing in the major leagues with white players, on an equal basis and with equal reward.

That, of course, didn't begin to happen until 1947, when Jackie Robinson broke the color barrier in Major League Baseball. Robinson's feat was historic for America. But it also marked the beginning of the end for the Negro Leagues, as first Robinson, then Larry Doby and other black ballplayers made the jump from the Negro Leagues to the major leagues. It would take more than ten years from Robinson's debut in Brooklyn until every major league roster included at least one black ballplayer—the Boston Red Sox, the last team in the majors to integrate, didn't play Pumpsie Green until 1959. By then, despite a few last barnstorming all-black teams, a critical chapter in baseball history had closed.

Using artifacts and memorabilia, including contracts, vintage uniforms and equipment, old photographs, film clips, and oral histories, the exhibits in the Negro Leagues Baseball Museum bring to life the story of teams like the Kansas City Monarchs, arguably the greatest of the Negro League franchises. It also highlights the exploits of great players like Paige and Gibson, Bell and Buck O'Neil, and Martin Dihigo (maybe the greatest all-around Negro Leagues player). Even Willie Mays and Hank Aaron, two black MLB legends whose careers are enshrined in Cooperstown, began their careers in the Negro Leagues. The exhibits—"The Early Years," "Pioneers," "Drawing the Line," "Hard Times," "Golden Years," "Emergence of Superstars," and "Changing Times" —wrap around the Coors Field of Legends. Two other exhibits, "Travelin' Men," which details the racial challenges that black ball teams faced as they went from one city to the next, and "Beisbol," which documents the role of the black Caribbean player, are equally insightful.

You can't leave the Negro Leagues Baseball Museum without recognizing two things: that black baseball remains a unique and indelible part of the history of the game; and that the Negro Leagues, despite the odious effects of racism, provided America with a fast and fun brand of baseball that every baseball fan wishes he could have experienced.

For hours, tickets, directions and other information pertaining to the Negro Leagues Baseball Museum, call (888) 221-NLBM. Or check its website at *www.nlbm.com*.

12 | LEARN TO KEEP SCORE ✦✦

Let's be honest: keeping score at a baseball game isn't necessary. Most MLB scoreboards today are large and complex and chock full of information about the players and the game. Then there are the pitching statistics, not usually shown on the jumbo screen, but still easily accessible. They're often found between grandstand levels, and track the number of pitches thrown, the balls and strikes, and the velocity of each pitch. There is also the traditional line score—an inning-by-inning account of the score, which back in the good old days of baseball, used to be hand-operated (and still is at a few major league ballparks).

So why then does keeping score at a baseball game rate a spot on the *Bucket List*? Tracking the action yourself instead of relying on contemporary scoreboards brings you closer to the game than most anything else. It forces you to pay attention to every batter, every pitch thrown. It gives you instant information about the game and the players in it. It encourages critical thinking of managerial decisions.

Scoring a baseball game goes back to the Civil War years, perhaps even earlier. Most of the game's historians give credit to Henry Chadwick, one of the so-called "fathers of baseball" for creating a basic scoring system that was useful and reliable. He published the first baseball box score in a newspaper. Since then, baseball, which is a game of numbers, has seen the art of keeping score grow, adding details along the way and increasing the clarity of the game.

Interestingly, there is a no single way for the baseball fan to keep score. If you've never done it—and today, there are many baseball fans who haven't—it's easy to begin. Most ballparks still sell scorecards for a dollar or two and include a small pencil in the price. Occasionally, these scorecards will come with a basic set of scoring instructions. Increasingly, however, the scorecard is being blended into the overall program sold at the game. The programs cost more, but they feature stories and players' biographies. The scorecard is usually located in the middle of the program, as are the instructions on how to keep score.

You'll see some fans disregard both the traditional scorecard and the program, and instead bring their own baseball scorebook. Official baseball scorebooks, available from most sporting goods stores, provide the opportunity to easily and efficiently document much more of the game, and collect, under one cover, scorecards for all the games you see in a season. Going that route is an investment you may or may not want to make. Best to begin with a simple scorecard bought at the ballpark and see if you enjoy the art of scorekeeping.

A Yankees–Red Sox scorecard.

Keep score with a pencil (with an eraser on it) instead of a pen. You're bound to make mistakes the first few times you keep score, and those pencils you get at the park don't always come with erasers. Get in your seat early enough so that you can insert into the scorecard the line-up for each team. If you're a novice, it's best to arrive at your seat even earlier so that you can familiarize yourself with the scoring suggestions printed on most scorecards and the different symbols such as "K" for strikeout and "BB" for a walk. Each position on the field has a designated number: the pitcher is 1, the catcher is 2, the first baseman is 3 and so on. You'll need to know these, no matter what style of scorekeeping you use.

Keeping score also provides you a memento of the game. Keep your scorecards and in, say, twenty years, you'll be able to recall exactly what occurred the first time you visited Wrigley Field or the first time you saw Albert Pujols play. Finally, by keeping score, you're keeping alive a tradition that is nearly as old as baseball itself.

To learn how to keep score, you can consult number of websites, such as www.baseballscorecard.com. The best scoring tutorial is Paul Dickson's wonderful book, *The Joy of Keeping Score: How Scoring the Game Has Influenced and Enhanced the History of Baseball*. (Walker & Co., 2007); it can be ordered from most bookstores or online booksellers. Read it before you go to the ballpark. Dickson supplies a short history of baseball scorekeeping and plenty of pointers for making it fun and accurate and a valuable tool for gaining greater understanding of baseball.

13 SEE SOME GRAPEFRUIT LEAGUE SPRING TRAINING GAMES

Each year, the baseball ritual begins right after the Super Bowl ends. Football is finished, and the crisp bite of winter doesn't sting so much anymore. February means pitchers and catchers are coming out of hibernation and beginning to throw and catch, leading up to March and the start of spring training for every team and player. It's the time of year when every baseball fan, no matter his age or gender, or where he lives, or what team he roots for, is smiling because baseball is back.

For many fans, spring training represents one of the best parts of the baseball season. Nearly all the games are played in warm, sunny weather, either in Florida or Arizona, and they aren't about wins or losses or a team's place in the standings. Spring training is about preparing for the real season. For fans and players alike, the atmosphere around the spring training complex is loose and jocular. Everyone seems to sense something good in his team. Perhaps it's an exciting rookie pitcher, or a veteran outfielder looking to make the team, or a new acquisition who's bound to make a difference. Optimism fills the air. "Next year" has arrived.

Tickets to spring training games are cheaper than regular season tickets. Players are more accessible, which means getting autographs is possible, even probable if you bring a kid. You can watch infield practice on one field and batting practice at another, and no one will bother you. You can sit in the warm sun and chat with other fans about the upcoming season and share your dreams about winning the pennant. You could say that spring training is more about false hopes than reality, since of Major League Baseball's 30 teams, only two will make it to the World Series. But October is a long way off, so in March most fans harbor a harmless baseball fantasy, and there's nothing wrong with that.

Two leagues comprise Major League Baseball's spring training. The Grapefruit League teams play in Florida, while the Cactus League games take place in Arizona (see *Bucket List* item #15). Because the Grapefruit League is older than the Cactus League, it gets a slightly higher *Bucket List* entry. Each spring training league fields 15 teams. Not surprisingly the East Coast clubs and the Toronto Blue Jays train in Florida, while the West Coast teams, including the Colorado Rockies, choose Arizona. The Midwest and Texas teams split up. The Detroit Tigers, Minnesota Twins, Houston Astros, and St. Louis Cardinals head to Florida, while the Chicago Cubs and White Sox, the Cleveland Indians,

Cincinnati Reds, Milwaukee Brewers, Kansas City Royals, and Texas Rangers play in the Cactus League.

The first pre-season game was played in Florida in 1908 and pitted the Reds against a local St. Petersburg team, the Saints. Then in 1913, the Cubs traveled to Tampa and the Indians to Pensacola to train, initiating a trend. The following year, the St. Louis Browns arrived in St. Petersburg, the Cardinals in St. Augustine, and the Philadelphia Athletics in Jacksonville. Teams began playing each other in March on a regular basis and the Grapefruit League was born. Only six Major League Baseball teams (the Angels, Brewers, Mariners, Padres, Rockies, and Diamondbacks—all of them clubs who debuted after 1960) have never been a part of the Grapefruit League.

Each spring, more than 1.5 million baseball fans head to Florida to attend the 250+ games on the Grapefruit League schedule. Florida is a big state, so unless, you're at spring training to only watch games played by your favorite team, be prepared to do some driving. One of the mandatory stops is Tampa, home of the New York Yankees' spring training complex. Whether or not you're a Yankees fan, a stop at George M. Steinbrenner Field (formerly Legends Field) in Tampa has to be on your itinerary. A replica of the old Yankee Stadium, Steinbrenner Field towers above other spring training sites in terms of quality and popularity. It's best to buy tickets well in advance.

A good way to experience the league is to travel the roughly 130 miles of U.S. 41 on Florida's West Coast, starting in Dunedin, home of the Blue Jays, and ending up in Fort Myers, where both the Red Sox and Twins train. In all, you'll hit the training sites of seven teams (including the Phillies in Clearwater, the Yankees in Tampa, the Rays in St. Petersburg, and the Pirates in Bradenton)— eight if you include a relatively short detour to Lakeland, where the Tigers play.

A spring training trip that takes in the Grapefruit League teams located on Florida's East Coast includes stops in Viera (Nationals), Port St. Lucie (Mets), Jupiter (Cardinals and Marlins), and Fort Lauderdale (Orioles). Finally, the area around Disneyworld in Central Florida hosts the Braves (Lake Buena Vista) and Astros (Kissimmee). But Mickey Mouse and Donald Duck compete with the excitement of spring training baseball, and for purists, this is tough to take.

> For more information on planning a Grapefruit League trip, check out the website www.floridagrapefruitleague.com or each Grapefruit League team's official website (just click "Teams" on the homepage of the league's website to find links to them all). Be sure to plan your spring training trip well in advance. Hotels close to the ballparks fill up fast, and you'll want to stay as close to the training complex as possible to go autograph hunting and watch practices, which take place most mornings. Being able to walk back to your hotel for a late morning rest is something you'll appreciate as well.

14 WATCH THE MOVIE, *BULL DURHAM*

Many movie critics and historians consider *Bull Durham* to be the best feature film ever made about baseball. In 2008, the American Film Institute, a keeper of the country's rich cinematic legacy, called *Bull Durham* one of the best sports films ever made. The praise for *Bull Durham* that appeared in *Sports Illustrated* went even further; in 2003 its writers ranked it as the greatest sports film of all time. That's a lot of applause for a film that was released in 1988, a time when the public's appetite for baseball movies had only been recently whetted again by the movie, *The Natural* (1984). Every studio passed on *Bull Durham*, except for Orion, which imposed a relatively small budget ($9 million), as well as strict limitations on actor's salaries and the film's shooting schedule.

As it turned out, the success of *Bull Durham*, along with another acclaimed baseball film released in 1988, *Eight Men Out*, created a baseball movie renaissance. Following on the heels on these two films came *Field of Dreams* and *Major League*, both released in 1989, and *A League of Their Own* in 1992. All of these great baseball movies are "must sees" and *Bucket List* items that get their own entries later in this book.

Bull Durham got classic performances from Tim Robbins, as the sex-crazed, can't-miss pitcher Nuke LaLoosh; from Susan Sarandon, as the seductive, minor league mistress Annie Savoy, who quotes Whitman, views baseball as life's ultimate metaphor, and knows more about the game than the players and managers she follows; and from Kevin Costner as Crash Davis, the nearly washed-up catcher who is sent down to the minors to tame LaLoosh and ready him for the big leagues, before being thrown onto baseball's scrap heap. Together, Robbins, Sarandon, and Costner made movie magic and enabled *Bull Durham*, a romantic comedy twisted up in the wild world of the minor leagues, to help kick the baseball movie revival into a higher gear.

Bull Durham is also one of the most risqué baseball films ever made. Although there's little flesh exposed, the love scenes are as charged as LaLoosh's fastball. At the start of each season, Savoy selects one player from the minor league Durham Bulls to be her summer sex toy. LaLoosh, who owns "a million-dollar arm and a five cent head," is her pick. In one scene, she tells LaLoosh, "When you know how to make love, you'll know how to pitch." She makes it with first the young pitcher and then with Davis, her ultimate catch, after a series of classic cat-and-mouse scenes that are as funny and as baseball savvy as they are rousing.

Written and directed by Ron Shelton, a former minor league player himself (which explains why so much of the baseball world portrayed in the movie feels so authentic), *Bull Durham* was both a critical and commercial success. It helped that Shelton hired a number of minor leaguers as extras to fill out the field, and that both producer Thom Mount and consultant Pete Bock were longtime minor league baseball men. Robbins had no baseball experience, but plenty of passion for the game, while Costner played baseball in high school and retained a lot of his throwing and hitting skills. But in the end, it was Susan Sarandon who stole, not just hearts, but also the movie. Her seamless portrayal of the ultimate baseball groupie and trivia expert (she says, matter of factly, that there are 108 beads in a rosary and 108 stitches in a baseball) coupled with a delightful Southern accent and charm (the film was shot and set in North Carolina), gave the baseball movie genre its most memorable character who wasn't a ballplayer.

The movie's original title was *A Player To Be Named Later*, but Shelton later re-named it *Bull Durham* after the Durham Bulls, a real minor league team, which at the time played in the Single-A Carolina League. (Today, the Durham Bulls play in the Triple-A International League.) The success of the movie made the Bulls one of the most popular minor league teams in America. Attendance at its games jumped and sales of Durham Bulls gear soared. Baseball fans even made the journey to Durham, North Carolina to see Durham Athletic Park, the old ball field that was used in the film and by the Bulls. The Durham Bulls got so popular that it outgrew Durham Athletic Park; in 1995 it moved into a brand new stadium, Durham Bulls Athletic Park where the team currently plays. The original Durham Athletic Park still stands, a tribute to the movie and to minor league baseball of yesteryear.

Bull Durham runs 108 minutes and received an "R" rating. It is available for purchase or rental from most movie stores and online merchants in VHS and DVD formats. A special 20th anniversary features extras, including documentary shorts on minor league baseball and the making of the film, plus audio commentary from Director/Writer Ron Shelton, along with stars Kevin Costner and Tim Robbins. Shelton based Robbins' character Nuke LaLoosh on his old minor league teammate Steve Dalkowski, reputed to be the fastest—and perhaps wildest—pitcher ever to play pro ball (though, unlike LaLoosh, he never made it to the majors).

15 SEE SOME CACTUS LEAGUE SPRING TRAINING GAMES ✵✵

The junior circuit of spring training, the Cactus League plays its games in Arizona. Where the Grapefruit League features Florida sun and humidity, the Cactus League is all about dry heat. In Arizona, there's no chance of an alligator meandering along the left-field foul line. But you might see a scorpion scurry away from the locker room. When it comes to geography, the two leagues couldn't be more different. However, on the baseball field each March things are exactly the same: major league players are shagging fly balls, taking batting and infield practice, and running sprints, all with the goal of getting ready for the long season ahead.

The first spring training game in Arizona dates back to 1929 when the Detroit Tigers played the Pittsburgh Pirates in Phoenix. Arizona had only been a state since 1912, so the facilities were spartan, and few fans of the Tigers and Pirates made the journey to see their teams play. It wasn't until the early 1950s that the Chicago Cubs, Baltimore Orioles, New York Giants, and Cleveland Indians began playing their spring training games in the desert. Baltimore and Cleveland didn't stay; they moved to Florida and trained there. Over the years other teams changed training sites as well. However, the idea of a permanent spring training league in Arizona took hold. By the early 70s, eight teams were playing spring ball in the desert. Today, the Cactus League rivals the Grapefruit League in terms of teams, popularity, and revenue.

Most of the Cactus League teams train in the greater Phoenix area, including the Cubs, San Diego Padres, Seattle Mariners, Milwaukee Brewers, Chicago White Sox, Oakland Athletics, Los Angeles Dodgers, San Francisco Giants, Kansas City Royals, Los Angeles Angels, Texas Rangers, Cincinnati Reds, and the Indians, which moved back to Arizona in 2009. Unlike in Florida, nearly all the teams' training complexes in Arizona sit within a 90-minute drive of each other. The easy commute between the fields means a spring training vacation made up of more games and less driving.

Tucson, an hour-and-a-half drive south of Phoenix, is home to two spring training clubs: the Arizona Diamondbacks and Colorado Rockies. Make Tucson a stop on your Cactus League visit, as two of Arizona's more interesting ballparks are located there. Tucson Electric Park, home to the Diamondbacks, possesses views of the nearby mountains that will command just as much

A billboard in the Tucson, Arizona area encourages fans to watch the Diamondbacks and Rockies play spring ball.

attention as what goes on at home plate. And if you're there at sunset, you'll see a postcard view that's unrivaled anywhere else where they're playing baseball in March. Expect to see a full house at Tucson Electric Park when the Diamondbacks are home. Phoenix fans of the team have little distance to travel to see their Diamondbacks play.

The Rockies play in Hi Corbett Field. Built in 1929, Hi Corbett, located in a public park, has all the charm you'd expect to find in a classic old ballpark. There's no telling how long either the Diamondbacks or the Rockies will stay in Tucson. The White Sox used to train there, but have since moved north to Phoenix. The Diamondbacks and the Rockies might do the same soon.

The Chicago Cubs play in Hohokam Stadium, with more than 13,000 seats, the largest of the Cactus League ballparks. Still, it's a good idea to purchase tickets to spring training Cubs games before you arrive in Arizona, since Mesa, where Hohokam Stadium is located, is filled each March with Cubs fans happy to escape the Windy City's blustery weather. Also expect big crowds at the Dodgers' spring training facility, Camelback Ranch in Glendale, Arizona, which they've shared with the

Plan your Cactus League visit early. Hotel rooms and car rentals get scarce come February, along with tickets to some team's games. Each Cactus League team puts spring training information on its main website right after the close of the previous season; you can find links to all the Cactus League team's websites at *www.mlb.com*. For hotel information, it's best to contact the Chamber of Commerce in the Arizona city where you're planning to start your Cactus League baseball excursion.

White Sox since leaving the legendary Dodgertown in Florida in 2008; the trip from L.A. to Glendale is a relatively short one, and a lot of Dodgers fans are happy to make it in March. The Indians and Reds, which share a complex in Goodyear on the outskirts of Phoenix, also have brand new facilities and plenty of Ohio fans now come to Arizona for a spring training vacation.

16 TAKE A KID TO HIS OR HER FIRST MAJOR LEAGUE BASEBALL GAME ✳✳✳

If you can recall your first visit to a major league ballpark, you'll understand why giving that same experience to a kid is a *Baseball Fan's Bucket List* entry. There is nothing quite like walking through a grandstand tunnel for the first time and coming upon the baseball diamond in all its major league majesty. Then there's the scoreboard, the people, the players, the music, the vendors, and the smell—the hot dogs, popcorn and outfield grass, all blended together in a perfect ballpark aroma. For a kid, it all adds up to something he or she won't ever forget.

Take note: bringing a kid to a minor league game, while admirable, doesn't count as a *Bucket List* check off. More and more, the minor league experience for kids is about seeing the mascot and waiting anxiously for between-inning gimmicks and giveaways. It's also about having fun in the playground just beyond the outfield, or whatever else the park might offer in the way of kids activities. Of course, there is nothing really wrong with any of this. Having and doing such things at minor league ballparks is a big reason for minor league baseball's booming success in the past twenty years. But all too often, it comes at the expense of experiencing the game itself. Admittedly, it's difficult for young kids to stay focused on a game that might last three-and-a-half hours. But with continued interaction with a parent or older sibling, the kid has a chance to cultivate interest in the game and gain a better understanding of it.

As a father whose memories of taking each one of his three kids to his or her very first major league game are some of my most precious, here are ten rules to follow to complete your *Bucket List* item. First, make the first game a day game, especially if the child is young, as in seven-or-under; he or she will stand a better chance of staying engaged and less a chance of growing tired or bored. Second, pick a game in which his or her favorite team is playing; if the child hasn't developed a favorite team yet, then take the kid to a game in which your favorite team is playing. Enthusiasm for the experience will be increased and make the game more memorable.

Third, get the best seats you can afford. Plopping a kid in the bleachers where you can hardly see home plate won't make it easy to sustain interest. Let the child see the action up close and hear the crack of the bat and watch foul balls land just a few rows away. Fourth, explain the game. Tell him or her why the manager is on the mound talking to the pitcher. Explain the meaning of a fielder's choice and an error and so forth. Remember, this is all about the child's experience. Do what it takes to make it a great one.

Fifth, keep the child stocked with food. Kids love to eat at ballgames; don't deny them that pleasure, even if, at home, the child eats organic lettuce and soy burgers. A hot dog is a must. Peanuts are also mandatory. By the time the game is over, you'll probably spring for ice cream and soda. Sixth, buy a souvenir. Whatever the kid wants: a cap, a miniature bat, a pennant. Remember, this is a very first baseball keepsake. Make it a memorable one. Seventh, stay at the ballpark at least until the seventh inning. However, if you're little guest tires of the game and wants to go home earlier than the seventh, then don't force the issue. Making him or her stay will ruin the good time. You want the child to want to come back to the ballpark. That won't happen if he or she regrets coming in the first place. Eighth, stretch during the seventh inning and sing "Take Me Out to the Ball Game." Teach him or her the words if you have to, but sing it—together.

Rules nine and ten apply to after the game. Number nine: talk about the game on the way home. Ask the kid's opinion of certain players and of certain plays. Get a baseball conversation going, not a lecture. And finally, number ten: the next morning, read the sports page together and explain the box score for the game. Check the standings. In the end, use the experience to make the child a fan of the game—just like you.

Go to *www.mlb.com* to find links to the site of the Major League Baseball team you want to take a child to see for his or her first big league ballgame. Contact the club for information on children's ticket prices and any special promotional day designed for children.

17 READ THE BOOK, *BALL FOUR* ✦✦

While many baseball historians and literary observers of the national pastime will call Roger Kahn's *The Boys of Summer* (see *Bucket List* item #23) the most eloquent and most beautifully written of all the baseball books published over the years, that same group will often cite former MLB pitcher Jim Bouton's memoir *Ball Four* as the most entertaining and most revealing work in the baseball library. Bouton's book, ripe with rare and funny insight into what really occurred behind-the-scenes in baseball back in the 60s, was a real eye-opener when it was published in 1970.

Not only did *Ball Four* forever change the nature of baseball book writing, it also shocked the baseball world and demanded that fans look at the game through a much different prism than they did before publication of the book. Much more than a baseball diary or "tell all" journal, *Ball Four* was like one of Bouton's artfully thrown knuckleballs—moving wildly and unpredictably toward the batter/reader, and in the end, plopping ever so neatly into the catcher's mitt for a nasty called strike.

The book was written during Bouton's 1969 season with MLB expansion team the Seattle Pilots and its farm system, and then his short stint with the Houston Astros before he retired from baseball in 1970. Bouton also wrote about his time as a member of the New York Yankees. In 1963 and '64, Bouton was a top-line starting pitcher for the Yankees, winning 18, then 21 games respectively. After that, arm trouble set in and in 1965, his record plummeted to 4-15. His career went into a tailspin that took him from being an elite starter for the MLB's top franchise to a struggling, knuckleball-throwing middle-reliever for the expansion Seattle Pilots in 1969.

The Pilots would last only one year in Seattle before the franchise moved to Milwaukee and became the Brewers. By that time, Bouton was ready to tell his story. If his arm didn't give out, he might have been run out of the league by fuming players, coaches, owners, and even Bowie Kuhn, the baseball commissioner at the time. Many believed that Bouton had broken an unwritten code: what goes on in the baseball locker room and beyond stays there.

There had only been a couple of credible baseball diary-type books before the publication of *Ball Four*, most notably a pair of pitcher Jim Brosnan's books, *The Long Season* (1959) and *Pennant Race* (1961). Other similarly styled baseball books were either dull and homogenized looks at baseball, with little to raise an eyebrow, or else penned by ghost writers who really didn't have enough information or freedom to tell an unabashedly honest story about the game.

In the best-selling *Ball Four*, Bouton held nothing back. He talked candidly about his and his fellow players' drug use (mostly amphetamines), drinking escapades, sex, and all-night parties. He let loose on former Yankees teammates Mickey Mantle, Whitey Ford, and Yogi Berra, blowing apart their Wheaties cereal box images and painting them as flawed baseball heroes. Much to Bouton's surprise, baseball fans devoured *Ball Four*. What they learned was that baseball players were human after all, that there were plenty of cracks in their off-field personalities. And that baseball didn't always act as "the national pastime," a game so pure and so American that it was beyond criticism and above controversy and vice.

As revealing as *Ball Four* was, it was also often hilarious. Bouton had a way with words, and his already left-of-center personality provided a viewpoint that illuminated the comic side of baseball and its players. Even though it was published in 1970, it remains a classic read, highly relevant in the age of steroid use and gargantuan egos. Although Bouton wrote a number of other books, and there have been a few editions of *Ball Four*, none of his other works have come close to replicating the commercial or critical acclaim bestowed on *Ball Four*. Bouton does, however, remain a baseball rebel. Most recently, Bouton has been involved in the revival of vintage, 19th century baseball, and creating waves at most every baseball turn.

> If you plan to purchase a copy of *Ball Four* for your library, buy it from Jim Bouton's website, *www.jimbouton.com*. Not only can you get it autographed, but you'll also be able to pick up copies of *I'm Glad You Didn't Take It Personally*, the 1971 sequel to *Ball Four*; *Strike Zone*, a 1994 novel co-written with Eliot Asinof about corruption in baseball; and *Foul Ball*, a 2003 book about Bouton's attempt to save old Wahconah Park in Pittsfield, Massachusetts. Bouton is a wonderful writer; all his books ought to be in your baseball library. Bouton enjoyed a brief acting career, landing one of the leads in Robert Altman's critically acclaimed *The Long Goodbye* (1973) and starring in a TV sitcom version of *Ball Four* that lasted just four episodes in 1976.

18 ATTEND A MAJOR LEAGUE BASEBALL FANTASY CAMP

Fantasy camp is the ultimate embrace of everything baseball: playing it, being a fan of it, chasing fly balls in a major league outfield, wearing a pro uniform, feeling like playing baseball is what you *do*. For approximately one week the distance between fan and player disappears. *You* become the player, the major league shortstop you've always dreamed of being, the hard-throwing hurler, the long-ball hitter. It's all there for you to savor. The memories you create will last a lifetime. The feeling of having experienced the life of a big leaguer, even if only for a fantasy week, is unequivocally real.

Most major league teams now feature fantasy camps. They usually occur just prior to spring training at a team's spring training complex. It's not cheap to attend a fantasy camp; expect to pay in the neighborhood of five thousand dollars for the privilege of experiencing it. But for true baseball fans, there can be no better way to get up close and personal with the national pastime—and do so in a big league way.

Former major league greats fill out the fantasy camp coaching staff. You're drafted onto a particular team after you've demonstrated your baseball skills. You don't have to be young to go to fantasy camp; in fact, the average age for most camps is over 40. Men and women can attend. You don't even have to be good, though if you've taken the time to throw and catch a bit and hit in the batting cages a few times before you arrive in camp, you'll have a more enjoyable week.

What you must do before you head to camp is get into some sort of shape. If you don't, you'll spend a good portion of the week on the trainer's table. Stretching is an absolute must. Hamstring pulls at any age will sideline even the best players. Unfortunately, they take a long time to heal, they hurt, and the older you get, the more you're apt to pull or even tear a "hammie." Three months before camp, start a disciplined leg stretching regimen. You'll quickly recognize those who didn't follow such advice; they're the ones sitting on the bench or limping around the dugout. They don't take the field much because they can't run.

When you arrive at fantasy camp, you're given an authentic major league uniform, the kind worn by the host team. You have access to major league instruction and locker room facilities. You play on major league fields, with out-

Cleveland Indians Fantasy Baseball Camp, 2008.

field grass like expensive carpet and infield dirt where you won't find even a piece of a pebble. Professional umpires call balls and strikes during the seven inning games, of which you'll probably play two per day. During the evening, you socialize with your teammates, seek out autographs from the baseball legends in camp, and listen to them tell stories about their playing days. Usually, one game you play will be against the former pro players in camp.

The best fantasy camp to attend is run by the Cleveland Indians organization. You don't have to be an Indians' fan to attend it, but it helps. Why the Indians? For starters, it's run by the ballclub and not a "for hire" outfit that specializes in sports camps. Secondly, the team goes out of its way to simulate a major league experience, without patronizing campers. Authenticity is its mantra, so that by the end of the week, you'll have fully experienced a week in the life of a major league ball player. Third, the amount of baseball goodies you get is unparalleled. Two full uniforms—a home and away, with your name sewn on the back of both. You get your own customized bat to hit with, plus another one with your signature engraved in it and full of autographs to hang on your wall at home. You also get a dugout jacket, hats, shirts, and socks to go with your uniform. Your own baseball card, complete with camp stats on the back, and your own DVD of your baseball accomplishments (and bloopers, too!) rounds out the mementos.

And if all that wasn't enough, the Indians feature a camp reunion in early summer in Cleveland when the Indians are playing away. That's when you get to play a game at Progressive Field as the culmination of your fantasy camp experience. Finally, a generous chunk of your fantasy camp fee goes to charity and is tax-deductible, a nice touch, considering the Indians could have pocketed the profits.

Fantasy baseball camp makes for a great birthday or anniversary gift. Father and sons often attend together, celebrating a special baseball bond. Don't be shy about hinting how much attending a baseball fantasy camp would mean to you. If you're a baseball fan and love *playing* the game as much as *watching* it, spending a week at a major league fantasy camp is a *Baseball Fan's Bucket List* classic.

> For more information on attending the Cleveland Indians fantasy camp, check the team's website at *www.clevelandindians.com.* You can get information about other team's fantasy camps on their official websites. For links to every team's website, go to *www.mlb.com.*

19 | WATCH THE MOVIE, *THE NATURAL* ⚾⚾⚾

The Natural might be the most complicated baseball movie ever made. Based on Bernard Malamud's novel by the same name, *The Natural* is as much a movie about the flaws and failings of the modern American male as it is about the mythic, romantic qualities of baseball. With Robert Redford starring as "the natural" (fictional slugger Roy Hobbs), it's easy to miss the movie's darker side. Redford's uncommon good looks and the movie's gorgeous cinematography (*The Natural* was nominated for four Academy Awards, including Best Cinematography) so sway the viewer's attention that you forget—or dismiss—how tragic a character Hobbs is throughout much of the movie.

Published in 1952, Malamud's first novel used baseball as the setting for a story about the rise, fall and redemption of Midwest baseball player Roy Hobbs, who had all the tools and confidence to fulfill his declared dream to become "the best there ever was." Hobbs also has a girl who loves him, Iris Gaines (Glenn Close), though he forgets her in a moment of misguided passion. On the train heading to his big league tryout with the Chicago Cubs, he meets another girl, shadowy and mysterious, and dangerously beautiful. He winds up in a hotel with her, where she shoots him, ending any hope he has of fulfilling his potential.

Set in the 1920s, the rest of the story deals with the redemption of Roy Hobbs, culminating with his pennant-winning home run for the fictional New

York Knights—one of the greatest sports moments Hollywood ever created. The final, full-circle scene of the movie shows Hobbs reunited with Gaines, playing catch with their son on the family farm—just like Hobbs did with his father at the movie's outset. The moral of the story: people make mistakes, even those as gifted as Hobbs, and fortunately life often gives us a second chance. Pay your penance, right yourself, and, like Hobbs, you, too can win in the end.

Malamud's novel was, in part, based on a real-life incident. In 1949, Eddie Waitkus, a first baseman for the Philadelphia Phillies, was shot by a lovesick 19-year-old female fan, whose violent obsession with the young All-Star nearly led to his death. Waitkus pulled through, but was never the same. Malamud, on the other hand, got just he needed—a real-life story on which to base his novel. The character Roy Hobbs also contained elements of Bob Feller's life as a boy growing up on an Iowa farm. Hobbs even had some traces of Shoeless Joe Jackson in him. A part of the film's plot deals with Hobbs and the temptation to throw a pennant game, a story not unlike what Jackson experienced with Chicago "Black Sox" in 1919.

Redford wasn't the first actor interested in the role of Roy Hobbs. Jon Voight, Michael Douglas and Nick Nolte all thought that playing Hobbs would be a rewarding experience. Redford, however, acted on his interest in Hobbs and *The Natural* by taking the script to director Barry Levinson, who agreed the make the film with him. Redford, a baseball fan who, as a kid, idolized Ted Williams, chose to wear number nine in the film as a tribute to his favorite ballplayer. Like Williams, it was Hobbs' goal to become the greatest hitter of all time.

Pop singer Randy Newman was brought onto the film project to write the movie's score. Not only did Newman's music get nominated for an Oscar and dramatically add to the emotional ebullience of *The Natural*, but since then pieces of it have been routinely used to create an aural portrait of baseball nostalgia. Newman's score ranks with the greatest baseball music ever composed.

The Natural didn't wow all the critics when it premiered in 1984. Some of them found the delicate balance between reality and fantasy, which ran throughout the film, not altogether successful. The importance of Hobbs' bat in the story was the most problematic. Named "Wonderboy," the bat was made from wood from a tree that was struck by lightning, giving it magical power. The film begs the question: was Hobbs' talent natural, or did it come from the bat? Today it's easy to equate "Wonderboy" with the alleged use of steroids used by a number of big league sluggers like Barry Bonds and Mark McGwire. However, no Congressional inquiry followed Hobbs' colossal, scoreboard-shattering home run at the conclusion of *The Natural*.

The way Levinson ended *The Natural* was far more uplifting than the way

Malamud ended his book, which was dark and not exactly triumphant. Read the book before you see the film. For your baseball movie library, buy the two-disc version of *The Natural*, which contains the director's cut that's 15 minutes longer than the original version of the film, along with a batch of extras.

> The film, *The Natural*, is available for rental or purchase from most movie stores and online merchants in VHS and DVD formats. The two-disc DVD version features the film's director's cut. The book, *The Natural*, remains in print in paperback. It can be purchased from most bookstores and online booksellers. An audio CD version of the book read by Christopher Hurt is available for check out from many public libraries.

20 VISIT RICKWOOD FIELD

Visiting Rickwood Field in Birmingham, Alabama allows you to take a big step back into baseball history. Built in 1910, before Wrigley Field (1914) and Fenway Park (1912), it is America's oldest surviving baseball park. It is a relic, an absolute treasure, and a *Bucket List* must—a place where baseball time has stood still and ghosts roam the outfield on hot summer nights.

During the Roaring Twenties, the Great Depression, and the war years, Rickwood Field was the home of the Birmingham Black Barons of the Negro Leagues and the Birmingham Barons of the famed Southern League, as well as a frequent stop for barnstorming teams. The names of the ballplayers, black and white, who played there sounds like a roll call from the National Baseball Hall of Fame. Babe Ruth, Ty Cobb, Christy Mathewson, Dizzy Dean, Grover Cleveland, Rogers Hornsby, Honus Wagner, Pie Traynor, Burleigh Grimes, Josh Gibson, Cool Papa Bell, Satchel Paige, Jackie Robinson, Willie Mays, and Hank Aaron—all played at Rickwood Field.

Located in a working class residential area just outside downtown Birmingham, Rickwood Field is still kept operational during the baseball season for use by area high school and college teams, and for special events. The Birmingham Black Barons, of course, are no more, while the Birmingham Barons moved to Hoover Metropolitan Stadium on the other side of the city in 1987. Once a year, however, the Barons, the Double-A minor league affiliate for the Atlanta Braves, don replica uniforms of the Black Barons and salute Rickwood Field's legacy by playing the Rickwood Classic. The game attracts locals and fans turning out to see the Rickwood Field grandstand full again. If you can, this is the time to visit Rickwood Field, since it is one of the very few times you'll still be able to see a professional baseball game played there.

Rickwood Field is only open to the public when games are scheduled. But a local group called The Friends of Rickwood Field occasionally conduct tours. However, if you visit Rickwood without previously joining a tour and a gate is open, walk in. Rickwood's rich legacy instantly comes alive, and you wonder what it must have been like to see a game there during the ballpark's heyday. Though some of its landmarks are actually replicas, many of which were paid for and put in by the Friends of Rickwood, the ballpark looks and feels the way it did in the late 1930s. Check out the manually operated scoreboard (a replica of the original, installed in the early 1990s) and the outfield fence that is home to faded advertisements and billboards. One sign along the first-base line reads: "No betting on games."

The field itself has elements inspired by Pittsburgh's Forbes Field and Philadelphia's Shibe Park, both long gone. A concrete outfield fence from 1928 is still standing, but it sits beyond the wooden one that currently encloses much of the park. Walk around and you can see where in 1948 Walt Dropo hit one of the longest home runs in Rickwood Field history; an "x" on the concrete wall marks where the ball landed, nearly 480 feet from home plate.

Four of the light towers are antiques; they were installed at Rickwood Field in 1936, thus enabling the ballpark to become one of the first in the South to feature night games. They stand tall above the grandstand and jut out, casting

Rickwood Field in Birmingham, Alabama—former home of the Birmingham Black Barons from the old negro leagues.

light onto the field. The press box is a gazebo (not original) on the roof behind home plate, and the vintage grandstand, though minus its original seats, looks like a Hollywood set for a classic baseball movie; a few have been made in Rickwood, including *Soul of the Game* and *Cobb*.

As glorious as Rickwood Field's tradition is, the sad fact is that the ballpark is in desperate need of renovation. Paint is peeling, concrete needs patching, wood is rotting, pigeons occupy every nook and cranny, and the outfield fence supports are falling down. There are plans to save Rickwood Field, but money, most likely in the millions, must be raised. By becoming a member of The Friends of Rickwood, you can help save a rare piece of baseball history.

> For information on special tours of Rickwood Field, or on how you can contribute to its renovation, visit the Friends of Rickwood website, *www.rickwood.com*. The site also provides information about the annual Rickwood Classic and other events scheduled for Rickwood Field.

21 | WATCH THE MOVIE, *FIELD OF DREAMS*

Field of Dreams created quite a stir when it was released in 1989. Based on the novel *Shoeless Joe* (see *Bucket List* item #122) by W.P. Kinsella, the movie starred Kevin Costner, fresh from his sterling performance a year before in another great baseball film, *Bull Durham*, in which he played a gritty minor league catcher trying to hold on to his fading baseball career. In *Field of Dreams*, Costner plays Ray Kinsella, a farmer who clears part of his Iowa cornfield to create a baseball diamond with the hope of attracting the great Chicago White Sox player, Shoeless Joe Jackson, and the rest of his teammates. The problem is that Jackson and his teammates are all dead.

Costner's Kinsella thinks he sees them, though they're ghosts, and he knows what he hears in his head: "If you build it, he will come." That line has since become one of the most memorable in baseball movie history. Walking through his cornfields, he decides to obey the command, despite the possibility of losing the farm. Full of great music, expert cinematography, a terrific screenplay by Director Phil Alden Robinson, and a fine cast, *Field of Dreams* captured the hearts and imagination of virtually everyone who saw the film. The fact that *Field of Dreams* was nominated for four Academy Awards, including Best Picture, and went on to gross more than $80 million offers proof enough of the film's impact.

Fans so embraced the movie's feel-good qualities that the Iowa farm where *Field of Dreams* was filmed has since become a universal baseball pilgrimage site (see *Bucket List* item #77). Located in the farming community of Dyersville, the *Field of Dreams* movie site gets visited by baseball fans from around the world each summer. It's for all those people who love the game, who believe that dreams do come true, and who seek a closer connection to a baseball movie that nostalgically floats them back to a time of American innocence and simplicity.

The *Field of Dreams* storyline is anything but simple. Kinsella (the author, not the character of the same name played by Costner), created an intricately woven plot that recalled one of the most infamous episodes of baseball history. In 1919, Shoeless Joe Jackson was forever banned from professional baseball due his alleged role in the Black Sox Scandal that saw eight members of the Chicago White Sox throw the 1919 World Series. Jackson was also one of the greatest players of his era, and Costner's Kinsella, an armchair baseball historian who appreciates Jackson's place in history, is anxious for Jackson to play on his baseball field.

Add to this, the story of a reclusive writer, Terrence Mann (played by James Earl Jones), and the need for Costner's character to reconcile with his late father. The fact that Jones' character was inspired by the reclusive real-life novelist, J. P. Salinger, author of *Catcher in the Rye* (a book, by the way, that had a character named Richard Kinsella), just makes things more intriguing.

Costner deals with baseball ghosts, a once famous writer who no longer wants any part of baseball, a ball field that requires tender care, a family that wonders if it'll be able to pay the mortgage, and a mission that he doesn't fully understand. He handles them all, and in the end, finds out that his real quest is one of self-discovery, culminating with the redemption of his relationship with his deceased father. The film ends on a perfectly pleasant note that left moviegoers believing that they had just seen a baseball classic, which they had.

> *Field of Dreams* is available for rental and purchase from most movie stores and online retailers in VHS and DVD formats. A special two-disc, 15th anniversary edition contains deleted scenes, commentary tracks and a pair of short films: "A Diamond in the Husk" about how the film's shooting location has become a baseball shrine, and "Passing Along the Pastime," a series of recollections from cast members and baseball legends about how the game played a role in their relationships with their fathers. In addition to Costner and Jones, the *Field of Dreams* cast includes Ray Liotta as Shoeless Joe Jackson, Amy Madigan as Annie Kinsella, and Burt Lancaster as "Moonlight" Graham, a former ballplayer who gave up the game to practice medicine.

The movie's tagline said it all: "All his life, Ray Kinsella was searching for his dreams. Then, one day, his dreams came looking for him." See the movie before reading *Shoeless Joe* and visiting the *Field of Dreams* movie site, both *Bucket List* items in their own right. Together, these three experiences will make you consider baseball's supernatural powers and wish that life's grand story was as rewarding as the one in *Field of Dreams*.

22 SEE THE DODGERS PLAY AT DODGER STADIUM ✫✫

Dodger Stadium, which opened in 1962, is the oldest Major League Baseball park after Wrigley Field and Fenway Park. The difference in age between Dodger Stadium and both Wrigley and Fenway—some fifty years—reminds us of how many early-20th century ballparks are now only memories. Classic ballparks like Ebbets, Forbes, and Crosley Fields, the Polo Grounds and the original Yankee Stadium live on only in books, documentaries, and museum exhibits. But Dodger Stadium still stands and continues to serve as one of the world's finest places to catch a baseball game.

Located in the sprawling city of Los Angeles, Dodger Stadium is surrounded by acres of parking lots—because taking a car is about the only way to get there. (As a city, Los Angeles still has a long way to go when it comes to effective mass transportation.) Sitting in Chavez Ravine, just north of downtown Los Angeles, Dodger Stadium claims no integration into the city's urban landscape, though when the smog isn't bad, the views of downtown L.A. from the south facing parking areas are worth a look.

Dodger Stadium doesn't have that grand exterior in the form of classic, red brick walls or adjacent streets where the aroma of sausage cooking and the hustle of souvenir buying fill the air. Once inside, you'll be surprised that Dodger Stadium has 56,000 seats, making it the largest of all major league parks. It feels smaller, mostly because the bleachers, with their trademark wavy sunroof, are compact, giving way to the San Gabriel Mountains in the background.

After the team's relocation from Brooklyn back in 1958, which set off an expansion of Major League Baseball beyond St. Louis and the Mississippi River, the Dodgers played at the cavernous Los Angeles Coliseum. Home at the time to the National Football League Los Angeles Rams and the University of Southern California Trojans, the Coliseum held nearly 100,000 fans. Playing baseball in such a vast setting seemed ludicrous. But L.A. baseball fans were all too happy to have a major league team to call their own, and they gladly cheered on the Dodgers at the Coliseum while patiently waiting for Dodger Stadium to be built on the other side of downtown Los Angeles.

The construction of Dodger Stadium was steeped in controversy, as the team displaced longtime residents of Chavez Ravine and razed their homes to make room for the ballpark, despite furious objections from locals and civic groups. Once it was finished, however, Dodger Stadium became the toast of Los Angeles, the most important symbol at the time that the City of Angels, which now had its own Major League Baseball club and a brand new ballpark for it to play in, had arrived.

Then, like now, palm trees sway in the breeze just outside the stadium. They complement all the other greenery around the ballpark that stands in stark contrast to the brown Elysian hills that border the ravine. All those plants, plus the sunshine and the mostly balmy temperatures, and the fact that there is hardly ever a rainout at Dodger Stadium, make it one of the most pleasant ballpark experiences in the major leagues.

One of the best things about Dodger Stadium, once you're inside, is the seat colors that scream early 60s—mild yellow and turquoise are dominant—and the park's welcome simplicity. Unlike so many other major league ballparks, especially the newest of them which sport gigantic scoreboards that practically overwhelm the action on the diamond and gaudy electronic billboards, Dodger Stadium is devoid of visual clutter. There is a video board in left field

> For more information about Dodger Stadium, including tours, directions, and game tickets, check the Los Angeles Dodgers' website at *www.dodgers.com*. Many L.A. fans arrive late for Dodgers games and leave early, due to traffic. If you want to take in a full nine innings, it's best to leave well ahead of game time and keep an ear to the radio for traffic reports. Also, don't plan anything for too soon after the game, so you can take your time getting out of the stadium area.

and a scoreboard in right. Neither is ostentatious. They include the essential baseball facts and bits of trivia that heighten your enjoyment of the game.

While seeing a game at Dodger Stadium for the first time, you'll want to try a Dodger Dog, one of the most famous of all ballpark tube steaks. Long and less meaty than the franks at many other major league parks, Dodger Dogs are grilled, not boiled. Eat one to say you've had one, but you'll be unlikely to say that Dodger Dogs match the tasty fare of Fenway or Citizens Bank Park in

Philadelphia, the two best ballparks to eat in the majors.

Despite five world championships, Hall of Famers like pitching greats Sandy Koufax and Don Drysdale, and the Brooklyn Dodger legacy that came with the team to California more than fifty years ago, there is little at Dodger Stadium that celebrates Dodger glory. There are plans, however, to build a Dodger Museum, plus adjoining shops and restaurants just beyond the Dodger Stadium outfield, along with a park-like "Green Necklace" that will be a meeting place for fans, and a large plaza. It'll all be called Dodgertown, the name of the old Dodgers' training facility in Florida that was considered one of the best spring training sites in baseball before closing in 2008. (The Dodgers now train in Arizona.)

23 | READ THE BOOK, *THE BOYS OF SUMMER* ✤✤✤✤

The Brooklyn Dodgers have been the source and inspiration of more books than any other team in Major League Baseball history, save the New York Yankees. And most fans of the baseball literary genre will agree that many Brooklyn Dodgers books stand on a shelf above even the best Yankees books in terms of quality.

Why did the Brooklyn Dodgers, the team that abandoned its city and fans in 1958 for Los Angeles (and inspired another New York-based National League team, the Giants, to do the same, thus forever changing the geography of baseball) become such a hot book topic? Old Brooklyn Dodger diehards will tell you it's because the city has never really quite gotten over the move, and so writing and reading about the team's time in Brooklyn serves as the best therapy available to them.

They'll also say, and it's probably true, that no team was so fully integrated into a city's soul and the daily fabric of its citizens' lives as the Brooklyn Dodgers. As wins and championships go, the Dodgers were hardly the toast of baseball, or even New York. The Yankees, those hated Bronx Bombers that played on the other side of the city, owned those accolades. But in the last decade of the team's time in Brooklyn, the Dodgers battled the Yankees, as well as their New York National League rivals, the Giants, winning one world championship in 1955, and helping create what many baseball fans and historians consider "the Golden Age of Baseball."

Add to all of that: one of the most beloved, most memorable ballparks, Ebbets Field; general manager, Branch Rickey, still recalled today as one of baseball's all-time best minds; Jackie Robinson, who, thanks to Rickey, broke baseball's color line in 1947, thus becoming the game's greatest hero; and finally, the Dodger fans, who often referred to their team as "da bums," but underneath, had such passion and love for their Dodgers that to live in Brooklyn in the 1940s and 50s and not be a rabid Dodgers fan was unthinkable, perhaps impossible.

Roger Kahn, a newspaper writer for *The New York Herald Tribune*, covered the Dodgers in the early 1950s, before moving on to the magazine world and the *Saturday Evening Post*. When the *Post* folded in 1969, Kahn embarked on a full-time career as a freelance writer. He authored two books, *The Passionate People* and *The Battle for Morningside Heights*, before penning his masterpiece and what many baseball literary authorities believe to be one of the best and most beautiful books ever written about the game, *The Boys of Summer*.

Published in 1972, *The Boys of Summer* not only rekindled memories of the Brooklyn Dodgers, it immediately elevated the standards of sports writing. This was a book that, for starters, took its title from a Dylan Thomas poem ("I see the boys of summer in their ruin..."). The book didn't long for the Dodgers' return in a way that made it seem sappy or sad, didn't lament their California success (the Los Angeles Dodgers promptly won two World Series on the West Coast after exiting Brooklyn). Instead, Kahn wrote *The Boys of Summer* as a celebration of a team and its relationship to its city and fans and as a memoir of his years covering the Dodgers.

Kahn grew up in Brooklyn and was a dedicated Dodger fan as a boy. He started with the *Herald Tribune* in 1948 as a copy boy. Four years later, he was covering sports for the newspaper, his favorite beat being the Dodgers. *The Boys of Summer* is as much about Kahn and life in Brooklyn in the 1950s and the game of baseball as it is about the Dodgers. Written with careful attention to details and artful descriptions of the times, *The Boys of Summer* reads like literature. His prose, fluid and precise, Kahn makes you feel for the Dodgers, even embrace them as your own. If you didn't live in Brooklyn in the 50s, you read the book and you wished you had.

In *The Boys of Summer* Kahn provided illuminating insight into the courage of Jackie Robinson and the day-to-day heroics of Duke Snider, Roy Campanella, Carl Erskine, Pee Wee Reese, Preacher Roe, Don Newcombe, and other Dodger greats from the 50s. But we also learn how baseball is the great metaphor for America and why Brooklyn was one of the very best places in the country to be a baseball fan.

Upon publication, *The Boys of Summer* went to the top of the *New York Times* bestseller list, ultimately selling over three million copies. A few years ago, *Sports Illustrated* named it the best baseball book ever written. Brooklyn Dodgers fan or not, *The Boys of Summer* is mandatory reading, a *Bucket List* "must."

The Boys of Summer remains in print and can be purchased from most bookstores and online booksellers, as well as checked out from many public libraries. A paperback edition was published by Harper Perennial Modern Classics in 2006. Kahn occasionally appears as a guest commentator on ESPN's *Who's #1* and *SportsCentury* shows. He also appears in the documentaries *Baseball's Golden Age* and *100 Years of the World Series*.

24 OWN A BASEBALL GLOVE

The bat, the ball, and the glove: baseball's blessed trinity of essential equipment. But bats break and balls grow old and unusable, or else become lost. However, the baseball glove, the tough piece of leather that molds to your hand over time and becomes an extension of the baseball "you," should remain in your possession for a long time and grow more meaningful as the years wear on.

If you've been fortunate to keep your first baseball glove, make a promise to yourself that you'll never get rid of it. It's the link between the lost years of youth and the reality of adulthood. Pick it up and you can't help but recall games, plays and friends. Work your fingers into your old glove, make a fist with the other hand, and punch the pocket, just like you did when you awaited the next hit, and suddenly the memories flow and summer comes roaring back even if it is the middle of winter.

The baseball glove is like no other piece of sporting equipment. Like a personal diary, the baseball glove is a keeper of dreams and a repository of your baseball life. About the only thing you should do with an old baseball glove if you don't keep it, is to pass it on to a son or daughter with careful instructions that it is to be safeguarded and respected and even loved, because, after all, what they hold in their hands is a little piece of you.

But what if you hadn't kept that old glove? Maybe it got lost or was sold in your mother's garage sale, or is hiding up in the attic or down in the basement, in a box, long neglected. How do you reconnect? You can do one of three things: refurbish your old glove and give it a new life; buy a brand new glove; or, buy an old, broken-in beauty that's fielded its share of line drives and grounders and give it a new home.

The glove, or mitt, came into the game after some players grew tired of the pain of catching a ball barehanded. The earliest use of hand protection occurred in 1870 when catcher Doug Allison of the Cincinnati Red Stockings, the first professional baseball club, began using "mittens" to protect his bruised hand. Rather than look upon such a piece of equipment as an innovation, other ballplayers and many fans ridiculed Allison for his lack of manliness.

Despite the negative reaction, the idea of using hand protection, especially for catchers and first basemen, eventually took hold. Wearing two mittens or gloves gave way to wearing just one. Then Albert Spalding, a pretty decent player who went on to become a sporting goods magnate in America, began featuring baseball mitts or gloves in his equipment catalogue. Gradually, infielders other than first basemen joined the baseball glove revolution as it became increasingly apparent that not only did such a leather piece protect your hand from the sting of a batted ball or throw, but by wearing one, you could also cut down on errors. Pitchers and outfielders were the last players to embrace the baseball glove, but a few years into the 20th century, virtually all players in the field were sporting gloves.

The first baseball gloves were just that—gloves, similar to the kind you'd wear to protect your hands from the cold. Early models had minimum padding, but when baseball players began throwing overhand, thus increasing the velocity of the ball and the sting of catching it, padding was added. Not surprisingly, specialty gloves soon surfaced. The catcher's mitt grew bigger and thicker than gloves used in the infield or outfield, while a first basemen's glove grew longer with a deeper pocket.

The modern baseball glove prototype was created in 1920 by pitcher Bill Doak and the Rawlings company. Not nearly as large as later gloves, the Doak glove featured a solid, padded pocket, a leather "hinge" that connected the thumb with the rest of the fingers, and had Doak's name on it. Despite Albert Spalding's pioneering efforts, many baseball historians consider Rawlings baseball gloves the best made in the first half of the 20th century.

After World War II, the name Wilson became associated with the top baseball gloves. In 1957, the company released the model A2000. Noah Liberman, in his fine book, *Glove Affairs: The Romance, History, and Tradition of the Baseball Glove* (Triumph, 2003), wrote, "With a bigger web, a better hinge, and a more ergonomic shape, the Wilson A2000 took the baseball world by storm in 1957, stealing the spotlight from longtime leader Rawlings."

The Wilson A2000 is still around today, and if you want a true American baseball glove classic, this one fits the bill. Since the 1950s, however, there have been a number of baseball glove innovations that have made the mitt even more efficient and streamlined. If you're still regularly playing baseball, such a piece of equipment might be in order. But for the true baseball fan, where history and authenticity count for more than anything else, owning a baseball glove classic is the way to go.

> You can purchase a Wilson A2000 at many sporting goods stores and online retailers. Classic gloves come up regularly for sale on *eBay* and at other auction sites. You can also scour garage sales and local second-hand stores, many of which offer classic gloves at bargain rates.

25 | SEE THE YANKEES PLAY THE RED SOX

The New York Yankees versus the Boston Red Sox ranks as the most heated rivalry in all of baseball. Whether it's a mid-season game at Fenway Park or Yankee Stadium, or a playoff game to decide the American League pennant, or the first game of spring training, every game counts to the players and the fans. When these two clubs go at it on the field, they define—and sometimes even redefine—the word "rivalry." You don't have to be a fan of either team to appreciate it. The competition on the field, the energy and passion in the stands, and the history and tradition of both teams makes a Yankees-Red Sox game an essential experience for every baseball fan.

How deep in this rivalry? Consider this: in 2008, during the construction of the new Yankee Stadium in the Bronx, workers found a David Ortiz Red Sox jersey buried in the ballpark's concrete foundation, apparently planted there by a Boston fan eager to curse the new stadium. The Yankees made certain the jersey was removed and the New York media had a field day with the incident, portraying it as a low-blow, clandestine attempt by the Red Sox Nation to jinx the Yankees' new, billion-dollar home. You could just imagine Boston fans smiling and saying, "Hey, all's fair in love and war and the Red Sox-Yankees rivalry."

The rivalry extends all the way back to 1903, the year the Boston Pilgrims (also known as the Americans and later the Red Sox) met the New York Highlanders (later the Yankees) for the first time, splitting a two-game series. Later that year, the Pilgrims defeated the Pittsburgh Pirates in the first World

Series. Boston went on to win four more World Series between 1912 and 1918, while the Yankees waited to claim their first.

Then, in early 1920, Boston sold the young Babe "The Bambino" Ruth to the Yankees for $125,000, plus a $300,000 loan—despite Ruth being one of the league's best pitchers and its top home run hitter. Not only did Ruth become the greatest and most popular player baseball has ever seen, he initiated the Yankees Dynasty, helping them earn their first World Series title in 1923, the year the club opened Yankee Stadium (also known as "The House That Ruth Built").

The Yankees went on to win three more World Series with Ruth and an astounding 27 through 2009, making them the most successful franchise in all of major North American sports. In the meantime, the Red Sox won...zero more world championships until 2004. Their 0-fer before then became attributed to "The Curse of the Bambino," and the mere mention of it to a longtime Red Sox fan can lead to a heated exchange. Boston almost ended "The Curse" in 1946, and then again in 1975, but came up just short. In 1978, Boston and New York played a one-game playoff for the American League East title at Fenway. The unlikeliest Yankee, shortstop Bucky Dent, hit a three-run homer to give the Yankees the lead and secure the team's trip to the World Series. In 1986, Boston fans watched a title roll through the legs of Red Sox first baseman Bill Buckner, allowing another New York team, the Mets, to stay alive and go on to win the World Series. Boston failed to reach another World Series for the rest of the century and was forced to watch the Yankees reestablish their dominance over the game as the Bronx Bombers claimed four World Series from 1996 to 2000. All Boston could do was wonder if the "Curse of the Bambino" would ever end.

It finally did in 2004 in remarkable, even incredible fashion. The Red Sox had their backs against the wall, down three games-to-none in the American League Championship Series against the Yankees. Then they staged one of the greatest comebacks in baseball history, winning the next four games in dramatic fashion to beat the Yankees and move to the World Series, where they swept the

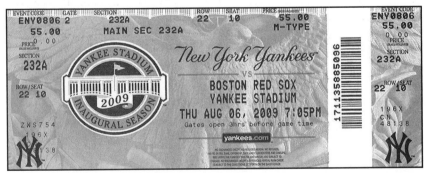

A ticket to baseball's greatest rivalry.

St. Louis Cardinals, finally ending "The Curse." It was a beautiful moment for baseball. It was a defining, historic, heroic moment for the Red Sox and their fans. Even the most fanatical Yankees fan had to tip his hat and begrudgingly admire what the Red Sox had done.

There is so much more history to the Yankees-Red Sox rivalry. The trades and free agent signings, the wars in the stands between fans, the differences between cities and ballparks, the media's never-ending thirst for Red Sox and Yankees controversy, the on-field brawls and special moments, the century-old history—it all adds up to a wonderful baseball tradition.

Catch a Yankee-Red Sox game wherever you can, but make your first choice Fenway Park, simply because the energy level feels more intense there. Tickets will be difficult to get, whether you see the Red Sox and Yankees battle in Boston or New York. You might have to rely on scalpers to get into the game, but you can't fully appreciate this beautiful baseball rivalry without experiencing it in person.

> For schedules and tickets to a Yankees-Red Sox game, check the teams' official websites, *www.yankees.mlb.com* and *www.redsox.mlb.com*. A number of fine books provide more information on the legendary rivalry. A good one is *The Yankees vs. Red Sox Reader*, edited by Mike Robbins (Carroll & Graf Publishers, 2005).

26 | GO TO THE COLLEGE WORLD SERIES

It isn't quite like basketball's March Madness or football's BCS (Bowl Championship Series), with all the fan frenzy, network television coverage, and millions of dollars in potential gain for the schools involved. But the Division I College World Series, held annually in Omaha, Nebraska, is nonetheless a great celebration of college baseball and an important "must" on your *Bucket List*. Each June since the College World Series moved to Omaha in 1950, students of the schools invited to play in the tournament and college baseball fans in general meet in the middle of the country to watch the best college baseball teams in America determine the NCAA baseball champion. It is amateur baseball at its very best.

Up to now, all of the games have been played in Johnny Rosenblatt Stadium, built in 1948. Originally called Omaha Municipal Stadium, the park

"The Road to Omaha" led the 2007 Oregon State baseball team to their second National Championship, celebrated here by the authors.

got a new name in 1964 in honor of former city mayor Johnny Rosenblatt, who helped bring the College World Series to Omaha just after World War II. Johnny Rosenblatt Stadium originally held 10,000, but its capacity has more than doubled to 23,000. At its entrance stands the baseball statue, "The Road to Omaha." Most fans don't leave the College World Series without snapping a picture in front of it.

If you want to see a College World Series game in Rosenblatt Stadium, you'd better do it fast. In 2011, the College World Series will begin play in a brand new baseball facility called TD Ameritrade Park Omaha, which will seat a minimum of 24,000 fans. Naming rights to the ballpark were purchased by this Omaha company for 20 years, and though it's a terrible name for a college ballpark, the $20 million earned from the naming rights went straight into the new ballpark's construction budget. The Triple-A Omaha Royals will also abandon Rosenblatt Stadium after 2010. So much for baseball tradition in Nebraska.

The College World Series isn't "a one-and-done" affair like March Madness, where if you lose a game, you go home. The double-elimination format makes it possible for fans of each team to watch more than one game and gives the College World Series an atmosphere where hope lingers. The fact that all the College World Series games take place in one city and at one ballpark concentrates the baseball excitement and energy and makes it easier to spend the week watching as many of the tournament games as possible.

The College World Series features Grand Opening ceremonies in the form of fireworks and the introduction of teams. Outside Rosenblatt in one of its parking lots, there is a fan fest that takes the shape of a Midwestern county fair. Aside from the booths selling World Series souvenirs, young fans can measure the speed of their fastball or work on their hitting, via hi-tech exhibits. You can get a close-up look at the NCAA College World Series trophy. Plenty of food concessions and sponsor tents and people walking around dressed in their team's colors complete the festive scene. It all makes for a baseball celebration that's a long way removed from the hustle and hassle of some larger sporting events, where the meaning of the game can get lost amid the excess of crass commercialism.

Eight teams play in the College World Series. Each of them is a Super Regional winner. The University of Southern California has won 12 baseball national championships—more than any other school. Led by their great coach, Rod Dedeaux (see *Bucket List* item #93), USC won five consecutive championships from 1970 through 1974. More recently, teams from Oregon State, Louisiana State, Texas, North Carolina, Rice, and Cal State Fullerton have had successful runs, but nothing like what USC accomplished more than thirty years ago. The closest any team has gotten to such a string of championships is the pair that Oregon State won in 2006 and 2007.

Getting tickets to the College World Series can be a challenge, but not if you're affiliated somehow with a team that's playing in it. Most universities set aside tickets for students and alumni. So get your World Series tickets through a school, if possible. If not, watch the College World Series website at *www.cwsomaha.com* for announcements of when tickets go on sale to the public. Finally, ticket agencies like *StubHub* also carry College World Series tickets, but at an inflated price.

27 WATCH THE MOVIE, *A LEAGUE OF THEIR OWN* ✹✹

Before *A League of Their Own*, one of the most original baseball movies ever made, hardly anyone knew American women played professional baseball at one time. Released in 1992, the film revived this little-known, largely-forgotten piece of baseball history: during World War II and the years just after it, the All-American Girls Professional Baseball League provided fans, mainly in the Midwest, the opportunity to follow baseball at a time when so many male professional players were serving in the armed forces.

The league was created in 1943 at the height of the war by Chicago Cubs owner Philip Wrigley and actually lasted until 1954. If ever there was a time when such a league could get going, it was the World War II years. Throughout the early- and mid-1940s, the country was all but depleted of young male athletes, who, thanks to the fighting on two fronts—Europe and Asia—were now throwing grenades instead of baseballs or footballs. At the same time, a new female image and sensibility surfaced in the U.S. Best represented by Rosie the Riveter, American women were suddenly empowered to do men's work. Carefully balancing feminine sexuality with a strong, toughened attitude that no man's work was too hard for a good woman, factories were suddenly staffed with females doing tasks that were always thought to be a man's job.

Baseball was no exception, as *A League of Their Own* so entertainingly celebrates. The superb cast featuring Tom Hanks as crusty manager Jimmy Dugan and Geena Davis as feisty catcher Dottie Hinson, plus wonderful performances by Madonna (Mae Mordabito), Lori Petty (Kit Keller, sister of Dottie) and Rosie O'Donnell (Doris Murphy) gave *A League of Their Own* quality up and down the lineup. Directed by Penny Marshall, the film was inspired by the story of the Rockford Peaches, a real team in the All-American Girls Professional Baseball League.

The movie's plot was simple: America can't let the war ruin its great tradition of baseball, so if young men weren't available to keep the game alive, then it was necessary to find young women who could. At first, the girls look pathetic in their skirts and cute hats as they try to field, throw, and hit. Manager Jimmy Dugan, a former big league player battling the bottle and other demons, is selected to lead the team based out of Rockford, Illinois. Not at all convinced that girls playing baseball is a good idea, he nonetheless takes the job, having little or no chance in managing men. One of the film's most famous lines, "There's no crying in baseball!" comes from Dugan as he tries to comfort his team when their emotions get the best of them.

The team is a colorful bunch. Madonna's character is city slick and sexy, while O'Donnell plays the role of a wisened bruiser. Davis's character comes from rural Oregon, but she is surprisingly sophisticated and a darn good ballplayer. In addition to working to hone their baseball skills, the players are forced to take an etiquette class. Such scenes provide *A League of Their Own* with some of its best humor. The girls learn to eat properly and apply make-up, something certain hayseed gals like Lori Petty's character, Kit, didn't know much about in the 1940s, a time when the difference between urban and rural America was like night and day.

Gradually, Dugan comes around as a manager. His team actually starts winning games and—more importantly—attracting fans. Catcher Hinson becomes the team's leader, and by the end of the film, the girls are in the championship series against the girls' team from Racine, Wisconsin.

A League of Their Own is more than just a great baseball film. It success inspired the National Baseball Hall of Fame and Museum to acknowledge the role women played in professional baseball with a now-permanent exhibit on the All-American Girls Professional Baseball League. It also accelerated the idea that young girls could—and should—play organized baseball, including Little League.

> *A League of Their Own* is available for rental or purchase from most video stores and online retailers in VHS and DVD. The "special edition" DVD lists runs 127 minutes with a PG rating. Brooke Shields accepted the role of Dottie Hinson before dropping out of the project. The scratches, scrapes and bruises the actresses sport in the film were the result of injuries received during training and filming, not effects concocted by makeup artists. The extras portraying the aged versions of the film's characters wandering around the Hall of Fame during the film's closing credits were actual players from the All American Girls Professional League. A year after *A League of Their Own* played in movie theaters, Marshall launched a short-lived television series by the same name, and after that, the Ladies Professional Baseball League was formed, but neither made it through a full season before folding.

28 SEE THE ORIOLES PLAY AT ORIOLE PARK AT CAMDEN YARDS ★★

When it opened in 1992, replacing old Memorial Stadium, Oriole Park at Camden Yards ushered in a new chapter in major league ballpark history. Built in downtown Baltimore on the site of a former railroad center called Camden Yards, Oriole Park was the first of the new ballparks to pay tribute to baseball and architectural tradition while offering a compelling, contemporary space to enjoy a Major League Baseball game.

Oriole Park was an immediate critical and commercial success. Located a short walk from Baltimore's Inner Harbor, another of the city's acclaimed projects meant to re-vitalize downtown, Oriole Park became known as simply "Camden Yards" to most locals and reporters. The ballpark quickly became the role model for how to create a modern ballpark with classic overtones that fans would love. It was designed by HOK (Hellmuth, Obata, and Kassabaum), a Kansas City sports architecture firm that believed that modern baseball stadiums didn't have to be like all the large, boring, multi-purpose bowls built in the 1970s.

HOK also realized that baseball fans, more than other American sports fans,

Orioles Park at Camden Yards has become a model ballpark for other newer parks across the country.

had a special relationship with ballparks. Maybe it was because baseball games were mostly played during the warm summer months and the ballpark became an urban oasis, a respite from the bustle of city life. Nostalgia played a role, too. Parents who took their kids to ballgames recalled memories of when their parents had taken them to their first games. The ballpark, like the game itself, had become an extension of its fans, a pleasant reminder of youth and innocence, fathers and grandfathers.

In short, HOK launched a ballpark revolution in America with Camden Yards. Though it has almost 49,000 seats, Camden Yards is nevertheless intimate and comfortable, and nearly every seat in the park is a good one. HOK used steel and brick, instead of the concrete preferred by stadium designers of the 1970s. The firm was aware of how fans in Boston and Chicago so loved Fenway Park and Wrigley Field. It studied the architectural nuances of old baseball landmarks (such as now-gone parks like Ebbets Field in Brooklyn, Crosley Field in Cincinnati, Forbes Field in Pittsburgh, and Shibe Park in Philadelphia) and incorporated as many design elements as it could into the creation of Camden Yards.

A main feature of Camden Yards was the integration of the old B&O Warehouse into the design of the ballpark. Rather than demolish the old brick building, HOK made it central to the look and feel of Camden Yards, suggesting that the ballpark had so integrated itself into the traditional architecture of the city that it was difficult to know where one began and the other ended. The warehouse wasn't used merely to complete the outfield design of Camden Yards; its old brick walls became the walls of the offices of the Baltimore Orioles, the team store, and more.

For information about tours of Camden Yards and tickets to Orioles games, check the team's website at www.orioles.com. You can also call (410) 685-9800. Before you visit the stadium, try to read any of the books about Camden Yards, including: Peter Richmond's *Ballpark: Camden Yards and the Building of an American Dream* (Fireside, 2007) or Thom Loverro's *Home of the Game: The Story of Camden Yards* (Taylor Trade Publishing, 1999); both available from most bookstores and online retailers. *From 33rd Street to Camden Yards* (McGraw-Hill, 2002) by John Eisenberg can be purchased from many used bookstores and online booksellers.

Orioles' fans and baseball fans from around America embraced Camden Yards the way they did Wrigley and Fenway. Attendance at Orioles games soared, making tickets to games hard to come by. It didn't hurt that Cal Ripken, Jr. was in the process of breaking Lou Gehrig's record for consecutive games played, his progress noted daily at Camden Yards. In the 1990s, Camden Yards became the toast of baseball, and major league cities around the country put plans in action to replace their old stadiums with new "retro" ballparks inspired by what Baltimore had erected.

Media and fan attention to Camden Yards subsided a bit with the debut of similar retro parks like Progressive Field (formerly Jacobs Field) in Cleveland (see *Bucket List* item #41), Coors Field in Denver (see *Bucket List* item #63), and Rangers Ballpark in Arlington (see *Bucket List* item #92). Still, Camden Yards remains a "must visit" ballpark. If you haven't been to any of the other Camden Yards-inspired parks, then visit it first.

29 | READ THE BOOK, *MONEYBALL* ☆

Few baseball books, if any, have been as influential or as enlightening as Michael Lewis's *Moneyball: The Art of Winning An Unfair Game*. Published in 2003, the book immediately became a baseball bestseller and initiated conversations throughout the baseball world about its main premise: that the 20th-century ways of evaluating ballplayers had become obsolete.

On-base percentage, a previously little known and rarely highlighted baseball statistic, is the unlikely focal point of *Moneyball*. But it took one clever general manager, the Oakland A's Billy Beane, to bring the statistic out of the shadows of more sexy stats, like batting averages and home runs. His story, and how he created a winning baseball organization playing "small ball," with relatively low-cost, high on-base percentage players filling out the Oakland A's roster, made *Moneyball* an instant classic and one of the great books written about America's pastime.

Having an intriguing story, with a fresh twist on something as American as baseball, is a good recipe for a book. The other necessary ingredient is a good writer, and Michael Lewis is certainly that. Lewis used his knack for creating a compelling narrative and his ability to generate enthusiasm for the less glamorous aspects of the game into a book that is hard to put down. "I wrote this book because I fell in love with a story," Lewis recollected in *Moneyball*'s preface. Most readers of *Moneyball* did the same.

Not many books have been written about the Oakland A's, a small-market team that plays in the Oakland Coliseum, arguably the worst ballpark in Major League Baseball. Oakland remains a predominantly football town where the Raiders rule. Yet, Lewis ignored all that to focus on Beane, who, despite the disadvantage of dealing with one of the smallest personnel budgets in either the American or National league, still managed to regularly field competitive teams with shots to go all the way to the World Series.

Beane's secret lay in his formula for building a roster: sign players who somehow, some way, get on base. On the surface, Beane's strategy was simple: getting on base meant you had a better chance of scoring than if you were on the bench. Not exactly an earth-shattering revelation. However, most of the other major league clubs paid far more attention to batting average than on-base percentage.

Beane's strategy might have seemed simple, but complex mathematical analyses lay underneath the premise. His most important tool wasn't a radar gun or a veteran scout, but rather a computer. Beane became a baseball numbers junkie, loading reams of baseball data onto his laptop in order to figure out what players to draft, to sign as free agents, or to trade for. Along the way, Beane revolutionized baseball strategy, which is why *Moneyball* became a book that every baseball fan must read if he or she wants to better understand today's game. Beane rose to the stature of baseball guru after *Moneyball*, and other teams hired general managers with the same baseball philosophy as his in order to emulate his success.

To be fair, Beane wasn't the first baseball man to celebrate numbers in a new way. That honor goes to Henry Chadwick (see *Bucket List* item #70), one of the fathers of baseball who, back in the mid-1800s invented the box score and made fans of the game more aware of the stats behind it. More recently, people like Bill James (see *Bucket List* item #83), whose baseball abstracts paved the way for Beane's brand of thinking, were using baseball numbers in novel ways. But James didn't run a baseball club; instead he was a writer, historian and numbers geek with a serious passion for baseball. Right after the success of *Moneyball*, James became part of the Boston Red Sox front office under the reins of Theo Epstein, a disciple of Beane's who had been hired as Boston's new general manager. How much credit for the Red Sox finally shedding the "Curse of the Bambino" and winning the World Series in 2005 should go to James and his numbers is debatable. But he was part of the winning team.

Today, most Major League Baseball general managers approach their jobs

> *Moneyball: The Art of Winning An Unfair Game* is available from most bookstores and online booksellers. The 2004 paperback edition was published by W.W. Norton. The book is also available in audio format. Lewis has written numerous other books, including *The Blind Side: Evolution of a Game* about football, and *Liar's Poker* about Wall Street.

differently than in the pre-*Moneyball* days. Human assessment, namely scouting reports, now exists side-by-side with numerical analysis and other data compiled and stored in computers. In the end, critical decisions will be made using both forms of analysis, but clearly there is a new way to identify talent and build baseball clubs. Billy Beane and *Moneyball* led the way to this 21st century baseball revolution.

 ## 30 SEE THE PIRATES PLAY AT PNC PARK

The Pittsburgh Pirates might be one of the least formidable teams in big league history. The small-market National League club has suffered through 17 straight losing seasons as of 2009. Not only is such futility a major league record, the Pirates' perennial woes have tried even the team's most patient and faithful fans. But Pittsburgh fans enjoy some significant consolation: their team plays in one of the very best ballparks in the majors. PNC Park in downtown Pittsburgh ranks number one among ballparks built in the post-Camden Yards era.

Why PNC Park? You'll know the minute you see it. No major league ballpark integrates itself so seamlessly into the look and feel and architecture of its city. Built in 2001 amidst a cityscape full of buildings, some of them over a century old, PNC Park is a masterpiece in urban ballpark design. Situated on the north bank of the Allegheny River, PNC Park offers great views of the Pittsburgh skyline if you sit behind home plate or along the first- or third-base lines. It's as if the buildings and the Clemente Bridge (named after Pirates star Roberto Clemente) in the background are actually a part of the ballpark. The scenery becomes particularly impressive at dusk during the summer when the sun falls in the western sky and its reflection lights up the city's buildings. HOK (Hellmuth, Obata and Kassabaum—the Kansas City stadium design firm that developed PNC Park, Oriole Park at Camden Yards, and many other recent ballparks) recognized the beauty of the Pittsburgh skyline and incorporated it into the outfield sightline, helping make PNC Park perhaps the firm's finest achievement in baseball architecture.

Taking a cue from Fenway and Wrigley, HOK also made certain that the fan experience at PNC Park extended beyond the ballpark. The restaurants and shops around the park are hopping before game time and infuse the area with an energy that fine ballparks like Dodger Stadium and Turner Field in Atlanta lack. Also, the city closes Clemente Bridge to auto traffic on game days, mak-

PNC Park in Pittsburgh might be a small park, but it is never dull.

ing it a pedestrian walkway. That means you can park in a downtown garage across the Allegheny River and walk across Clemente Bridge, admiring the views of PNC Park as you go. It only takes minutes once you park your car in a local garage to walk across the bridge and get to an entrance to the park.

Another reason to love PNC Park is its size. Holding a shade over 38,000 fans, PNC Park is the very definition of an intimate Major League Baseball experience. The only other major league ballpark with less capacity is Fenway Park in Boston and not by much. Every seat at PNC Park is a good one because you can't get too high in the grandstand or too far back in the infield seat section not to feel close to the action on the field. Remarkably, the highest seat at PNC Park is just 88 feet from the field—less than the distance between home plate and first base. Add to this the fact that, unlike Fenway, tickets to Pirates games are affordable and readily available. If you have young kids, no major league park offers the economy and accessibility of PNC Park. It's a great place to take your kids on their first ballpark road trip.

Yet another reason to love PNC Park is its substantial tribute to the Negro Leagues and Pittsburgh's two great Negro Leagues teams—the Pittsburgh Crawfords and the Homestead Grays. PNC Park has life-size bronze statues of former Negro League greats Satchel Paige, Cool Papa Bell, Josh Gibson, Oscar Charleston, Judy Johnson, Buck Leonard, and Smokey Joe Williams. Interactive kiosks next to each statue show a video summarizing the career of each legend. There's also a 25-seat mini-theater that presents a short film narrated by Hall of Famer Joe Morgan celebrating the Negro Leagues, and a "chatting wall" where visitors can hear testimonies from Negro Leagues players as well as fans.

PNC Park features some classic architectural elements—the home plate entrance, for instance, recalls the entrance to old ballparks like Fenway, Wrigley and Forbes Field, where the Pirates once played. The masonry archways add another nice touch. But what you won't find at PNC Park are the cookie-cutter nods to yesteryear. PNC Park references the great ballparks of the golden age of baseball without imitating them. Made of limestone with exposed steel trusses, PNC Park rates as one of the most handsome stadiums in the majors. Intimate, instead of imposing or cathedral-like, PNC Park lets you know right away that baseball is played there. And unlike so many contemporary ballparks, PNC forgoes the corporate sponsorship eyesores and visual gimmicks.

The only thing PNC Park lacks at the moment is a winning ball club. It's been a long, long time since the team dominated the NL East in the 1970s with the "Lumber Company," one of baseball history's most feared hitting lineups. That the Pittsburgh Pirates are a small-market team means their front office will have to be spot on when it comes to player development and trades while implementing a clear, strategic vision for building a new winning tradition. Maybe some day. In the meantime, Pittsburgh boasts some of the most loyal fans in baseball and one of its finest stadiums, PNC Park.

> For information on Pirates tickets and tours of PNC Park, check the team's website at *www.pirateball.com.*

31 | WATCH THE DOCUMENTARY, *VIVA BASEBALL* ✦✦

Despite all the baseball books and films out there, you'll have to look long and hard to find a good one about the Latin contribution to the game. Latin ballplayers from the Dominican Republic, Cuba, Venezuela, and other countries in the Caribbean and Central and South America populate major league rosters in increasing numbers. Nearly one quarter of all players in the major leagues are of Latin descent, and some of the game's biggest stars are Latinos. Yet baseball authors and filmmakers have only rarely tackled the role of Latin players in their work.

Dan Klores' documentary film, *Viva Baseball*, captures the remarkable story of Latin baseball players. Like black players before them, early Latin players endured racism, cultural differences, and economic oppression—along with the biggest barrier of all, language—to make their mark in the major leagues. Released in 2005 to glowing reviews, *Viva Baseball* offers interviews with a number of Latin players, both past and present, including Rod Carew, Fernando Valenzuela, Luis Tiant, Orlando Cepeda, Juan Marichal, Alex Rodriquez, Pedro Martinez, and Carlos Beltran.

One striking part of the Latino baseball story told in *Viva Baseball* pertains to the poverty that engulfed so many Latin players as youngsters. Whether growing up on an island in the Caribbean and playing baseball with a stick masquerading as a bat and rolled up cloths held together by rubber bands taking the form of a ball, or in a rural village in Venezuela, where baseball diamonds were cut from sugar cane fields, most non-U.S. Latin major league players overcame serious economic hardships, in addition to the other challenges, to play professional baseball. The individual stories in *Viva Baseball* are illuminating, but the tales of the common, formidable obstacles these individuals had to overcome will enlighten the minds of many a North American reader and increase their appreciation of the Latin players they watch play.

Klores traces the popularity of baseball in Spanish-speaking countries in the Western Hemisphere back to Cuba in the mid-19th century and then charts the region's growing obsession with the game as fan bases swelled, leagues formed, and stars emerged. Despite the baseball craze in Latin America, it took Spanish-speaking ballplayers even longer than American black players to get signed by major league teams. The first true Latin player of note is Orestes "Minnie" Minoso, who made his MLB debut with the Cleveland Indians in 1949. Although Minoso went on to be named to seven All-Star teams, win three Gold Gloves and become the only man to play professional baseball in five different decades, his role as a trailblazer for Latin players receives a tiny fraction of the attention paid to Jackie Robinson, who broke through the color barrier for blacks when he debuted in the major leagues two years before Minoso. Interviews with Minoso, Vic Power (another early Latin player), and such Latin players who became big league stars in the 1960s as Orlando Cepeda and Juan Marichal, reveal that Latin players' integration into Major League Baseball was just as difficult and dangerous—and not nearly as glorified—as that of American black players.

Not surprisingly, *Viva Baseball* spends a considerable amount of time recalling the story of Roberto Clemente, who is not only viewed as one of the greatest Latin players of all time, but as a man of great courage and a humanitarian hero. Clemente has come the closest of any early Latin player to achieving the legendary status of Jackie Robinson. Clemente died in a plane crash while delivering emergency supplies to Nicaragua after a hurricane had devastated the country in 1972—the same year he had made his 12th All-Star team, won his 12th Gold Glove in right field and surpassed 3,000 hits. It was one of the worst tragedies baseball has endured and a major blow to Latin baseball fans everywhere.

After viewing *Viva Baseball*, it is hard not to come away wondering why there aren't more exemplary films made about Latin players and the vital role they play in professional baseball. *Sugar* (see *Bucket List* item #114), a feature film released in 2009, is an excellent movie and a good follow-up to *Viva Baseball*. And there are more base-ball books being published with Latin themes. Still, there is plenty more to explore when it comes to Latin baseball history and cul-ture. Hopefully, the wait for more excellent books and films about Latin baseball players won't be a long one.

> The documentary film *Viva Baseball* is nar-rated by Latino pop singer Marc Anthony and can be purchased or rented from many video stores and online movie merchants. Produced in 2005 by SpikeTV, the film also occasionally reruns on television.

32 WATCH THE MOVIE, *EIGHT MEN OUT*

"Say it ain't so, Joe, say it ain't so." That's what a young Chicago fan begs infa-mous White Sox outfielder Shoeless Joe Jackson, played by D.B. Sweeney in the John Sayles' movie *Eight Men Out*. The kid is referring to how a group of White Sox players threw the 1919 World Series against Cincinnati, not only breaking the hearts of White Sox fans, both young and old, but also tarnishing the tra-dition of baseball and jeopardizing its very existence as a legitimate professional sport. As a wallop to the jaw, only the recent steroids scandal rivals what the 1919 White Sox (now known to history as the "Black Sox") did to baseball. Shoeless Joe, the premier player on the Sox and maybe in all of baseball at the time, could not give the kid in the movie a straight answer because Jackson was either part of the fix, or at least knew that many of his teammates had indeed thrown the Series.

Making a film about baseball's dark side was no easy task for director John Sayles, who also wrote the script, yet he triumphantly pulled it off after spending over a decade trying to get financial backing for the film. He based his script on Eliot Asinof's 1963 book by the same name, a critically acclaimed account of the 1919 World Series. There has always been debate, among baseball fans and historians, about how many of the White Sox were actually involved in the scandal and what role, if any, Jackson played in it. Though the eight charged Sox players were acquitted by a jury, then–Commissioner of Baseball Judge Kenesaw Mountain Landis banned them forever from Major League Baseball, ending the careers of Jackson and the others and permanently relegating them to the gutter of baseball history.

Rather than producing a simple tale of greed, Sayles, like Asinof in his book, makes the scandal more complex by shifting a significant portion of the blame onto White Sox owner Charles Comiskey, a notorious skinflint who really did give his players flat champagne to celebrate their 1917 World Series triumph. At times in the film, the players appear to be the victims rather than the culprits, mere pawns of cheap owners on one side and the gangsters and hoods that stood to make a killing off the fix on the other. Most viewers will actually sympathize with the underpaid players, despite their guilt. We see them as flawed humans, not baseball gods-turned-devils. As one reviewer of Asinof's book wrote, "In many ways, the scandal, as the book shows, was an indictment of American mores." Perhaps. But then, so isn't the steroid scandal? And does that make the guilty any less guilty? Should we sympathize with A-Rod? Roger Clemens? Barry Bonds?

Unlike virtually every other baseball film, there are no heroes in *Eight Men Out* and there isn't a happy ending. The closest anyone comes to such a role is infielder George "Buck" Weaver, played by John Cusack. The movie contends that Weaver wasn't involved in the conspiracy to intentionally lose the series, though he was charged. Tirelessly he tried to clear his name, pointing to, among other

Originally released in 1988 by MGM, *Eight Men Out* is now available from most movie retailers for rental or purchase in VHS and a special 20th anniversary DVD format. The film runs 119 minutes and 48 seconds, just 12 seconds under the two hour-limit imposed by MGM on Director John Sayles, who had to constantly urge his actors to talk faster during filming. Shot in various locations in Ohio, Indiana, Kentucky and Illinois, *Eight Men Out* staged its baseball scenes in Indianapolis' Bush Stadium, which has since been torn down and converted to a racetrack. Several prominent non-actors show up in cameo roles: author Studs Terkel plays Chicago sportswriter Hugh Fullerton and Sayles himself plays famed humorist and baseball writer Ring Lardner (see *Bucket List* item #94), while former White Sox outfielder Ken Berry plays a heckler.

things, his .321 World Series batting average. At the end of the film, Weaver, years later, is watching a baseball game in New Jersey when someone wonders out loud if the hitter who just smacked the ball wasn't Shoeless Joe Jackson playing under an assumed name. Weaver hesitates, then remarks, that no, it wasn't Jackson, though he knew it was. It's a sad ending to a sad story and the saddest episode in baseball history.

Some baseball fans, along with a number of critics, consider *Eight Men Out* to be the best baseball film of all time. There are no flights of fantasy or overt nostalgia as in *The Natural* or *Field of Dreams*. It isn't a film where what happens in bed rivals what goes on at the ballpark, as in *Bull Durham*. It isn't a baseball tearjerker like *The Rookie* or *The Pride of the Yankees*. Instead, *Eight Men Out* is about a piece of baseball history that for years was better left alone. That Sayles took up the challenge and managed to tell the story in such a compelling way make this a "must-see" film and at least a contender for top baseball film honors.

33 | SEE THE CARDINALS PLAY THE CUBS

The rivalry between the Chicago Cubs and the St. Louis Cardinals has, over the years, been a National League version of the American League's Red Sox-Yankees rivalry. Like the Red Sox in much of the 20th century, the Cubs have been a study in baseball frustration, a team beloved by its fans and its city and yet, year after year, they came up short in their quest for a World Series title. While their rival, the St. Louis Cardinals, practically made it a habit of winning pennants in the post-war years, so much so that the team is often referred to as the National League version of the Yankees.

The Red Sox-Yankees rivalry gets a lion's share of media attention every baseball season because New York is the media capital of the world and, of late, both teams have been very good, furiously battling for the American League pennant, while their fans, equally frenetic and often fight-happy, kept the competition going in the stands. But baseball fans shouldn't let the Red Sox-Yankees rivalry overshadow the one between the Cubs and Cardinals, even if the latter is a bit more civil and the stakes aren't usually as high.

The Cubs-Cards rivalry has come to be known as "The I-55 Series" in honor of the 300-mile stretch of highway between the two cities. But the feud between the franchises kicked off back before they were even known as the

Cubs and Cardinals. In 1885, the National League pennant-winning Chicago White Stockings (who would change their name to the "Cubs" in 1903) and American Association champs the St. Louis Browns (who would change their name to the "Perfectos" in 1899, then the "Cardinals" the following year) met in an early forerunner of the World Series known as "The Championship of the United States" or "World Championship Series." A controversial—and even at times bizarre—affair, the seven-game series took place in four separate locations. It featured a game called on account of darkness and another forfeited when the Chicago manager ordered his players off the field to protest a call. And though the series ended in a 3-3-1 draw, St. Louis claimed they had won the title.

Since then, the two teams have faced each other well over two thousand times, and while the Cubs hold a slim lead in wins, the Cards hold a significant lead in world championships. Currently, the Cardinals have won ten, while the Cubs have claimed only two, the last coming over a century ago. With Boston's "Curse of the Bambino" finally put to rest, the Cubs now stand as baseball's greatest sufferers of "wait 'til next year" malady.

Why a rivalry between the Cubs and the Cardinals? Close proximity for starters. St. Louis sits on the western edge of the Mississippi River in Missouri, while Illinois sits on the eastern side. Traditionally, St. Louis has claimed a lot of Illinois fans, especially during its championship seasons. That infuriated Cubs fans in Illinois. They believed that if you lived in Illinois and were a National League baseball fan, you should be rooting for the Cubs. Sometimes families would split their loyalties—some members would root for the Cubs, while the others sided with the Cardinals. This has only intensified the rivalry. That St. Louis and Chicago are the two best baseball towns in America has added even more fuel to the rivalry fire.

The greatest moment in the Cubs-Cards rivalry occurred not when the two teams were locked in a close battle for the National League pennant, but when two players—the Cards' Mark McGwire and the Cubs' Sammy Sosa—were locked in an epic battle for the major league single-season home run record in 1998. It didn't hurt that the two teams met in September that year with McGwire and Sosa both chasing Roger Maris' record of 61 home runs, a mark set all the way back in 1961 (see *Bucket List* item #54). The Cubs and Cards played two games in St. Louis, a short series. In game one, McGwire smacked home run number 61, tying the Maris mark, and in game two, he hit number 62, breaking the record. That he did it against the Cubs made it even sweeter for Cards fans. However, in a classic display of baseball sportsmanship, Cubs outfielder Sammy Sosa left the dugout after McGwire hit his record-breaking shot and congratulated him at home plate with the rest of the Cardinals' players and coaches.

The McGwire-Sosa competition perfectly encapsulated the Cubs-Cards rivalry. Intense, on occasion. Passionate, almost always. But it's rarely been a no-holds-barred grudge match, the way the Red Sox-Yankees rivalry has turned out. Cards fans don't have to fear for their lives when they wear their colors to Wrigley Field. The same is true for Cubs fans when they sit in Busch Stadium in St. Louis. Getting tickets to a Cubs-Cards game isn't impossible, either. But you'll have to act early and secure your tickets when they first go on sale in order to avoid paying scalper's prices on game day. Where you see the Cubs play the Cards is your choice: Wrigley Field or Busch Stadium. Either site will treat you to a great *Baseball Fan's Bucket List* experience.

> For more information on tickets for Cubs-Cards games, check the teams' websites, *www.cubs.mlb.com* and *www.cardinals.mlb.com*. For more information on the rivalry, check out *The 1-55 Series: Cubs vs. Cardinals* (Sports Publishing LLC, 1999) by George Castle and Jim Rygelski.

34 TOUR THE LOUISVILLE SLUGGER MUSEUM AND FACTORY ✻✻✻

You can't miss the Louisville Slugger Museum and Factory in downtown Louisville, Kentucky. In front of it stands a 120-foot replica of Babe Ruth's model R43, affectionately known as "Big Bat." Not only does the giant bat serve as an ideal site for a photo for the more than 200,000 baseball fans who visit the museum each year, it also acts as a tribute to John A. "Bud" Hillerich, who made the company's first baseball bat in 1884. In addition to the giant bat, the site holds the family-owned factory where more than 1.8 million baseball bats are made annually. You can tour the factory and check out the theater and film that celebrate the grand legacy of the game, and a museum that depicts the history of the baseball bat and the Louisville Slugger's role in its evolution.

Exactly how important was that role? Consider this: over 80% of the players inducted into the National Baseball Hall of Fame in Cooperstown, at one time or another during their careers, used bats made by Hillerich & Bradsby Co., the manufacturers of the Louisville Slugger. Today, despite the widespread use of aluminum bats in amateur baseball and the establishment of numerous other wooden baseball bat companies, Hillerich & Bradsby Co. remains the biggest and some say best bat maker in the world. Today, over 60% of Major League Baseball players choose the company's Louisville Slugger over competing brands.

The site's museum and the factory's 30-minute tour will fill you in on the rest of the story of the Louisville Slugger and the part it's played in baseball history. You'll learn how a bat begins its life as a rough piece of either ash or maple; how the wood has to be at least eighty years old and from a forest in New York or Pennsylvania; and witness the process that turns that wood into an object that holds the very essence of baseball in its handsome form.

A few things worth noting: far more ash bats than maple bats are "turned," as they say, because maple breaks easier than ash and is more expensive. More and more Major League Baseball players are choosing maple over ash, however, because it's a harder wood, and therefore, capable of more "pop." On the tour you'll also learn that the strongest part of any bat is where the wood's grains are closest, namely in the fat of the bat; that most contemporary baseball bats are either 31 or 32 ounces, lighter than the bats of yesteryear because a lighter bat leads to faster bat speed, a key component in a hitter's success at the plate; and that it takes approximately 30 seconds to make a "recreational" bat, while nearly double the time, 50 seconds, to turn a pro bat.

On the tour you'll see lathes in action, where information on approximately one thousand bat models are stored, including height and weight of the bat, wood type, bat knobs, handles, barrels, wood grain, and color. Look closely and you'll see bats being made for particular major league players, who, on average, go through more than one hundred bats per season at a cost of anywhere from $50 to $100 per bat. While special attention is given to the creation of major leaguers' bats, those that players swing in the minor leagues and below are mass-produced. Occasionally, players will stop by the Louisville Slugger factory to discuss customizing their bats, but most of the time, such talk occurs during spring training, where Louisville Slugger bat makers are on hand to work with hitters.

At the end of the tour, visitors receive a complimentary mini-bat as a memento of their factory experience. The tour ends where the museum begins, leading you into displays of photos, equipment, autographs, artifacts, and interactive materials. You'll see Babe Ruth's bat, complete with notches for each home run he hit with it, and the one used by Joe DiMaggio in 1941 during his 56-game hitting streak. One exhibit deals with the history of the baseball bat. Another celebrates the great hitters, including Ruth, Ty Cobb, Joe DiMaggio, and Ted Williams, along with more contemporary hitters such at Ken Griffey, Jr. You'll also be able to hold bats used by Mickey Mantle, Jim Thome, David Ortiz, and other great hitters.

From the museum, head to the theater that shows the film, *The Heart of the*

Game, a look at the glories of baseball and its role in American history as the national pastime. You can then stop by the batting cages to take a few cuts, followed by a visit to the gift shop to order your own personalized Louisville Slugger. Kid-friendly and informative, even for the veteran baseball fan, a tour of the Louisville Slugger Museum and Factory will deepen your appreciation of baseball and one of its essential pieces of equipment.

For information about tours and times, refer to the factory's website at *www.sluggermuseum.org*. For a more in-depth look at the Louisville Slugger and the history of the baseball bat, you can check out *Sweet Spot: 125 Years of Baseball and the Louisville Slugger* (Triumph Books, 2009) by David Magee and Phillip Shirley, with a foreword by Ken Griffey, Jr., and *Crack of the Bat: the Louisville Slugger Story* (Sports Masters, 2000) by Bob Hill.

Serving America's Pastime since 1884—
The Louisville Slugger Museum and Factory.

35 | SEE THE GIANTS PLAY AT AT&T PARK

San Francisco Giants fans are understandably proud of AT&T Park. With a setting that celebrates downtown San Francisco and its beautiful bay, AT&T is one of the nicest ballparks in the majors.

Before moving into their new home on the waterfront, the Giants played in Candlestick Park, south of the city, sharing it with the NFL San Francisco 49ers. It is a difficult place to get to and, with winds gusting and temperatures fluctuating, it was an uncomfortable place to watch and play baseball.

When the Giants finally committed to a new ballpark, engineers and weather experts helped minimize the impact of wind and other weather problems. Despite being on the bay, AT&T offers the best baseball experience that San Francisco Giants fans ever had. And the fact that AT&T Park was built without public funds, a Major League Baseball feat not accomplished since the opening of Dodger Stadium in 1962, gives citizens of the city an extra reason to feel proud about the place.

AT&T Park has 41,503 seats, making it one of Major League Baseball's smaller parks. Yet it feels considerably larger. Sitting in seats behind or near home plate, you're treated to a wide-open view of San Francisco Bay, with passing freighters and sailboats dotting the seascape. Seats along the baselines offer less impressive bay views, while bleacher seats offer none.

If there is one thing about AT&T Park that tarnishes its reputation among traditional baseball fans, it's the excessive commercial landmarks behind the left-field bleachers. A large Coca Cola bottle with adjoining playground slides and a giant replica of a 1920s era baseball mitt slants toward the water. Adjacent to these sits a miniature AT&T Park that kids can play in. There is also a San Francisco cable car. Rusty, a large robotic ballplayer used to stand in the right-field bleacher area, impeding fans bay views, but thankfully, he's gone, presumably to a warehouse or the dump. A ballpark as attractive as AT&T Park doesn't need all these unsightly extras.

For your first visit to AT&T Park, plan to arrive at least an hour early and stroll the park's perimeter, which is filled with tributes to Giants' players and team history. There is little celebration of the time the Giants played in New York (the team moved to San Francisco in 1958, the same year the Dodgers moved from Brooklyn), and much about the team's time on the West Coast. AT&T Park's official address is 24 Willie Mays Plaza, in honor the great Giants center fielder's retired number, and not surprisingly, features a bronze statue of

One of the Major League's most unique parks, AT&T Park in San Francisco, CA.

the "Say Hey Kid" at the park's home plate entrance, as well as 24 swaying palm trees.

A necklace of four other statues graces the outside of AT&T Park, three of which honor Orlando Cepeda, Willie McCovey and Juan Marichal. The fourth, located at the park's ferry plaza (yes, you can get to AT&T Park by ferry), depicts a seal balancing a baseball on its nose—a tribute to the Pacific Coast League's San Francisco Seals, the city's top baseball attraction before the arrival of the Giants.

Walk around the red brick and green steel ballpark and behind the bleachers to visit McCovey Cove, a protected basin where Barry Bonds would regularly blast home run balls and kayakers would scurry to grab them. Make sure you also visit the nearby walkway filled with sidewalk plaques honoring feats by Giants players, including Bonds' historic home run number 756 that eclipsed the record held by Hank Aaron. Then walk across the Third Street Bridge to the bay side of McCovey Cove. Here you'll find bronze home plates for every year since 1958 that detail that season's Giants roster, pitching staff, batting and pitching leaders, and Opening Day line-ups. The Willie McCovey statue is located here at the tip of McCovey Point.

Inside AT&T Park offers more tributes. On the upper deck along the left-field line are the retired numbers of New York and San Francisco Giants, including Bill Terry, Mel Ott, Carl Hubbell, Willie Mays, Juan Marichal, Orlando Cepeda, Willie McCovey, and Gaylord Perry. Jackie Robinson's

Brooklyn Dodger #42, which is retired and celebrated in all major league ballparks, hangs there as well, along with the retired "uniforms" of manager John McGraw and pitcher Christy Mathewson, both of whom were Giants in the pre-number era.

To some, especially archrival Dodger fans, AT&T Park might seem like an outdoor baseball museum where they just so happen to play games as well. You can't fault the park for honoring the team and the players who call it home, even if at times, it might seem a bit much. And the fact is, you won't find a better place to watch a Major League Baseball game than AT&T Park.

For information about AT&T Park tours and tickets to Giants games, check the Giants website at *www.sfgiants.com.* You can also call the club's offices at (415) 972-2000.

36 ATTEND THE WORLD BASEBALL CLASSIC

Is there anyone who doesn't know that baseball is America's national pastime? Nearly everyone agrees that the game is an indelible part of our culture and a true reflection of the American spirit. But judging from the intentions of Major League Baseball with the creation of the World Baseball Classic, you might get the impression that the league wouldn't mind if one day, baseball became the entire planet's favorite pastime. Think of it: baseball, the Official Sport of the Global Village. It has a very 21st-century ring to it. Try to get used to it, because we might indeed be heading in that direction.

American baseball traditionalists might shudder at the idea. Why do we have to share what has been a precious American sports tradition with countries in a different hemisphere? The truth, of course, is that it's much too late for that kind of thinking. Baseball is now played in dozens of countries, including China, a sleeping baseball giant if there ever was one. In a number of nations—Canada, Cuba, Japan, Korea, the Dominican Republic, Venezuela, Mexico—they play it very well. All it takes is a quick glance at major league rosters, with their growing number of international players—and not just Latin players at that—to realize that baseball is already an international sport. Doesn't it stand to reason then that the World Baseball Classic is a natural result of

The 2009 World Baseball Classic, Los Angeles, CA.

the world's growing love affair with baseball?

There have been two World Baseball Classic tournaments thus far. The first was held in 2006 and the most recent in 2009. Japan won both, the latter in an extra-inning thriller against its rival, South Korea, at Dodger Stadium in Los Angeles in front of nearly 55,000 fans. The best that the United States could do was to reach the semi-finals, and we didn't even get that far in 2006. That, too, tells you that America's world domination of the sport is on shaky ground, at best.

The World Baseball Classic begins before the start of spring training and ends before the start of the Major League Baseball season. Most of the games are played in America—in Florida, Arizona and California where the weather in February and March is suitable for baseball. But expect the next Classic, which will occur in 2013, to feature more games abroad and involve more nations than the 16 that played in the 2009 tournament. Expect, too, that Los Angeles, with its melting pot population, heavy with Asian and Latin fans, will become the permanent home of the World Baseball Classic championship round.

The World Baseball Classic features some interesting rules. For starters, the WBC has a "mercy" rule, meaning that the head umpire will end any game that occurs in the first two rounds of play if one team is leading by ten or more runs.

Another interesting rule twist: if a game goes into extra innings and reaches the 13th inning, each team will begin its turn at bat with runners on first and second base in order to promote scoring and bring an end to the contest. This rule, however, does not apply to the championship game. Here's another: in order to preserve the arms of pitchers, many of whom are professional players in the U.S. or abroad, hurlers can only throw a maximum of 70 pitches in round one; 85 in round two; and 100 in the semi-final and final rounds. Half of the umpires enforcing these rules come from Major League Baseball in America while the other half get their mail at international addresses.

The World Baseball Classic rates a *Baseball Fan's Bucket List* entry because every true baseball fan ought to experience the unchecked passion in the stands and the special style of baseball performed on the field. The Asian teams, for instance, exhibit near flawless baseball fundamentals. Their fans, overly nationalistic and into every pitch with cheering, singing, and flag-waving, make their games all the more exciting. As the *Los Angeles Times* pointed out in its coverage of the 2009 championship game at Dodger Stadium, not once did the scoreboard have to remind fans to "make some noise."

The Latin fans are equally enthusiastic and festive. At times, you're not quite sure whether you're at a baseball game or a giant pep rally where the cheers are all in Spanish. American fans, too, turn it up a notch. American flags fly and chants of "USA! USA! USA!" fill the air whenever the U.S. team does something notable on the diamond. Unfortunately, that didn't happen quite enough for Team USA to claim victory beyond the opening rounds in '06 and '09.

To witness the World Baseball Classic is to witness the future of baseball. Go to a game and you'll be struck with the feeling that baseball is now and forever more a game that will be played with great skill and enthusiasm beyond our national boundaries.

For more on schedules, tickets and other information about the World Baseball Classic, go to *www.worldbaseballclassic.com*. The website also features a store where you can extend your collection of jerseys, caps, cards and other baseball collectibles from around the world.

37 READ THE BOOK, *BASEBALL: A LITERARY ANTHOLOGY* ✦✦

Baseball boasts a great literary tradition. Its history is rich with novels, short stories, poems, plays, and non-fiction pieces—a number of them written by America's most gifted writers. Reading the entire gamut of baseball literature, while a most admirable goal, would take years, maybe decades. To make things more manageable, the *Bucket List* includes only the best baseball fiction and non-fiction books. Read them all and you'll extend your appreciation of baseball well beyond its current bounds. To experience a sweeping survey of baseball's longstanding literary legacy, from its earliest days on, you can acquire a compact "library" called *Baseball: A Literary Anthology*, and over time, read everything in it.

Published in 2002 and edited by Nicholas Dawidoff, *Baseball: A Literary Anthology* is part of the acclaimed Library of America series that celebrates America's literary legacy. The author of *The Catcher Was a Spy: The Mysterious Life of Moe Berg* (1994), a book about baseball's only-known undercover agent during World War II, and *The Crowd Sounds Happy* (2008), a baseball memoir, Dawidoff did a masterful job of selecting pieces for the anthology. A true baseball fan, Dawidoff's passion for America's pastime is obvious, as is his knowledge of baseball literature. You'll especially see it in his insightful introductions that frame each selection. Whether they're small samples from large novels or simple pieces of poetry, nearly every one of Dawidoff's picks is an important piece of baseball writing. You'll enjoy reading all of them.

Don't be intimidated by the size or scope of *Baseball: A Literary Anthology*. Yes, it is a massive tome with dozens of selections spread over 715 pages. But there's no need to read them all at once. Like all good anthologies, you can pick it up and read a few pieces, then put it down and read a few more some other time. But you should eventually read all of the entries. If this sounds like labor, it's not. Get yourself started, and you'll see what I mean.

The collection begins with Ernest Lawrence Thayer's "Casey at the Bat," baseball's most famous poem. Written in 1888, it first appeared in the *San Francisco Examiner*. After it was recited onstage in New York a few months later, "Casey at the Bat" became a sensation, a piece of verse that every baseball fan has encountered some time in his or her life. As great literary poems go, "Casey at the Bat" doesn't exactly rank with the writings of Robert Frost (who's also represented in *Baseball: A Literary Anthology*). But no collection of baseball writings would be complete without it.

From there, Dawidoff takes us on a warm and wondrous baseball journey as we touch bases, catch sharp one-hoppers, hit homers, and slide safely through some of baseball's wittiest and most poignant pieces. From baseball's early days come selections from Ring Lardner and Damon Runyon. Literary giants Carl Sandburg, William Carlos Williams, and Thomas Wolfe are represented, as is the humorist James Thurber. There is a selection from Bernard Malamud's classic *The Natural* and from the play *Damn Yankees*. The book also features works by contemporary writers, including Richard Ford, Annie Dillard, Stephen King, and Don DeLillo. And then there are fine pieces from baseball's great non-fiction writers. The two Rogers—Kahn and Angell—are represented, as are George Plimpton, Roy Blount, Jr., Pat Jordan, and A. Bartlett Giamatti.

In the end, these writers and all the others represented in *Baseball: A Literary Anthology* have succeeded in contributing something beautiful and of consequence to America's pastime, not just because of their literary genius, but also because of their love of baseball. Throughout each and every piece, you'll find nestled in the carefully crafted sentences, the artful descriptions, and the bold language, a genuine passion for the game. To read their work is to re-affirm your own deep affection for baseball.

> You can find *Baseball: A Literary Anthology* at most public libraries. It can also be bought directly or ordered from most bookstores. Or you can order it from online booksellers.

38 SEE A TRIPLE-A PACIFIC COAST LEAGUE GAME

The Pacific Coast League is one of three Triple-A leagues in the minors. (The other two are the International League, located mostly in the East, and the Mexican League, all of whose teams reside south of the border.) Before 1958, when the Brooklyn Dodgers left New York for Los Angeles and the New York Giants followed its National League rival by heading to San Francisco, thus bringing Major League Baseball to the West Coast for the first time, the popular Pacific Coast League provided Left Coast fans with the highest caliber of professional baseball.

Stretching from San Diego in Southern California to Seattle in Northwest Washington, the Pacific Coast League in its heyday featured such young stars as Joe DiMaggio and Ted Williams. During the 1950s, the golden age of professional baseball in America, Pacific Coast League teams like the Los Angeles Angels, the San Francisco Seals, and the Seattle Rainiers filled their ballparks with fans and made certain the national pastime was alive and well west of the Rocky Mountains.

Emboldened by their success at the gate and the fact that people were flocking to California to relocate in the post–World War II years, Pacific Coast League team owners nudged Major League Baseball for the opportunity to become a third major league, joining the American and National Leagues as the premiere baseball leagues in the U.S. Most major league owners, however, loathed the idea. Why share profits with a minor league and break tradition by upsetting professional baseball's balance of power? Expansion was a far more acceptable alternative, and when the Dodgers and Giants established themselves on the West Coast, the possibility of the Pacific Coast League becoming a major league died.

Despite the presence of Major League Baseball in Los Angeles and San Francisco—and eventually in other cities west of the Mississippi River—Pacific Coast League baseball survived, but struggled. Classic ballparks like Wrigley Field in Los Angeles, built and owned by the same family that put its name on the home of the Chicago Cubs, were torn down. Attendance at Pacific Coast League games dropped as fan attention focused on the Giants and Dodgers and the other new major league teams now playing in former Pacific Coast League cities like San Diego, Oakland, and Seattle.

In 1997, the Pacific Coast League absorbed teams from the Triple-A minor league American Association, which had collapsed. Suddenly the PCL was double its original size and included teams as far east as Nashville and as far south as New Orleans. The league divided itself into four divisions: the American North and American South, and the Pacific North and Pacific South.

The PCL's timing was right on the mark. Under the leadership of Branch Rickey III, grandson of Branch Rickey, the man who had created baseball's farm system and had integrated the game by signing Jackie Robinson to a Dodgers' contract in 1947, popularity in minor league baseball grew, and then exploded. Rickey employed one of the successful strategies Major League Baseball had adopted: build new ballparks that were fan-friendly and family-friendly.

Although brand new minor league parks were sprouting up all over the minor league system, in the late 1990s and early 2000s, a few Pacific Coast League teams retained their older or original parks. While, for instance, the Memphis Redbirds moved into Autozone Park, a new and comfortable stadium right in the middle of downtown Memphis, the Portland Beavers kept its connection to PG&E Park, a beautiful, old classic in downtown Portland that begs to be visited.

So, if possible, make Portland and PG&E Park the place you go to fulfill this *Bucket List* item. Although the Beavers play on artificial turf (a field surface that, thankfully, has all but disappeared in most other major and minor league parks) because of the rainy Oregon weather, PG&E Park, built in the 1920s, possesses all the classic park charm you'll find at McCoy Stadium in Rhode Island, Bowman Field in Pennsylvania, and Bosse Field in Indiana.

Currently, the Pacific Coast League contains the following teams: American Conference Northern Division: Iowa Cubs (Des Moines, IA), Memphis Redbirds (Memphis, TN), Nashville Sounds (Nashville, TN), and Omaha Royals (Omaha, NE). American Conference, Southern Division: Albuquerque Isotopes (Albuquerque, NM), New Orleans Zephyrs (Metairie, LA), Oklahoma Red Hawks (Oklahoma City, OK), and Round Rock Express (Round Rock, TX). Pacific Conference, Northern Division: Colorado Springs Sky Sox (Colorado Springs, CO), Portland Beavers (Portland, OR), Salt Lake Bees (Salt Lake City, UT), and Tacoma Rainiers (Tacoma, WA). Pacific Conference, Southern Division: Fresno Grizzlies (Fresno, CA), Las Vegas 51s (Las Vegas, NV), Reno Aces (Reno, NV) and Sacramento River Cats (Sacramento, CA).

Triple-A baseball is infectious. Although the level of play is not quite up to major league standards, it is the highest you'll find in the minor league system. Also, seats are cheap, concession prices lower than at major league games, and the parks smaller and more intimate. Don't be surprised if you find yourself creating a new baseball fan bucket list that includes visits to all the Triple-A parks.

> For more information about the Pacific Coast League, check its website at *www.pclbaseball.com*. For schedules and ticket for individual teams, click on the link to the team's website at the top right of the league's homepage.

39 | WATCH THE MOVIE, *THE ROOKIE*

A Disney movie based on a true story, *The Rookie* is the ultimate feel-good baseball film. Released in 2002, it stars Dennis Quaid as Jim Morris, a former minor league pitcher turned high school teacher and baseball coach in Big Lake, Texas, an old oil town whose rusting wells are all that's left of a former prosperity. If Disney hadn't taken Morris's story as the basis for *The Rookie* and instead made it up, neither reviewers nor filmgoers, and certainly not baseball fans, would have bought it. Another Disney fantasy, many would say. Fact is, with the exception of the requisite Hollywood embellishments here and there, the Morris story did indeed happen the way director John Lee Hancock laid it out in the film. For proof, read *The Oldest Rookie* (Little, Brown, 2001) by Jim Morris and Joel Engel, Morris's memoirs of a most incredible baseball story.

And just what was that story? Coaching a losing high school baseball team in Big Lake, a town crazed for Texas high school football, Morris makes a pact with his players: win the district championship—a near impossible feat for a team that had won just one game each of the past three seasons—and he'd try out one more time to pitch in the big leagues. Morris, struggling financially to get by with a wife and three kids to care for, uses the pact as an unlikely incentive, a way to get his team to play better. He never believed that his players would actually fulfill their end of the deal, but, miraculously, they do.

Morris is now forced to hold up his end. He realizes that his fastball, which he once threw in the mid-80s before blowing out his arm, now is clocking at 96 and even 98 mph. As pitching arms grow old, they're supposed to become slower, not faster. What the 35-year-old Morris experiences then is unexplainable. Whether it's due to an act of God, or nature gone crazy, Morris and his arm have defied baseball logic and human biology.

Morris heads to a local tryout with the then-Tampa Bay Devil Rays. To his shock, he is offered a contract and begins minor league play. Over the course of the baseball season, with his wife and kids at home, Morris begins a second life as a rookie minor league baseball player on a team filled with guys nearly half his age. If the story stopped there, it would be still hard to believe, but it doesn't. Morris works his way from Double-A, to Triple-A and then to the big leagues, where he strikes out the first batter he faces. *The Rookie* ends with Morris realizing the dream that he had long thought lost.

It's hard to watch *The Rookie* and not suffer a case of teary eyes. It's a story, after all, about not giving up, even if what you're chasing is out of sight and seemingly unreachable. Inspirational and uplifting, *The Rookie* is also a wonderful family movie in grand Disney fashion. It offers a nice subplot about the relationship between Morris and his father (Brian Cox), a military man who denied his son the love he craved as a boy—and still craves as a man. Quaid, who performed without a double in most of the pitching scenes, is both effective and believable as Jim Morris. Rachel Griffiths also turns in an impressive performance as his wife. Director Hancock creates a Texas landscape that is dry, barren, and mostly desolate, yet comes to life thanks to a baseball dream that finally comes true.

Don't let the fact that *The Rookie* is not often bunched with the best baseball movies ever made, or that critics didn't thumb through a thesaurus to find new adjectives to describe the film's merits. *The Rookie* might not rank with baseball film classics made in the past few decades like *Bull Durham* (see *Bucket List* item #14), *The Natural* (see *Bucket List* item #19) and *A League of Their Own* (see *Bucket List* item #27), but it comes close. It's a film that you won't mind going back to every couple of years or so, finding plenty of value and inspiration in the time spent watching it.

> Released in 2002 and filmed in various locations around Texas, *The Rookie* is available on DVD in full-screen and original widescreen from most video retailers and rental stores. *The Rookie* marks the second time a fine baseball film has been directed by someone named John Hancock, the first being *Bang the Drum Slowly*, (see *Bucket List* item #95), which was directed almost 30 years before by John D. Hancock, who is not related to *The Rookie*'s John Lee Hancock. The real-life Jim Morris and his wife Lorri show up in cameo roles as fans cheering from behind the backstop during the scene in which Morris' high school team wins the district championship.

40 SEE A TRIPLE-A INTERNATIONAL LEAGUE GAME

The International League, along with the Pacific Coast League and the Mexican League, make up the Triple-A level of minor league baseball. While Mexican League teams all hail from south of the border and Pacific Coast

League teams come mostly from the West Coast, Midwest, and South, the teams of the International League hail from the East Coast, as well as the Midwest and South.

The level of play in the International League rivals that of the Pacific Coast League and together the two leagues represent the highest caliber of baseball you'll find in America, outside, of course, the majors. In recent years, the International League champion has played the Pacific Coast League champion for Triple-A bragging rights. Formerly known as the Bricktown Showdown, the title matchup was rechristened the Triple-A Baseball National Championship Game in 2009. The game usually takes place in late September at the AT&T Bricktown Ballpark in Oklahoma City, home of the city's Triple-A RedHawks.

The International League's origins extend back to the 1880s. For more than a century the league has not only readied young ballplayers for the major leagues, but also provided professional baseball to towns and small cities that lacked a major league franchise. While it's not uncommon for minor league teams to change ownership, location, major league affiliation, and nicknames, Triple-A leagues have proven more stable over the years than clubs in the lower levels of the minor leagues.

The International League has a North, South, and West division. The Northern Division consists of the Scranton/Wilkes Barre Yankees, Syracuse Chiefs, Pawtucket Red Sox, Lehigh Valley Ironpigs, Rochester Red Wings, and Buffalo Bisons. The Southern Division fields the Durham Bulls, Norfolk Tides, Gwinnett Braves, and Charlotte Knights. The Western Division features the Louisville Bats, Toledo Mud Hens, Indianapolis Indians, and Columbus Clippers.

The Governor's Cup, the series that determines the International League champion, features the winners of all three divisions, plus a wild-card team with the best record of the second-place finishers. The Governor's Cup began in 1933 and remains one of the most anticipated minor league playoffs. Catch the Cup, if you can, because not only will you check off this *Bucket List* entry, you'll also have an opportunity to see a number of the International League's best players before their call-up to the majors.

The International League boasts two storied franchises with famous ballparks: the Pawtucket Red Sox and the Durham Bulls. The Red Sox play out of Pawtucket, Rhode Island in one of the grandest and oldest minor league ballparks, McCoy Stadium. The Durham Bulls, perhaps the most famous of all minor league baseball teams, thanks to the success of the 1988 classic baseball film *Bull Durham*, play out of Durham, North Carolina. The Bulls play in the classy, modern, yet wonderfully retro Durham Bulls Athletic Park, not the older, more historic Durham Athletic Park where *Bull Durham* was filmed (though you can visit the old park before catching a Bulls game). The Durham franchise also features one of minor league's most famous mascots, a bull whose nostrils flare with smoke and whose tail wags whenever a Bulls player hits a home run.

Seeing either the Pawtucket Red Sox at McCoy Stadium or the Durham Bulls in Durham Bull Athletic Park is a great way to sample the culture and history of International League Triple-A baseball. Another recommended International League stadium to visit is in Louisville. Located a couple of miles from the Louisville Slugger Museum and Factory in downtown Louisville, Kentucky, Louisville Slugger Field, a retro red brick ballpark, is home to the Louisville Bats. You can make it a baseball day in Louisville by first visiting the Louisville Slugger Museum and Factory and then catching the Louisville Bats, knocking off two *Baseball Fan's Bucket List* items.

> For more information on the International League, check its website at *www.internationalleague.com.* For more information on the Durham Bulls, see *www.durhambulls.com* or check out *Bucket List* item #108, while you can find out more about the movie *Bull Durham* from *Bucket List* item #14. To find out more about the Pawtucket Red Sox, go to *www.pawsox.com.* You can learn more about the Louisville Bats at *www.batsbaseball.com,* and more on the Louisville Slugger Museum and Factory from *Bucket List* item #34.

41 SEE THE INDIANS PLAY AT PROGRESSIVE FIELD

The Cleveland Indians provide a perfect example of what a new ballpark can do for a franchise on the ropes and a city in need of something to cheer about. In 1954, the Indians went to the World Series. Heavily favored after winning 111 games during the regular season, the Tribe got swept the by the then-New York Giants. After that, it was pretty much all downhill for the Indians for the next 40 years. Bad personnel moves, questionable talent, poor leadership, and the cavernous Cleveland Municipal Stadium—which held 74,000 but had trouble attracting enough customers to fill one-tenth of its seats—made baseball in Cleveland little more than a joke. Remember the movie *Major League*? For a long time, the real Cleveland Indians were nearly as bad as their Hollywood counterparts.

There was even talk that the Tribe, a charter member of the American League, would leave Cleveland. That's when local businessman Richard Jacobs stepped in and bought the club. Jacobs promised to keep the Indians in Cleveland and a build a new ballpark. Jacobs Field opened in 1994, and a year later the Indians were back in the World Series, losing to the Atlanta Braves. With the Tribe's amazing turnaround (the team would also go to the World Series in 1997, losing this time to the Florida Marlins) and with Jacobs Field providing a beautiful addition to weary downtown Cleveland, fans responded in a big way. From June 1995 to April 2001, the Indians sold out 455 consecutive home games—an incredible achievement for any team, especially a small market club with a dubious history. At the ballpark today, the Indians celebrate the retired numbers of the team's greatest players—along with the number 455, a fitting tribute to Cleveland fans and their loyalty.

Jacobs Field name changed to Progressive Field in 2008 after Progressive Insurance bought the naming rights. But from the beginning, it was considered one of the best ballparks in the major leagues. Oriole Park at Camden Yards in Baltimore, the first ballpark to be built in the new "retro" era, opened in 1992, and immediately became the toast of Major League Baseball for its revolutionary design and downtown location. But Jacobs Field was every bit its equal.

Where the authors' love for the game of baseball started, Progressive Field in Cleveland, Ohio.

Camden Yards celebrated baseball history with a look and feel that reminded baseball fans of the old classic ballparks. Though designed by HOK (Hellmuth, Obata, and Kassabaum), the same architectural firm that crafted Camden Yards, Jacobs Field features a contemporary ballpark design that possesses just enough retro nuances to acknowledge Cleveland's long standing as a great American baseball city. The result represents a perfect balance of baseball yesterday, and baseball today.

With a beautiful beige and blonde limestone and brick façade, lots of exposed steel painted white, sightlines that take in the picturesque Cleveland skyline, and the old style vertical light poles, Progressive Field boasts an impressive baseball aesthetic. It holds some 43,000 seats, an ideal size for Cleveland (except during the 1990s glory years when even another 20,000 might not have been enough). Speaking of seats, you won't find a more comfortable ballpark to sit in when watching a game. You'll be surprised by Progressive's generous legroom and the width of its aisles, and you'll curse all the ballparks in the majors that practically pin you to your seat. Finally, you'll also admire the innovative, angled position of the seats beyond the dugouts in the lower and upper decks that offer better views of the batters and minimize neck cramps.

When you visit Progressive Field, be sure to come early enough to wander around Heritage Park, a classy tribute to the Tribe's greatest players and moments. Located behind center field, it opened in 2007 and features bronze plaques set against a backdrop of brick that recalls the spirit of Cooperstown. Those honored include the great Indians pitchers Bob Lemon, Early Wynn, and, of course, the legendary Bob Feller—all three National Baseball Hall of Fame inductees. Feller also rates a bronze statue located at the E. 9th Street entrance of Progressive Field. The Cleveland Indians might have had a checkered past, but neither the team, nor its fans, have forgotten the good times, many of them courtesy of the players in Heritage Park.

For information on Progressive Field tours and tickets to Cleveland Indians' games, check the team's website at www.indians.com. For more information about Bob Feller, see *Bucket List* item #97. You can find out more about *Major League*, a fictional film about the Cleveland Indians, from *Bucket List* entry #73.

42 COACH A SEASON OF LITTLE LEAGUE BASEBALL ✬✬✬✬

Playing Little League baseball offers kids a great introduction to the game. They can learn the rules as well as sportsmanship. Taught properly, they can eventually develop into young ballplayers, some of whom go on to play high school baseball, then college baseball. Some even go further. Many major league players today got their start in Little League baseball organizations.

Coaching Little League baseball offers adults a great way to give back to the game. It gives you the chance to help make your sons, daughters and neighbors' kids into better baseball players and better people. You'll gain the satisfaction of passing along America's pastime to younger generations, and of establishing yourself as a role model. You'll also gain an opportunity to advance your knowledge of the game and gain a greater appreciation of baseball by experiencing it from a new perspective.

Little League is a national organization that applies strict standards on how they bring coaches aboard. A potential coach must pass a background check, available at any city hall in any city across the U.S. Then you will need to review the rules, because a good Little League coach must know the rules. Don't think because you've followed baseball your whole life that you know all its rules well enough to teach them to a group of kids, especially Little League rules, some of which differ from the rules applied in the major leagues. League coordinators often pass out rulebooks to coaches before the start of the season. If that doesn't happen, go to *www.littleleague.org*, and you'll find the rules there.

Get yourself in shape. The last thing your team needs is a coach who can't run or hit grounders to infielders or throw batting practice without hurting himself. Begin a stretching and exercise program that builds up your stamina and baseball muscles at least a couple months before the start of practice. Work on building up your patience as well. Remember, you might be coaching the Yankees, but they're not the New York Yankees.

Along with knowing the rules and being in shape, a Little League baseball coach must understand how to teach the fundamental skills youngsters require to become baseball players. And remember: knowing how to do something doesn't necessarily mean you know the best way to teach a group of children how to do it. Most Little League organizations offer seminars to review things like the proper way to throw, field, and bat. It's a good investment of time,

Major League Baseball's next generation of stars and fans.

especially if it's been a long time since you've actually played baseball.

The most important thing you'll want to pass onto your team is a love of the game. Playing Little League baseball needs to be fun for kids, or they probably won't continue with the game. So make sure everyone on the team gets to play. Always show encouragement and be optimistic, especially toward the kids who may not be as talented and skilled as your team's best players. At this level, it isn't about winning baseball games, but winning kids over to the joys of playing baseball.

If you teach kids baseball fundamentals, insist on fair play and sportsmanship, don't emphasize winning games over participation and fun, and give each kid a chance to succeed to the best of his or her ability, you'll be surprised at the positive impact you have on these kids' lives and the role you played in making them young baseball players—not to mention the impact you have on your own love and understanding of the game of baseball.

> To get involved, contact your local Little League or local Parks and Recreation Department and express your desire to coach. You can find the nearest Little League by going to the national organization's website *www.littleleague.org*. Most coaches are assigned teams in January, so contact them right after the first of the year at the latest.

43 WATCH THE MOVIE, *FOR LOVE OF THE GAME* ✗

Released in 1999, *For Love of the Game* completed Kevin Costner's baseball trilogy and marked him as the game's greatest Hollywood actor. With *Bull Durham* (see *Bucket List* item #14) and *Field of Dreams* (see *Bucket List* item #21), two of baseball's best films behind him, Costner turned in another stellar performance as Detroit Tigers' pitcher Billy Chapel.

For Love of the Game didn't garner rave reviews and box office success, like Costner's other two baseball films. Perhaps it was because movie fans had grown weary of Costner in a baseball uniform, or that the film hit movie theaters in September, too late in the season to attract much attention from baseball fans as they focused in on the final days of the pennant races and the upcoming World Series. But don't believe the lack of hype—this is a very fine baseball film that offers strong performances and a compelling and believable story, along with some of the most authentic-looking on-field action ever filmed. It offers a loving tribute to the game while also revealing some of the harder truths about baseball and baseball players that usually get glossed over. That Costner, a former ballplayer, brought solid baseball skills and knowledge to the role made his Billy Chapel character that much more believable and involving.

Based on a book by the same name written by Michael Shaara and directed by Sam Raimi, *For Love of the Game* tells the story of Billy Chapel, a career-Detroit Tiger and Hall of Fame-bound pitcher suffering through a disappointing season. Scheduled to pitch against the Yankees at Yankee Stadium in one of the final games of the season, a meaningless one for the Tigers since they are out of the pennant race, Chapel wakes up the morning of the game to find out that his girlfriend is leaving him and moving to London, that the Tigers are being sold, and that he is on the trading block unless he decides to retire at the season's close. On top of all this, his arm, which has taken him through 19 seasons, is tired and aching.

The film unfolds Chapel's story through a nine-inning game, mostly in flashbacks, as he bears down and retires Yankee batters—all of them. At the end, Chapel, who can barely muster enough strength to overcome the increasingly intense pain in his arm, finishes the game—a perfect game—and decides to retire, "for love of the game." Along the way, we learn of Chapel's on-again, off-again relationship with writer Jane Aubrey (Kelly Preston), who could never quite come to grips with Chapel's fame as a star major league pitcher. The relationship, unlike the game, is far from perfect.

For Love of the Game depicts Costner's character as an occasionally flawed, self-centered athlete who doesn't always understand the implications of his actions. When, for instance, Jane turns down his invitation to join him at spring training, but then at the last moment decides to surprise him in Florida, Chapel answers the door of his condo and behind him another woman, fresh from a shower, walks down the stairs. Chapel tries to explain that she is his masseuse and the fact that she spent the night with him wasn't any big thing. He wonders why Jane can't understand that as she runs back to her car and returns to New York, shattered. The professional baseball life can be brutal on personal relationships, something *For Love of the Game* understands all too well.

For most of the movie, the baseball scenes in *For Love of the Game* are realistic and accurate. Impressed enough with the script and the movie's intentions, as well as its casting of Costner in the leading role, Major League Baseball permitted the filmmakers to use real Tigers and Yankees uniforms, while then-Yankees owner George Steinbrenner allowed for much of the film to be shot in Yankee Stadium. The authenticity didn't stop there. Legendary Dodgers' broadcaster Vin Scully appears as the play-by-play announcer and even the umpires—Rick Reed, Jerry Crawford, and Rich Garcia—were true major league umps.

For Love of the Game has a happy ending of all accounts. Chapel does what every pitcher dreams of doing and bows out of baseball at the pinnacle of achievement. He also gets his girl. As for the film itself, there's a timelessness and a warmth to it that makes it a baseball classic. Not enough people have seen *For Love of the Game*, but every serious baseball fan should.

For Love of the Game is available for rental and purchase from most online movie retailers and video stores. It is rated PG-13 and runs 137 minutes. In addition to Costner and Preston, the film also stars John C. Reilly as Chapel's longtime friend and catcher. Costner's real parents make a cameo appearance as Chapel's parents. As Costner closes in on his perfect game in the ninth inning, he says to himself, "Think, Billy, don't just throw"—the opposite of the advice Costner's character in *Bull Durham* gives to the simpleminded pitcher Nuke LaLoosh.

44 OWN A PIECE OF VINTAGE BASEBALL CLOTHING ✴✴✴

It's difficult to say exactly when or how "vintage" first entered the baseball lexicon. The opening of Oriole Park at Camden Yards, the first of the retro baseball parks, certainly had something to do with it. Movies like *The Natural* and *A League of Their Own*, which reveled in romanticism and nostalgia, further spiked interest in baseball's past. Old was "new" and look-backs at baseball history and culture grew in popularity.

It didn't take long for true baseball fans, already enamored with the sport's long and colorful past, to want to own some of that history. And what better way to express your fondness for baseball days gone by or for a once-beloved but now defunct team, like the Brooklyn Dodgers or the St. Louis Browns, than to wear a vintage team cap, jersey, or dugout jacket?

Around this time, a longtime Philadelphia sporting goods store, Mitchell & Ness, tapped into the "vintage" groundswell. Frank Mitchell and Charles Ness opened Mitchell & Ness Sporting Goods in 1904, specializing in high-quality tennis products. (Mitchell was a former AAU tennis champion.) By the mid-1920s, the store expanded into uniform manufacturing, specializing mostly in football. Colleges and high schools in the Philadelphia area contracted Mitchell & Ness to make their football jerseys and create their varsity sweaters. Word spread about the durability and quality of Mitchell & Ness sporting goods. In 1933, the city's new professional football team, the Eagles, bought its maiden uniforms from Mitchell & Ness, followed by the city's professional baseball teams, the Athletics and the Phillies. Mitchell & Ness was on its way toward carving out a small space in American sports culture.

Along the way, the company changed ownership, but continued to make high-quality sports uniforms. When it came to wool and flannel—the preferred fabrics of major and minor league baseball teams—Mitchell & Ness had few equals. Eventually, however, these fabrics, which wore well but were hot and uncomfortable in baseball's summer months, gave way to synthetic polyester. Baseball modernized its look in the 1970s—the decade most vintage baseball fans like the least—and mothballed the traditional look and feel of the game.

Then in 1983, Mitchell & Ness discovered reams of flannel in its warehouse. The company had no use in its contemporary line for the material, which was taking up valuable storage space. But instead of sending the flannel roles to the trash heap, the company decided to create vintage flannel baseball jerseys, replicating details and specifications of the uniforms of the glory days of baseball.

At first, the vintage baseball jersey business grew mostly by word of mouth among hardcore baseball fans. But then in 1988, *Sports Illustrated* published a feature on Mitchell & Ness entitled "Baseball Flannels Are Hot." That same year, Major League Baseball sold Mitchell & Ness the license to produce historical baseball uniforms under the Cooperstown Collection label. Baseball fans have looked to Mitchell & Ness for authentic baseball clothing ever since.

So what piece of vintage clothing should you buy to check off this *Bucket List* item? Depends on your tastes in clothes, teams and players. Owning the jersey of your favorite player from when you were a kid will do the trick. Not surprisingly, Mitchell & Ness sells its share of Mickey Mantle, Ted Williams, and Joe DiMaggio jerseys, mostly to Baby Boomers. Lou Gehrig and Babe Ruth jerseys are also popular. All the jerseys come with embroidered replicas of each player's autograph and the uniform year at the base of the jersey, along with the uniform number of each respective baseball legend. You can, for instance, own a Mantle rookie year (1951) jersey, or one from the 1960s. Both are stunning in

Mitchell and Ness is a specialized sporting goods store in Philadelphia, PA, dating all the way back to 1904.

their detail and authenticity; both are "must owns" for the many fans who grew up worshipping Mantle during baseball's golden age.

Purchasing one of the Mitchell & Ness beauties is not cheap. An authentic vintage baseball jersey can cost around $300. Classic wool baseball caps are considerably cheaper (in the $35 range), but not personalized like the jerseys. Other attractive pieces of vintage baseball clothing created by Mitchell & Ness and the other vintage baseball clothing companies include jackets, sweaters, and other classic garments, and wool or felt pennants. But none of these compare to a vintage baseball jersey. If you can afford it, that's the piece of vintage baseball clothing to invest in.

For more information about the Mitchell and Ness vintage baseball clothing line, check out their website *www.mitchellandness.com*. But to appreciate the full quantity and quality of vintage jerseys and other traditional baseball clothing manufactured by Mitchell & Ness, you need to visit its store in downtown Philadelphia at 1318 Chestnut Street. (Mitchell & Ness also has a satellite shop at nearby Citizens Bank Park, home of the Philadelphia Phillies.) Bring your wallet. Unlike shopping online, going to the Mitchell & Ness flagship store means getting up close and personal with the best authentic outfitters of baseball history. For most baseball fans, it's hard to walk out of the store without a stuffed Mitchell & Ness bag or two in hand.

 45

VISIT THE LEGENDS OF THE GAME MUSEUM

As baseball sites and destinations go, Legends of the Game Baseball Museum falls under a lot of fans' radars. That might have something to do with its location: Arlington, Texas, where it's attached to Rangers Ballpark, home to the American League Texas Rangers. Many mistakenly believe that the museum features only exhibits on the Rangers. But Legends of the Game is not a team museum as such. Rather, it's one of the best baseball museums in America, a smaller version of the National Baseball Museum up in Cooperstown, New York, but without its heralded Hall of Fame and all the hoopla and tradition that surround it.

The museum annually draws about 80,000 visitors (compared to the more than 300,000 that visit the National Baseball Hall of Fame). With three floors and more than 24,000 square feet of exhibition space, there is plenty of room at Legends of the Game to tell more than just the story of the Texas Rangers, and that it does. A big part of the museum's success comes from its special relationship with the National Baseball Hall of Fame, which has loaned Legends more than 100 artifacts—significant pieces, such as Babe Ruth's jersey and his King of Swat crown; the trophy presented to Lou Gehrig upon his teary retirement in 1939; items that celebrate the majestic careers of Hank Aaron, Roberto Clemente, Ty Cobb, and many others—plus plenty of historic bats, balls, and gloves, and enough historic uniforms, special exhibits and displays to keep you occupied for a couple of hours. No other museum in America, save the one in Cooperstown, tells the full story of baseball better than Legends of the Game. (The Negro Leagues Museum in Kansas City is a top-notch baseball museum and a "must" destination, but its main concern is the black baseball experience in America.)

You can take care of two *Baseball Fan's Bucket List* items—visiting Legends of the Game and taking in a game at Rangers Ballpark (see *Bucket List* item #92)—with one trip to Arlington, Texas, located between Dallas and Fort Worth, by planning your day carefully. Arrive early at Rangers Ballpark so that you can be on the first tour of the park, which occurs daily when the Rangers are on the road or else playing a home night game. After the tour, spend the better part of the day going through Legends of the Game, and then in the evening, take in a Rangers' game.

In order to see everything, plan a good two hours in Legends of the Game. One of the wonderful things about the museum is its presentation. Rather than simply display the historic baseball artifacts without much in the way of context, Legends is artfully laid out so that the stories behind the artifacts become as important as the artifacts themselves—the sign of a quality museum. The exhibits have the look and feel of Cooperstown. Everything from the exhibit colors to the artifact captions contain a nod to baseball's tradition and history, something that the National Baseball Museum and Hall of Fame mastered long ago and Legends emulates.

Famous baseball artifacts aside, Legends of the Game also features exhibits on the Texas League, formed in 1888, long before the arrival of Major League Baseball in the Lone Star state. There are small, but concise displays on the Negro Leagues, great managers, umpires, and women in baseball and excellent accounts on baseball equipment, namely bats, balls, gloves, and catcher's masks. Baseball card and press pin displays also have a place in Legends. Other exhibits celebrate ballparks and baseball game broadcasters, particularly those, who before the advent of live "play-by-play," recreated the sounds of the game with special effects. On the third level is the Legends interactive education center, where kids can "catch" a pitch thrown by Nolan Ryan and learn about the science of baseball.

For more on hours, directions and admission fees and other information about Legends of the Game Museum, visit its website at www.museum@texasrangers.com or call (817) 273-5600. To find out more on when the Texas Rangers are playing at home and tours of Rangers Ballpark, go to www.texasrangers.com.

46 SEE THE MARINERS PLAY AT SAFECO FIELD

Safeco Field, home to the American League Seattle Mariners, is a delightfully modern, yet retro ballpark. Opening in 1999, it quickly established itself as one of the best parks in the majors—and not just because it had replaced one of the worst, the Kingdome (known to many locals as "the world's largest chia pet" due to the moss growing on its leaky roof). Safeco Field gave Seattle a legitimate major league presence that it hadn't enjoyed since the team's inception in 1977. Located in Seattle, where rain is part of the culture, Safeco Field has a retractable roof, or "umbrella," which merely covers the field rather than fully enclosing it, allowing the fresh air coming over the Olympic Mountains and Puget Sound to flow through the ballpark, even on the wettest of days.

Safeco has some 47,000 seats. Like so many of the newer major league ballparks, it is remarkably intimate, sacrificing wide open views of downtown Seattle or the beautiful vista of the mountains and water to the west, to create one of Major League Baseball's coziest places to watch baseball. When the roof is open, you can get spectacular views at Safeco, especially if you sit in right field's upper deck when the summer sun is dropping behind the mountains. Unfortunately, almost all the other seats in the park deprive you of postcard perfect views. Seattle is one of the prettiest of all U.S. cities and the Puget Sound area rates as one of the nation's most naturally stunning. Why not celebrate it in your ballpark design? The quick answer, of course, is the roof. It would have been difficult at best to build a weatherproof field within a ballpark featuring the wide-open architecture of some of the newer ballparks. But would it have been impossible? That depends on what architect you're talking to.

Safeco's signature "sound" is that of a train whistle. Train tracks run past the ballpark on its east side. Dozens of trains go by the stadium in a 24-hour span. During a game, slow moving trains let go a few whistles to warn fans outside the park of an approaching locomotive and to say "hi" to the Mariner faithful inside. It adds a nice touch to the Safeco experience.

Safeco has all the requisite characteristics of a retro park: brick walls and exposed, dark green steel, plus a hand-operated scoreboard. The private and corporate suites are named after Hall of Fame players, none of which, by the way, played for Seattle. Because Seattle lacks what many of the other ballparks celebrate: a grand baseball team history.

The Mariners weren't the first Major League Baseball club in Seattle. That honor belonged to the Pilots, which began—and ended—play in 1969, moving the next year to Milwaukee and re-naming themselves the Brewers. The Pilots were dismal that one year, and so were the Mariners for much of their early history. It took the team 15 years from its inception to achieve its first winning record in 1992. In the mid-1990s, the Mariners harnessed the managerial skills of Lou Pinella and the exciting play of Ken Griffey, Jr., Alex Rodriquez, Randy Johnson, Jay Buhner, and Edgar Martinez to make a series of runs at the American League pennant, but kept falling just short. In 2001, the Mariners won 116 games, an American League record, but failed again to reach the World Series. Pinella left after the following season, and not much of note has happened with the Mariners since. All those lean years means there's precious little Mariners glory to celebrate at Safeco, and except for the few banners in the upper deck rafters, you're not going to be swept away by Mariner baseball tradition at the ballpark.

Rather, it's the food at Safeco Field that will draw more of your attention. Because of Seattle's large Asian population, a number of concession stands sell Asian food, including sushi. Every first time visitor to Safeco should experience an Ichi Roll, a special egg roll named in honor of Mariner great, Ichiro Suzuki. As for more traditional ballpark fare, like hot dogs, you'll find they pass muster. But try the stands just outside Safeco, where the competition for business is keen and vendors sell fine-tasting hot dogs, complete with onions, sauerkraut, and spicy mustard, if that's your preference.

For information about tours of Safeco Field and tickets to Mariners' games, contact the team's website at *www.seattlemariners.com*. For an overview of Mariners' brightest year, you can check out *Sweet 116: The 2001 Seattle Mariners History-Making Season*, available on DVD from movie stores and online retailers.

One last thing you'll notice about Safeco Field: it boasts the nicest and most polite fans in the majors. No need to worry about wearing an opposing team's jersey or cap at Safeco. If you're hassled, it'll almost always be a good-natured ribbing. This is, after all, the ballpark where team officials during a visit by the Yankees tried to prevent some fans from wearing "Yankees Suck" t-shirts to the game, claiming it wasn't in good taste. Imagine how that would fly in Boston.

47 LEARN TO FIGURE IMPORTANT BASEBALL STATISTICS ✭✭

This *Bucket List* entry will be a done deal for some; if you've ever coached baseball on a level beyond Little League, chances are you know how to determine batting averages, earned run averages, on-base percentages, and other basic baseball stats. But a lot of other fans couldn't figure them out if their playoff tickets depended on it.

Fortunately, you can easily learn how to figure out five essential baseball statistics—three for batting, one for fielding, and one for pitching. Your newfound mathematical skills will not only help you become a more knowledgeable fan, you'll also be able to showcase your abilities whenever the baseball discussion turns to numbers.

Every baseball fan should know how to determine a batting average, the primary statistic to measures a player's batting performance at the plate. If you don't, here's how: divide the number of hits a batter has made by the number of his official at-bats. Remember, sacrifices, walks, and hit by pitches don't count as at-bats; if a player reaches base on an error, count it as an at-bat, but not as a hit.

So, let's make this simple. If a player has batted three times and made one hit, he's batting 1/3 = .333. It doesn't matter if that hit is a single, double, triple or home run. When it comes to the batting average, all hits carry equal weight. If a player is hitting better than .300, he's having a good year. If he's above .333, he's having a very good year. If a player hits .400 or more for a full season with enough at-bats to qualify for official records, he's probably on his way to the Hall of Fame. The last player to bat over .400 was Ted Williams, when he hit .406 in 1941.

A slugging percentage determines how effective a player is at making extra-base hits. Whereas doubles, triples, and home runs mean no more than singles when calculating a batting average, they gain additional weight when determining a slugging percentage. You figure a slugging percentage by dividing the total number of times at bat into the total number of bases achieved during at-bats. A single counts for one base, a double for two bases, a triple for three bases and a home run for four. So let's say a batter has made ten singles (10 bases), two doubles (4 bases), one triple (3 bases) and two home runs (4 bases x two=8 bases) for a total number of 25 bases. Let's say this same player has a total of 50 at-bats. His slugging percentage would be 25/50 = .500.

The on-base percentage has received a lot more attention ever since the 2003 publication of the book *Moneyball*, (see *Bucket List* item #29). To figure out a player's on-base percentage, you tally the number of times he got on base through a walk, hit or by being hit by a pitch. Then you divide that by his number of official at-bats, plus sacrifices. So, if a player made ten outs, walked five times, got five hits, was hit by a pitch twice, and made two sacrifice flies, his total number of at bats is 24. Then divide that by 12 (the sum of those same five walks, five hits and the two times he was hit by a pitch) for an on-base percentage of .500, which would be pretty darn good.

For pitchers, aside from their won-loss record, the statistic that counts most is the ERA (Earned Run Average). It figures the average number of "earned" runs that are scored on a pitcher over the course of nine innings. An "unearned" run due to an error made by one of his fielders does not count in a pitcher's total. You figure a pitcher's ERA by dividing the number of innings pitched into the number of earned runs scored, then multiplying that number by nine, and taking it two decimal points. Let's say a pitcher has given up nine earned runs over the course of 30 innings. Divide the 30 innings pitched into the nine earned runs and multiply the dividend by 9. This particular pitcher has an ERA of 2.70. An ERA of less than 3.00 over the course of a season will get a pitcher raves from his manager and teammates, and probably a big raise.

> For more on baseball's long and intense relationship with statistics like batting averages and on-base percentages, you can read *The Numbers Game: Baseball's Lifelong Fascination With Statistics* (St. Martin's Griffin, 2005) by Alan Schwarz (with a foreword by Peter Gammons), which is available from most bookstores and online booksellers.

The final basic baseball statistic is fielding percentage, used to help determine a player's effectiveness as a fielder. You figure a fielding percentage by dividing a player's total number of put-outs and assists by his total put-outs, assists and errors. So, if a player fielded 100 balls that resulted in 40 put-outs, 58 assists, and 2 errors—you'd divide that number

(100) into the successful number of put-outs (40) and assists (58), which is 98. Thus, the player's fielding percentage is .980.

There are other baseball statistics to ponder and to learn how to calculate, but these are the more essential ones. Remember, baseball is a game of numbers. If you don't like numbers, it's hard to like baseball. Learning to figure these basic stats will help you gain a greater appreciation for both.

---

48 | BECOME A MEMBER OF SABR ✦✦✦

Statistics remain more important in baseball than in any other major sport. Numbers rule, so appreciate them. And tell your kids or grandkids to pay attention in math class if you want them to grow up to become serious baseball fans.

Baseball fans who want to delve further than basic stats like on-base percentages and earned run averages can check out an organization commonly known as SABR (the Society for American Baseball Research). Stats become things of beauty at SABR, where formulas are created to measure the ratio of left-field foul balls to players who played their college baseball in the Pac-10 or to quantify the physics mysteries of what precisely happens when a ball thrown 95 mph meets a 32-ounce bat.

You may be surprised to find that SABR's membership isn't dominated by geeks with coke-bottle, horn-rimmed glasses who have always analyzed the mathematical aspects of the game instead of picking up a bat and glove. Okay, the organization was founded in 1971, in Cooperstown by Bob Davis, who, at the time, worked for the Atomic Energy Commission. But a number of baseball writers are members of SABR, along with some former players and commentators. Not surprisingly, one of SABR's most famous members, Bill James, popularized "sabermetrics" in his now-famous "Abstract" books.

So why do you need to become a member of SABR? Read the now-classic book, *Moneyball*, (see *Bucket List* item #29) and you'll know why. Today, the statistical side of baseball is more important than in any other era of baseball history, and it's bound to play an even a greater role in the future. *Moneyball* showed how one general manager (Billy Beane) of a small-market club (the Oakland Athletics) used statistics, particularly one undervalued statistic (on-base percentage), to build a small-market club with almost no money into a perennial pennant contender. The book was a bestseller, and Beane's disciples are now found throughout baseball, where every general manager, it seems, is never too far away from a laptop computer. That baseball's numbers guru Bill James (see *Bucket List* item #83) was hired by the Boston Red Sox as the team's sabermetrics advisor tells you just how far this stats thing has gone in baseball.

There are nearly six thousand members of SABR, and once a year many of them gather for three days at the organization's convention to eat, sleep, and especially talk about baseball. Members present papers, mathematicians explain theories, historians revise history—all of these things happen at the annual SABR convention. You don't need to be a presenter or big time researcher. You can just sit and listen and learn a lot. One year, Bill James served as the convention's keynote speaker. Another year, former Yankees pitcher Jim Bouton, author of the classic baseball book *Ball Four* (see *Bucket List* item #17), was the featured guest. In the audience at any SABR convention you might catch political and sports commentators George Will and Keith Olbermann, or St. Louis Cardinals Hall of Famer Stan Musial. Everyone is there because of their love for baseball and all the numbers and formulas that help us better understand the game and the performance levels of those who play it.

> To find out more about the Society for American Baseball Research, check out its website at *www.sabr.org*. The site includes information about joining SABR, its annual convention, news and upcoming events, plus updates on the latest in baseball scholarship.

49 VISIT THE CINCINNATI REDS HALL OF FAME AND MUSEUM ✦✦

While the Atlanta Braves and a few other ball clubs honor their past in small museums or displays at the ballpark, or celebrate players by inducting them into their teams' halls of fame, no major league club pays tribute to its past the way the Cincinnati Reds do. The Cincinnati Reds Hall of Fame and Museum is the standard bearer of major league team museums. It is comprehensive, large, engaging, and exceedingly well done. You don't have to be a Reds fan to enjoy it. This is a first-class baseball experience, one that fans of all stripes must visit.

It's appropriate that of the 30 Major League Baseball teams, the Reds have the most impressive museum facility. After all, the Reds are the oldest professional baseball club still in existence. The Red Stockings, as the team was known during the first phase of its history, first started paying its players in 1868, just a few years after the end of the Civil War. The team joined the National League in 1876 at the league's inception, and have been a part of it ever since. And because the Reds' story spans the history of professional baseball in America, the museum will help you see how the game became the nation's pastime—even if you are looking at its evolution through Reds-tinted glasses.

If you're serious about your baseball history, plan on spending at least two hours at the Reds Hall of Fame and Museum. Located on the west side of Great American Ballpark (see *Bucket List* item #118) in downtown Cincinnati, you could come early to the ballpark, visit the museum and then attend a Reds' game (checking off two *Bucket List* entries in one day). However, it's better to visit the museum on a day when there's no baseball being played. With up to 100,000 visitors a year—many of them coming before Reds' home games—the museum can get crowded.

The museum's first floor features a rotating exhibit gallery highlighting a particular piece of Reds' history or Cincinnati baseball culture. One temporary exhibit celebrated Crosley Field, home of the Reds from 1912 to 1970, before the team moved to Riverfront Stadium in 1970 and then on to Great American Ballpark in 2003. Crosley Field was famous for its terraced outfield. There was no warning track at the park; outfielders knew they were getting close to the

The Cincinnati Reds Hall of Fame and Museum.

wall when they began running uphill to catch a fly ball. In addition to viewing artifacts from Crosley, the exhibit enabled fans to experience what it was like for opposing players not familiar with Crosley's contours to deal with its odd outfield terrain. Adjacent to the temporary exhibit area is a wonderful theater that replicates the grandstand of Palace of the Fans ballpark, where the Reds played from 1902 to 1911. The theater shows a film celebrating the Reds baseball tradition. There is also a smaller temporary exhibit area on the second floor.

Many Reds fans buy an annual membership to the museum, which allows for unlimited visitation for one year to the Reds Hall of Fame and Museum AND the National Baseball Hall of Fame and Museum in Cooperstown AND two View Level ticket vouchers to a Reds game. Membership fees begin at around $40. Talk about a great deal.

Though its temporary exhibits can be fascinating, most fans come to the museum to check out the Reds Hall of Fame and the permanent exhibit honoring "The Big Red Machine"—the legendary Reds' dynasty that won three world championships in the 1970s and included the likes of Johnny Bench, Tony Perez, Joe Morgan and Pete Rose. Speaking of Rose, the Reds' Hall of Fame and Museum subtly honors the hometown boy known as "Charlie Hustle," despite the alleged gambling habit that got baseball's all-time hits leader disqualified from consideration for induction into the National Baseball Hall of Fame. At the Reds' museum, Pete Rose is honored as a baseball hero. There's even a "Rose" garden just outside the museum. Notice the single white rose in it. That's where Rose's 4,192nd single landed at the old Riverfront Stadium, breaking Ty Cobb's long-standing all-time hits record.

Begun all the way back in 1958, the Reds Hall of Fame features bronze busts and plaques similar in design to the ones at Cooperstown. All the Reds greats, save Rose, are represented, including the above mentioned members of the Big Red Machine, plus Frank Robinson, Vada Pinson, Joe Nuxhall, Johnny Vander Meer, Ernie Lombardi, Ted Kluszewski and other Reds' greats.

If all this wasn't enough, visitors to the Reds Hall of Fame and Museum will have a ball, literally, in the interactive area where fans can pitch, experience what it's like to be an umpire calling strikes and balls, and try to catch a home run before it goes over the fence. Multi-media displays showcase Reds greats like Johnny Bench giving pointers on the fine art of being a catcher. You can even sit in the Reds dugout with manager Sparky Anderson as he contemplates game strategy.

> For information about admission fees, hours, and membership for the Cincinnati Reds Hall of Fame and Museum, go to *www.reds.mlb.com* and click on "Great American Ballpark," then the museum link.

A great place to enjoy how much a Major League Baseball club can mean to its city, the Cincinnati Reds Hall of Fame and Museum has helped inspire a number of other major league ball clubs to plan similar facilities to honor their team's history. It's worth going out of your way to see why, even if you're not a Reds fan.

GO TO THE MIDNIGHT SUN BASEBALL CLASSIC

The game starts—not ends—at 10:30 p.m. It's usually over sometime around two in the morning. And they never use lights. Never. They don't have to. Mother Nature provides enough natural light to play baseball for the Midnight Sun Baseball Classic, an annual event that's been a part of the Summer Solstice celebration in Alaska for over a century now. You might not think baseball when you think of Alaska. But for one game every year in June, Fairbanks, Alaska ranks as the capital of the baseball universe.

A one-of-a-kind baseball game, the Midnight Sun Baseball Classic takes place a mere 160 miles south of the Arctic Circle. It begins around the time the sun is setting and ends when it's rising. Except that the sun never completely sets or rises at the height of the Alaskan summer. Instead, you experience something roughly akin to dusk as the sky gradually turns shades of purple, orange, and gray. But it never gets dark enough to turn on the lights at Growden Park. And even if it did due to dark clouds, you get the feeling that the grounds crew wouldn't flip the switch anyway. That would break with tradition.

The first Midnight Sun Baseball Classic occurred in 1906. That's 53 years before Alaska became a state. Not surprisingly, the game's origins are steeped in legend. The man most responsible for it was Eddie Stroecker, a Californian who had come to Alaska, like so many others, to get rich. Alaska was still feeling the effects of the Klondike Gold Rush and mining fever still burned in many a man's soul. Stroecker didn't strike gold, but he did make a few bucks selling liquor to the locals. His drinking establishment was called the California Saloon, and from it, a baseball team was formed. They called themselves the Californians, and in 1906 on a sunny evening in Fairbanks, they beat another Fairbanks team, 7-4.

The identities of the other participants in the first (yet-to-be-named)

Midnight Sun Baseball Classic are lost to history. But the tradition of playing baseball in the middle of the night in Fairbanks on June 21—the Summer Solstice—took hold, and has continued ever since.

The U.S. Air Force and Army bases close to Fairbanks stocked with young men who play baseball provided enough teams over the years to keep the Midnight Sun Baseball Classic going. In 1960, an amateur team out of Fairbanks called the Goldpanners was formed and joined the Alaska Baseball League. Similar to the celebrated Cape Cod League that showcases some of the top college ballplayers in the nation on the other side of the continent, the Alaska Baseball League attracts many of the best college baseball players on the West Coast. The league currently fields teams in Anchorage, Juneau, and towns around the state. But none of the other Alaska teams enjoy as deep a connection to the Midnight Sun Baseball Classic as do the Goldpanners, who are recognized as the event's perennial home team.

Over the years, nearly two hundred eventual major league ball players got the opportunity to take the field during a Midnight Sun Baseball Classic. Rick Monday, Graig Nettles, Andy Messersmith, Bill Lee, Dave Kingman, Floyd Bannister, Alvin Davis, Harold Reynolds, Jason Giambi, Travis Lee, Jacque Jones, and Ryan Garko are all Midnight Sun Baseball Classic veterans. So are Hall of Famers Tom Seaver and Dave Winfield. Even Barry Bonds has his name linked to the Classic.

Baseball at Midnight? Only in Fairbanks, Alaska, during the Midnight Sun Baseball Classic game played on the summer solstice each year.

During the Alaska Baseball League season the Goldpanners attract a few hundred fans for an average home game. For the Midnight Sun Baseball Classic, nearly 10,000 show up. And they come from all over the country. As a way of celebrating all that sunlight on the longest day of the year, Fairbanks throws a grand Summer Solstice party, complete with music, food, displays, contests, and demonstrations that reflect the city's proud heritage. Around 9 p.m., fans make their way over to the stadium. The beer flows and hot dogs become early morning snacks. No one really cares who wins. It's all about the game's tradition. As baseball goes, the Midnight Sun Baseball Classic is on par with a good Single-A minor league game. But many fans keep score, knowing that they are seeing a few players on the field who will one day become major league stars on a night when they won't see any stars in the sky.

> Catching a Midnight Sun Baseball Classic means planning ahead. Travel arrangements to Alaska can get complicated. Hotel rooms in Fairbanks fill up fast as the event nears and tickets to the game grow scarce. Your best bet is to order your game tickets well in advance. To find out more about tickets and the game, go to its website at *www.goldpanners.com/midnightsungame*. For more information on lodging and other amenities in Fairbanks, visit *www.fairbankschamber.com*.

51 PLAY IN AN ADULT BASEBALL LEAGUE

The best way to stay connected to baseball is to keep playing it. But up until a few years ago, an adult amateur baseball player's only opportunity to play the game—or more accurately, to play a watered-down version of it—was to join a softball league. Nowadays, the adult baseball enthusiast who's not ready to hang up his glove enjoys numerous opportunities to continue playing the real thing. You can attend a fantasy baseball camp hosted by your favorite Major League Baseball team (see *Bucket List* item #18), or join a vintage baseball league and play by 19th century rules (see *Bucket List* item #119). But for the baseball fan that yearns to compete through a full season of regular baseball and play the game as it's played today, joining an adult league is the way to go.

The Men's Senior Baseball League/Men's Adult Baseball League (MSBL/MABL) and the National Adult Baseball Association (NABA) offer the most popular adult baseball outlets. Both leagues field teams across the U.S. and include thousands of players. They offer fully structured league play overseen by professional umpires. Each features a postseason, with huge national tournaments each fall that often take place on Major League Baseball spring training fields in Florida and Arizona.

The leagues are structured into age divisions to ensure players compete against their generational peers. That way, if you're, say, a fit 50-year-old who still loves to play the game, you're not facing a 20-something pitcher just out of college whose fastball hits the catcher's mitt at 85 mph. Some seniors in their upper 60s continue to play in 55+ leagues under the MSBL banner. However old you are, you play against people roughly your own age, which tends to level out the competition and makes for a fun time on the diamond.

Take note: the MSBL/MABL are not "beer leagues"—informal get-togethers where players toss around a baseball on a lazy Sunday afternoon with a can of beer by their sides. Adult league players come from all professions and walks of life, drawn together "by a common passion for playing and enjoying baseball." They take the game seriously.

The National Adult Baseball Association organizes itself around a similar attitude and core structure, but also offers leagues that aren't just broken up by age, but also by experience and skill level. For instance, you could play in a 35

Preserving baseball history, one argument at a time.

& Over league that offers AAA, AA, and A levels of competition. Most players in AAA boast past college and even pro experience. The intermediate AA level usually attracts guys who played high school and perhaps some college baseball, while A is more recreational and "provides an opportunity for players whose love of the game perhaps exceeds their level of experience." Everyone must wear a uniform. Stats are kept. Games are usually nine innings long. The attitude is serious and spirited, but fun.

If you do plan on playing in an adult baseball league, do yourself a favor and prepare for it. In the off-season, get in baseball shape. Go to the batting cages and throw a ball on a regular basis. If you're a pitcher, find someone to pitch to from a mound at your local high school field a couple times a week. Most importantly, stretch daily. One of the most common injuries suffered by adult baseball players is a pulled, or worse, torn hamstring. Not only is a hamstring injury painful, but it'll cost you plenty of playing time. The older you are, the more time it takes to heal. You could pull a hamstring the first time you run at full speed from home plate to first base and end your adult baseball season just as it was beginning.

If you're a true baseball fan with some competitive fire left in your baseball soul and a desire to be more than just a spectator, you'll be surprised at how much fun playing in any of these leagues can be. And the couple described here aren't your only options. Independent adult baseball leagues have sprouted all over the country. It doesn't really matter which one you choose to join. The idea is to get off the couch and onto the field, glove in hand and play again the greatest game in the world.

Contact your local Parks and Rec department to find the nearest adult baseball league. You can join an established local league under the banner of the Men's Senior Baseball League/Men's Adult Baseball League or the National Adult Baseball Association. You can also organize players in your community and start your local team or even league, then join either the MSBL/MABL or NABA. There is plenty of information on how to do either on the websites of the MSBL/MABL (*www.msblnational.com*) and the National Adult Baseball Association site (*www.dugout.org*).

52 ATTEND A FAN FEST

If you're not fortunate enough to head to Florida or Arizona to take in the fun and sun that is spring training, then Fan Fest is the next best way to begin the new baseball season. Even if you're a spring training regular, Fan Fest is still a "must do" experience, especially if you have kids, and rates a spot on the *Bucket List*. These days, most major league clubs, along with an increasing number of minor league teams, create a festive, family atmosphere at Fan Fest that not only reconnects fans with their favorite team after a long winter of no baseball, but also celebrates the game itself.

Fan Fest usually occurs in either January or February, just prior to spring training. When the idea of Fan Fest first surfaced a few years ago, the event was free. Teams used it as a marketing ploy to sell tickets for the upcoming season. Today, you're more apt to have to pay for the Fan Fest experience, and teams still use it to push tickets. However, what once entailed a few autograph signings with rookies, base coaches, and bench players, pictures with the team mascot and games for the kids, has evolved into a full-fledged baseball love fest. Like most everything else in baseball, the cost of being a fan has risen, but so has the depth of the experience and it all starts each year with Fan Fest.

For adult baseball fans, the best part of Fan Fest is the player meet and greets and the opportunity to expand your autograph collection. More and more team stars are making appearances at Fan Fest, and getting a few of their autographs can more than make up for the price of admission. Bring your own baseballs for signings; if you buy them at Fan Fest, you'll pay a premium for them. Also, be advised that the biggest names draw the biggest crowds and the longest lines. Pick your players wisely. Arrive early and have an autograph plan.

Another fun part of most Fan Fests are the player interviews, during which one of the team's media relations people or a local sportscaster or sportswriter chats with players and takes questions from the audience. Then there are the baseball skill demonstrations. Learning more about the art of bunting, the different kinds of slides available to base runners, and the proper way to throw a curve ball will broaden your baseball knowledge. If you bring the kids, they'll learn a few things, too, and have fun in the process.

In addition to demonstrations, the events offer the opportunity to test your baseball skills in the Fan Fest area. Most teams' Fan Fests include simple skill tests that, for instance, measure your ability to throw a strike, or to call one as a home plate umpire. However, more and more teams are using increasingly sophisticated interactive technologies that enable fans to simulate all kinds of game situations without ever having to step out onto the field.

Museum-like exhibits that detail the history of the team make up another part of Fan Fest. You'll usually find old jerseys, trophies and awards, vintage equipment, and other club and player memorabilia on display. Tours of the ballpark are also often offered, usually for an extra fee. And then, finally, there are all the freebies, ranging from team schedules and rally towels, to posters and player pictures. If Fan Fest sounds like a full, busy day, it is. But you're assured of leaving the event entirely jazzed for Opening Day and the rest of the baseball season.

> Every Major League Baseball team hosts a Fan Fest in January or February. For information about your favorite team's pre-season Fan Fest, check the team's website. You can find a full list of every MLB teams' website, along with a link at *www.mlb.mlb.com/team*

53 MAINTAIN A BASEBALL CARD COLLECTION ✦✦✦✦

Baseball cards provide a lot of fans with their earliest and most enduring connection to the game. Kids who weren't even ready for sandlot or Little League have been collecting cards featuring paintings, pictures and stats of major leaguers for over a century. Earlier generations used to stick the cards in the spokes of their bikes to create an interesting sound effect when they pedaled around the neighborhood or remember the sweet smell of the bubble gum that used to come with each pack of cards. Others began collecting during the baseball card wars of the 80s and 90s when new companies challenged Topps' hold on the baseball card market. Thousands have maintained their collections in old shoeboxes or specialized plastic holders. Other than our first glove, our youthful baseball card collection is the one item we lifelong baseball fans are most likely to keep hold of throughout our lives.

Baseball cards date all the way back to 1869. At first, the cards were used to sell tobacco products. History's most famous and valuable baseball card, the Honus Wagner T206, is a tobacco card. Due to the great Pittsburgh Pirates

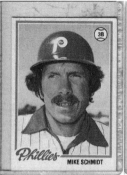

shortstop's insistence that the tobacco company stop using his likeness to market their products, only a few Honus Wagner T206s ever made it into circulation. Today, a Honus Wagner T206 in good condition can fetch over $1 million at auction.

The Wagner controversy didn't stop the tobacco companies from using other players to help sell their products, and the idea of the baseball card lived on. Beginning in the 1920s, candy and gum companies began packaging baseball cards (then commonly called "picture cards") as a means to reach the youth market and boost sales of their products. Collecting baseball cards, however, didn't take off until after World War II when Bowman, then Topps and other companies began manufacturing baseball cards en masse and marketing them to young Baby Boomers during what is generally considered "The Golden Age of Baseball." Trading cards in the school yard, or flipping them in playground competitions, or jumping for joy when the pack of cards you bought contained your favorite player remain cherished memories in the minds of many Baby Boomer baseball fans.

It was great fun to collect baseball cards as a kid, and it remains great fun for many adults. Though as an adult, you'll probably want to go about it in a more organized manner. So select a card collecting strategy. You can make it a part-time hobby, a full-time avocation, or even a business. But even if you really dive into collecting, it's still best to determine what you want to collect and set your spending limits. Otherwise, baseball card collecting can overwhelm your time and fiscal resources. Baseball card collecting offers a world of possibilities, so carefully choose which avenues of it you want to explore.

For purposes of satisfying this *Bucket List* item, you can and probably should narrowly focus your initial efforts. You can collect cards from a certain year (maybe the year you were born or the year you started watching baseball). Or limit your collecting to cards of your favorite team or favorite players. Choose an approach and get going on a collection, maintain it and upgrade it as you can. Enjoy the process, but don't let it run your life. Another tip: if you're interested in collecting baseball cards that grow in value, go after rookie cards; when a player develops into a superstar, you'll be surprised at how the value of his rookie card escalates.

As with so many other things these days, the best place to shop for cards is the Internet. Start with *eBay* and go from there. You can also join a card collector's group, either online or at your local card or memorabilia store. Some fans like to get their baseball cards autographed by players. Spring training is the best place to do that.

Finally, you'll enjoy your cards best when they're most accessible. Stocking them in boxes and stacking them in your closet is not recommended. Instead, buy a few ringed binders and keep your cards in plastic holders. Then you can easily use the cards for what they are—pieces of baseball memorabilia meant to help you recall and share your favorite baseball players and memories.

For more information on baseball card collecting, you can turn to a number of books. Written for kids, *Collecting Baseball Cards* (Millbrook Press, 2000) by Thomas S. Owens and the Running Press 1998 update of David Plaut's *Baseball Cards (Start Collecting)* still provide kids and adults with good overviews of the hobby and history of card collecting. For a more comprehensive look at the hobby, you can try Beckett's 1999 book *300 Great Baseball Cards of the 20th Century* by Mike Payne or *Cardboard Gems: A Century of Baseball Cards and Their Stories 1869-1969* (Maestro, 2008) by Khyber Oser. Beckett also publishes annual price catalogues and a monthly magazine on card collecting that you can purchase from most magazine sellers.

54 | WATCH THE MOVIE, 61*

A generation before the exciting, but steroid-tainted, home run battle between Mark McGwire and Sammy Sosa in 1998, another race for the single-season home run record riveted baseball. In 1961, two New York Yankees teammates, Mickey Mantle and Roger Maris, raced neck-and-neck for most of the season to surpass the record of 60 home runs hit in a single season set in 1927 by another New York Yankee, the great Babe Ruth. Baseball fans in New York and everywhere else were forced to choose who to root for: the incredibly popular, ten-year Yankee veteran Mickey Mantle, or the quiet, often brooding Roger Maris, who came to the Yankees just a year earlier when he won the American League's Most Valuable Player Award.

Most Yankee fans rooted for Mantle. Many thought he was living testimony to what it meant to be a Bronx Bomber, a man made for those celebrated Yankee pinstripes, the one who succeeded the Yankee Clipper Joe DiMaggio in center field, and went on to become one of the most popular Yankees ever. Maris, on the other hand, was a newcomer; some even vilified him as an intruder on Yankee tradition. He didn't own Mantle's magnetic charm. He was a rough fit in the Yankee clubhouse.

It all made for great baseball talk that magical 1961 season, and a great film 40 years later from director Billy Crystal. As a kid growing up in New York, the future comic and actor Crystal was a rabid Yankee fan. For Crystal, like many other young Baby Boomers, the Mantle-Maris home run race was a defining baseball moment.

You don't have to be a Baby Boomer or a Yankees fan who lived through the 1961 season to enjoy *61**. Released in 2001 by HBO, *61** digs deep into the storied competition between Maris and Mantle (or "the M&M Boys," as they were called). The film also presents a fascinating study of the dynamics of the major league locker room, the relentless pursuit by the media of a big baseball story, and the relationship between two of the game's biggest stars, playing for baseball's most popular team and chasing the game's most coveted record. Barry Pepper (Maris) and Thomas Jane (Mantle), turned in superior performances as the two leads, and Crystal's love of the story and baseball itself, along with his first-hand knowledge of the events, infuses *61** with a rare authenticity.

61* could have been suffocated by syrupy nostalgia and a Baby Boomer longing for the legendary days of "The Mick" and "Rog." Instead, Crystal painted flawed portraits of both ball players that detail their off-field problems as fascinating counterpoints to their on-field heroics. Mantle was a womanizer, carouser, and heavy drinker who, because of his importance to the Yankee line-up and his engaging personality, caused Yankee players and management, and even the media, to look away and excuse his wayward behavior. Maris, a family man, had a short fuse and was often aloof and antagonistic, especially when hounded by reporters. The two forged a necessary baseball friendship, though as men, they were worlds apart.

Beset by injuries, Mantle eventually fell out of the race, ending the season with 54 homers. Maris soldiered on and broke Ruth's record on the last day of the season. But controversy erupted almost immediately. The much-adored Babe Ruth had accomplished the feat of hitting 60 home runs in a 154-game season.

In 1961, the major league season expanded to 162-games, and it took Maris all of them to break Ruth's record. Which is why Ford Fricke, baseball's commissioner at the time, mandated that an asterisk be forever attached to Maris's 61-home runs record.

Crystal frames the story of Mantle and Maris as one big flashback; he begins the film with Mark McGwire closing in on Maris' record and ends it with the Maris family in the stands when McGwire breaks it. Some day, a film about McGwire's and Sosa's historic run at baseball's home run record will be made. When it is, the filmmakers will need to rise to home-run heights to fly higher than *61**.

> The film *61** is available in DVD for rental or purchase from most video stores and online movie sites. The film stars Thomas Jane as Mickey Mantle and Barry Pepper as Roger Maris. It also features supporting turns from the great character actors Richard Masur, Bruce McGill and Seymour Cassel. The film was released in 2001, the same year Billy Crystal and co-author Ron Smith released a book entitled *61**: The Story of Roger Maris, Mickey Mantle and One Magical Summer (McGraw-Hill). The book remains available from many used bookstores and online sellers.

55 | SEE THE PADRES PLAY AT PETCO PARK

Home of the National League's San Diego Padres, Petco Park ranks as one of the most unique ballparks in the major leagues. Although it debuted in 2004, just after the opening of numerous red brick retro-parks around the majors, the Padres took a wholly different tact in establishing the look and feel of their new ballpark. Petco doesn't dwell on tradition or nostalgia, though there are certainly hints of them at the park. Rather, Petco is pleasantly contemporary, bright, and spacious. Everything about it shouts San Diego and southern California, from the sunny colors to the close proximity of the harbor. You'd never mistake Petco for any other major league ballpark.

No big league ballpark integrates itself so seamlessly into its city or more successfully engages its visual and cultural surroundings. Much of the outfield opens up to downtown San Diego, so that views of the city's buildings complete Petco's panorama. Beyond the outfield wall sits "The Park in the Park," a green area that naturally merges the ballpark with the rest of the city. There you'll find a statue of Hall of Famer Tony Gwynn, winner of eight National League batting titles and the Padres greatest all-time player. On game days, the grass hill on which the Gwynn statue stands is usually filled with picnicking Padres fans sprawled out on blankets. Families with small children take advantage of the open space. Kids can roam and play, wander over to the mini-diamond to play whiffle ball or dig in "The Beachers," a sandy stretch behind the center field fence.

Petco Park's exterior, particularly the sharp lines and angles of its walls and office space, recall the Mayan and Aztec heritage of neighboring Mexico, whose border sits just a couple of miles away. Comprised of light natural stone and stucco draped with vines and indigenous plants and palm trees that sway in the sea breeze, Petco Park avoids the conventions of other major league ballparks. Baseball traditionalists might frown on Petco's distinctive features, but since the Padres only came into the National League in 1969, this isn't a team with a long history or a rich legacy of pennants and world championships.

For those baseball fans looking for a connection to the past in Petco Park, look no further than the Western Metal Supply Company building. You'll spot it adjacent to the left-field foul pole. After renovations, the historic building, with its red brick exterior, was incorporated into Petco's design. The integration not only acknowledges old San Diego, it pays tribute to Oriole Park at Camden Yards, the first great retro park and the one that popularized the integration of existing historic buildings into new stadium architecture.

Inside the Western Metal Supply Company building, you'll find the Padres team store, suites, a restaurant, and a small area that tells the story of San Diego

Petco Park in the heart of San Diego, California.

baseball. In 1936, San Diego became the home of the Pacific Coast League's Hollywood Stars; the club changed its name to the San Diego Padres after it arrived. The PCL San Diego Padres gave way and gave their name to the National League San Diego Padres when Major League Baseball granted the city an expansion franchise in 1969. The club played its home games in Jack Murphy Stadium (later renamed Qualcomm Stadium) until 2004, when it moved into the newly-built Petco Park.

Petco Park holds some 42,000 seats. Most offer good views of the playing field. Behind the seating area in the stadium's concourse area, you'll find plenty of concession stands, some of which sell surprisingly good seafood and Mexican fare, connecting Petco Park to San Diego's beach and Latino cultures. But all the smiles and pleasantries coming from Petco Park employees may still impress you more than anything else about the place. If Angel Stadium, located up the freeway in Anaheim is the American League's most friendly park, Petco wins the honor in the National League.

When talk among fans and other baseball people turns toward the best ballparks in the major leagues, Petco Park isn't an automatic part of the conversation, but it should be. With its architecture, food, good views and friendly folks, Petco Park will treat you to a very pleasant day of baseball.

For information about tours of Petco Park and tickets to Padres games, check the team's website at *www.padres.com*. With its pleasant year-round weather, San Diego makes for a good *Bucket List* visit early in the baseball season, when some other Major League Baseball cities are still enduring bouts of chilly, rainy weather. Check with the San Diego Chamber of Commerce for information about hotels, restaurants and other local amenities and attractions at *www.sdchamber.org*.

56 ATTEND A THEATRICAL PRODUCTION OF *DAMN YANKEES*

The musical *Damn Yankees* probably isn't the best baseball play you'll ever see, but it is undoubtedly the most popular. When it premiered on Broadway in 1955, New York baseball was at its zenith, with the Yankees, Brooklyn Dodgers, and New York Giants battling it out for Big Apple bragging rights, along with the world championship, practically every year. And then, pretty much like now, everyone who wasn't a Yankees fan, didn't just root against the ball club, they hated it. If nothing else, at least the title of the musical was right on the money.

So what makes *Damn Yankees* so memorable? Mostly, it's the music by Richard Adler and lyrics by Jerry Ross. At least two of its songs—"(You Gotta Have) Heart" and "Whatever Lola Wants"—are stage classics, with the former practically becoming the theme song of anyone in search of a brighter day. First sung on the stage by Gwen Verdon, the songs are lyrically rich and melodically infectious, though a bit dated, and helped the play win the 1956 Tony award for Best Musical. Through more than one thousand Broadway performances in the 1950s and another 718 during a mid-90s revival on Broadway, not to mention countless touring and local theater performances, *Damn Yankees* and its soundtrack worked its way into American popular culture and baseball history.

As for the story, well, *Damn Yankees* is hardly original. Based on the Douglass Wallop novel *The Year the Yankees Lost the Pennant*, the musical offers a standard Faustian tale of a forlorn sucker who sells his soul to the Devil for an earthly delight he would otherwise have no hope of ever enjoying. In the case of *Damn Yankees*, it's the story of Joe Boyd, a middle-aged, down-in-the-dumps Washington Senators fan (Senators fans were always down-in-the-dumps, and with good reason—their team pretty much lived in the American League cellar). Boyd meets a suave salesman, Mr. Applegate, who is actually the Devil. In conversation, Boyd says he'd do pretty much anything to "win the pennant from the damn Yankees." Applegate recognizes Boyd's frustration and offers him a deal: the chance to be the baseball hero on the World Series-winning Washington Senators in return for his soul.

> To find a stage production of *Damn Yankees*, check your local arts calendar or call your area theater company. If you're planning a trip to New York City and hope to catch the musical, check www.ibdb.com to see if it's being staged on Broadway in another revival. The recording featuring the original Broadway cast remains in print and can be ordered from most record stores, though make sure to distinguish it from a record by the rock band Damn Yankees. The original 1958 version of the film is available in VHS and DVD format and can be rented or purchased from many outlets. You can find all the lyrics to *Damn Yankees* original songs at www.thebroadwaymusicals.com/d/damnyankees.htm.

Boyd agrees and is transformed into Senators' rookie, Joe Hardy, a young slugger capable of taking the club all the way. Despite Hardy's heroics on the field, Boyd misses his wife and family and begins to second guess his deal with the Devil. To make sure Boyd doesn't back out, the Devil calls on Lola, the ultimate seductress, to keep Boyd's mind on baseball and something else Lola has to offer. In the end, of course, good triumphs over evil, Boyd recognizes his mistake and with the help of Lola, outwits the Devil, returns to his family, and saves his soul.

The stage version of *Damn Yankees* was so successful that Hollywood took a shot at the musical in 1958 when Warner Brothers bought the film rights and got Gwen Verdon and Tab Hunter to star in it. Hunter, at the time a teen heartthrob, barely cut it as Joe Boyd. But the popularity of the play helped carry the movie and the soundtrack recording. Since then, countless local and regional productions of *Damn Yankees* have hit stages across America, and another version of the film is scheduled for release in 2012 to bring the story to a brand new generation of filmgoers, baseball fans and Yankee haters.

57 ATTEND THE HALL OF FAME CLASSIC WEEKEND IN COOPERSTOWN

For 68 years, the Hall of Fame Game pitted two major league teams against one another on Father's Day on Doubleday Field in Cooperstown. But that game, which occurred in the middle of the Major League Baseball season, proved too disruptive to the participating team's regular season schedules. So although the game sold out every year and boasted a history dating back to the National Baseball Hall of Fame and Museum's earliest days, Major League Baseball opted to end the tradition in 2008.

The Hall of Fame Classic was born the following year as a new way to fill up the Hall of Fame induction weekend schedule and pay tribute to the players being enshrined each year. Instead of a game between two major league teams, the Hall of Fame Classic fields two teams made up of retired players and Hall of Famers. The quality of play isn't the same as what fans saw in earlier Hall of Fame games; for instance, the inaugural Hall of Fame Classic in 2009 featured 90-year-old Bob Feller (Hall of Fame Class of 1962) on the mound, albeit briefly. Also, the game is seven, not nine innings long. And there are plenty of light moments that make the game more a celebration of baseball nostalgia than a true competitive contest. But that's its allure. The Hall of Fame Classic is like no other game you'll get to see, save Old Timer's Day games. And when you make the trek to Cooperstown to see the Hall of Fame Classic, you can visit the National Baseball Hall of Fame and Museum and tour the village of Cooperstown, checking off a total of three *Bucket List* items in one memorable weekend.

The Hall of Fame Classic Weekend is attraction enough. In addition to the game, it offers a parade on Main Street preceding the ballgame on Sunday when bands from the Cooperstown area march down the biggest street in the village, followed by the legends who will be playing in the Classic. After the parade, fans are invited to watch the Hitting Contest at Doubleday Field. All the players participating in the contest and the game make themselves available for autographs and pictures, giving fans access to baseball greats without having to pay for the privilege.

The day before the game, the National Baseball Hall of Fame and Museum hosts numerous special events, including talks by baseball experts, book signings by authors with new baseball books, and programs produced by the museum's education staff. One of the best events is called "Voices of the Game." It features a half-dozen or so Hall of Famers discussing their careers and answering questions from the audience in the museum's Grandstand Theater. Some of these events are for museum members only, so signing up as a museum member is a good idea before attending a Hall of Fame Classic Weekend. That way you can register in advance for these programs and be certain to take advantage of all that is offered at the museum during the weekend.

The Hall of Fame Classic Weekend is the perfect time to visit Cooperstown with your family, especially if you have young children. The Father's Day connection aside, there are plenty of activities for kids during the weekend, including skills clinics, playing catch on Doubleday Field, and running its bases after the game. Doubleday Field, which featured the first Hall of Fame Game back in 1940, is a classic ballpark. Located just down the street from the National Baseball Hall of Fame and Museum on Main Street, its cozy environment and history make it a must-see ballpark. So many great players have played at Doubleday and there is something about watching a game there or playing catch on the field that will touch your baseball soul.

> To find out more about the Hall of Fame Classic Weekend, check out the museum's website at www.baseballhall.org or call 1-888-HALL-OF-FAME. Father's Day is a popular time to visit Cooperstown, so buy tickets and make your hotel reservations early. Check the Cooperstown Chamber of Commerce website (www.cooperstownchamber.org) for information about local lodging and restaurants.

58 | SEE AN INTERLEAGUE GAME

Teams from the American and National Leagues began playing each other during the regular season in 1997. But the argument over whether or not this was a good idea carries on. Not surprisingly, most traditionalists view interleague play the same way they view the use of the designated hitter: with disdain. Baseball was good enough before the American League took the pitcher out of the offensive game, so the thinking goes; why mess with something that worked for well over a century? And for at least as long, American and National League teams were kept separate until the pennant winners squared off every October in the World Series. Why mess with that, too? The answer to both questions: money.

With its great tradition and mystique, we sometimes forget that Major League Baseball is a business. It is about making money, lots of it. In 1997, owners saw the opportunity to drum up more fan excitement by fostering new interleague rivalries and scheduling games between teams that never played each other before in the regular season. Three years earlier, a player's strike paralyzed baseball, and fan interest in the game, so the owners thought, was fading. What the game needed was something new to get fans back to the ballpark. So interleague play was born.

Hardcore traditionalists aside, it didn't take most baseball fans long to get used to the idea of interleague play. It now stands as an annual baseball ritual that begins in mid-May and lasts until the All-Star break in early July. At first, interleague play was limited to games between teams from corresponding divisions in the American and National Leagues. That is, teams from the American League East would only play teams from National League East, and so on. However, by 2002, interleague play tossed out these restrictions. Now it's possible to see all kinds of interleague match-ups each season.

Which interleague games are the best? Clearly, the ones that involve inter-city and interstate rivals rise to the top of the list. The New York Yankees vs. the New York Mets draws a lot of attention in the Big Apple and beyond. When the Chicago Cubs square off against the Chicago White Sox, it's the North side of the Windy City against the South side. The San Francisco Giants and Oakland A's battle for Bay Area bragging rights, while the Florida Marlins fight for Sunshine State supremacy against the Tampa Bay Rays. Then there is the Astros-Rangers in Texas, the Royals-Cards in Missouri, and the Indians-Reds in Ohio. All are interesting to watch. Even more interesting is the way rival fans interact, meaning sometimes the real fun is in the stands.

If there has been a downside to interleague play, it's been in the post-season. The exclusive, interleague nature of the World Series is gone. No more wondering what a match up between the Philadelphia Phillies and the New York Yankees might be like, or the Dodgers and Red Sox. Sooner or later, these teams will play each other in May or June, even if it isn't for all the marbles. But, then again, given that only two teams make the World Series each season, and many teams go decades before putting in an appearance, you could have waited the rest of your life and not had the chance to catch some American League vs. National League match-ups that now occur regularly thanks to regular season interleague play.

> To find a full schedule of all the interleague games every season, go to *www.mlb.com*. You can check out the interleague schedule for your favorite team by going to the site and clicking through to your favorite team's website. Interleague games often sell-out, so get your tickets early.

59 SEE THE DODGERS PLAY THE GIANTS

Today, it's hard to imagine a baseball rivalry more intense than the one between the New York Yankees and the Boston Red Sox. But through the years and changing zip codes, the competition between Dodgers and Giants has come close.

That both teams originally played in the same city, New York, and in the same National League, gave the rivalry its original vigor. And when the Brooklyn Dodgers headed west in 1958 for the sunshine of Los Angeles and the promise of a new ballpark, the Giants immediately followed, settling in the cooler climes of San Francisco. Had the Giants not left New York with the Dodgers, the rivalry might have stalled and withered. Instead, it took a California twist, one that West Coast fans wasted little time embracing and, in some ways, even escalating.

The two California cities engaged in a multi-faceted rivalry before Major League Baseball arrived. Southern California vs. Northern California. Sun vs. Shade. Hollywood and Hedonism vs. Hipsters and Hell's Angels. Beginning in 1958, two transplanted Major League Baseball teams joined the fray.

The California rivalry reached a bloody boiling point in 1965. With Dodger pitcher Sandy Koufax on the mound and catcher Johnny Roseboro behind the plate, Giants pitcher Juan Marichal, who had already hit two Dodgers batters in the game, stepped into the batter's box. Intimidation has always demanded a place in baseball, and Roseboro, wanting to rattle Marichal, threw Koufax's pitched ball back to the mound. The problem was that the throw back nearly nicked Marichal's ear. Words were exchanged, then violence ensued. Incredibly, Marichal whacked Roseboro in the head with his bat, causing a nasty gash. Blood flowed down Roseboro's face. Benches cleared. More fights erupted. The rivalry intensified. The incident remained fresh in the minds of both teams for years to come.

> For more information about tickets and dates for upcoming Dodger-Giants games, check the teams' websites: www.dodgers.mlb.com and www.sfgiants.com. To learn more about the history of the rivalry, you can read Andrew Goldblatt's book *The Giants and the Dodgers: Four Cities, Two Teams, One Rivalry* (McFarland and Co., 2003). HBO's *Brooklyn Dodgers: The Ghosts of Flatbush* (2007) also highlights the Giants-Dodgers rivalry, and does a good job of encapsulating its most famous moment: Bobby Thomson's "Shot Heard Round the World."

That might have been the nastiest moment of the Giants-Dodgers rivalry, but its greatest moment occurred in 1951, back in New York. That year the National League pennant race seemed all but over in mid-August. The Dodgers held a commanding 13½ game lead over the Giants. Dodger manager Chuck Dressen boasted that "The Giants is dead." Whether it was that remark that sparked the Giants or the dazzling play of their rookie center fielder Willie Mays, or the pulling together of the entire team, or all of the above, the Giants surged. By the time the season ended, the Giants had miraculously pulled into a tie for first place with their crosstown rival, prompting a three game play-off to determine what team would represent the National League in the World Series.

One can only imagine the baseball fervor that filled the autumn air in New York that September. The Giants won the first game, but the Dodgers came back to take the second. In the bottom of the ninth inning of Game 3 with the Dodgers clinging to a one-run lead, Giants outfielder Bobby Thomson stepped to the plate with a man on base. With each pitch, the excitement at the Polo Grounds grew. And then Thomson hit "The Shot Heard Round the World"—a home run to win the pennant. Thomson's clutch homer regularly lands atop lists of the most famous and dramatic moments in baseball history. And at the bottom of Dodgers' fans lists of their least favorite and most heartbreaking moments.

Today, the Dodgers-Giants rivalry remains robust. Both teams compete in the National League's West Division and square off 18 times each regular season, nine times in each team's beautiful home ballpark. Catch a game at either AT&T Park or Dodger Stadium, and you'll feel the competitive tension in the air.

60 READ THE WRITINGS OF A. BARTLETT GIAMATTI ⚾⚾

Ordinary baseball fans might not recognize the name A. Bartlett Giamatti, a Renaissance scholar and former president of Yale University who was also president of the National League and served briefly as Commissioner of Major League Baseball before his untimely death in 1989. Giamatti was in the latter role for just five months, from April to September, but his time in baseball was significant. He was the one, for instance, who banned Pete Rose from baseball for betting on major league games. Giamatti, a fan of baseball as much as a leader of it, was also the game's most compelling scholar and philosopher, and one of its most unique writers.

The political and baseball essayist George Will once wrote that "Giamatti was to the Commissioner's office what Sandy Koufax was to the pitcher's mound: Giamatti's career had the highest ratio of excellence to longevity." Another great baseball writer, Roger Angell, wrote of Giamatti, "As exceptions are measured, he belonged on Mt. Rushmore." And finally, the late baseball historian David Halberstam wrote that Giamatti "loved baseball, he loved history, he loved ideas, and he loved words."

A. Bartlett Giamatti was far from a typical baseball figure. He had a degree in English and a Ph.D. in Comparative Literature from Yale University. He taught literature and Italian at Yale and Princeton, before becoming president of his alma mater in 1978. He wrote scholarly books such as *Earthly Paradise and the Renaissance Epic* (1966), *Play of Double Senses: Spenser's Faerie Queene* (1975), and *Exile and Change in Renaissance Literature* (1984). A lifelong Red Sox fan, Giamatti also wrote about baseball, mostly thought-provoking essays on the essence of the game and its meaning in American culture. In 1986 he was appointed president of the National League. Three years later, he became Commissioner of Major League Baseball, but died suddenly before the season was over, sending shock waves through baseball. Everyone in baseball knew the game had lost the caretaker of its soul and its most eloquent poet.

Despite his scholarly background and intellectual tomes, Giamatti's baseball writings are crisp and clear and surprisingly accessible to the average fan. Perhaps that's what was best about Giamatti's essays. The ideas might have been complex, the kind that don't occur naturally in the minds of most fans. Yet the manner in which Giamatti presented them made his ideas understandable to all who longed to think more deeply about the national pastime, but hadn't been shown the way.

To learn more about A. Bartlett Giamatti's thoughts on baseball, start with *A Great and Glorious Game*, a collection of Giamatti's baseball essays that was published posthumously in 1998 by Algonquin Books and edited by Kenneth S. Robson. It features some of Giamatti's best pieces, including "Tom Seaver's Farewell" (*Harper's Magazine*, 1977), an essay that Giamatti wrote after learning that the New York Mets had traded their greatest pitcher; "Men of Baseball, Lend an Ear" (*New York Times*, 1981) a piece about baseball's labor strike; "Baseball and the American Character," a paper presented to the Massachusetts Historical Society in 1985 that brought together the history of baseball with that of America and revealed how the two were intricately connected; and perhaps his most famous piece, "The Green Fields of the Mind," which appeared in November of 1977 in the *Yale Alumni Magazine*—exquisitely written, this short musing on the inherent beauty of baseball strikes the heart of most everyone who reads it.

Another collection of Giamatti's writings is contained in *Take Time for Paradise* (Summit, 1989). Not exclusively about baseball—Giamatti also ponders the role of sports and play, in general, in American culture—*Take Time for Paradise* features "Baseball As Narrative," a challenging, but powerful essay about how the game brings meaning to our lives. Finally, *Bart: A Life of A. Bartlett Giamatti by Him and about Him*, compiled by Anthony Valero for Harcourt, Brace, Jovanovich in 1991, contains biographical bits and pieces, plus quotes and interviews, either by Giamatti or those he touched. It's a quick, easy read, but it will give you a good sense of Giamatti, who, aside from some of the great players, might be the most missed man in all of baseball.

> A. Bartlett Giamatti's *A Great and Glorious Game* remains in print and can be ordered from most retail and online booksellers. *Take Time for Paradise and Bart: A Life of A. Bartlett Giamatti by Him and about Him* can be purchased at many used bookstores and online booksellers. All three can be found at many libraries.

VISIT THE YOGI BERRA MUSEUM AND LEARNING CENTER

61

Far more than just a tribute to a long and wildly successful career in Major League Baseball, the Yogi Berra Museum and Learning Center teaches area youth valuable life lessons. It also tells visitors the story of the New York Yankees, with a particular emphasis on the glory years of the 1950s, when the Big Apple was baseball and vice versa. During this exciting, post-war decade, three New York teams—the Yankees, the Brooklyn Dodgers, and the New York Giants—battled, not just for the baseball hearts of New Yorkers, but for baseball supremacy in America.

New York teams, with a couple of exceptions, owned the World Series in the 1950s, and Yogi Berra played in most of them. America focused on New York baseball because it had the best teams and they played in the media capital of the world. The New York-based baseball men in this chapter of the game's history are legendary: Jackie Robinson, Mickey Mantle, Willie Mays, Duke Snider, Whitey Ford, Pee Wee Reese, Leo Durocher, Monte Irvin, Phil Rizzuto, Gil Hodges, Don Newcombe, Don Larsen, Roy Campanella, Casey Stengel and, of course, Yogi Berra—names etched into the memories of nearly every baby boomer who grew up a baseball fan in the 1950s.

The museum is located on the campus of Montclair State University in Little Falls, New Jersey, next to Yogi Berra Stadium, home of the New Jersey Jackals (a club in the Canadian American Association of Professional Baseball). A half hour's car ride from Manhattan, the Yogi Berra Museum and Learning Center is one of the best "small" baseball museums in America. And you don't have to be a Yankees fan to enjoy it (though, it undoubtedly helps). Because, while Berra was a longtime wearer of pinstripes, few baseball fans of any stripe would deny the importance of his contributions to the game and the warmth and humor of his character. In fact, there may be no more beloved player in the history of baseball than Yogi Berra.

As the museum points out in concise, colorful displays, Berra was born in St. Louis into an Italian-American family, and fell in love with sports, especially baseball. He served in World War II, participating in the D-Day invasion of France in 1944, and went on to spend 18 seasons as an integral part of the New York Yankees. He hit 358 career home runs and batted .285, while playing the demanding position of catcher for most of his career. In all, Berra played in 14

Word Series and earned ten world championship rings, more than any other player in the history of Major League Baseball.

Longtime Yankees fans know of Berra's many accomplishments on the field. However, when the rest of America thinks of Yogi, they instantly conjure up an image of a small, folksy character with a five o'clock shadow who innocently uttered some of the most memorable malapropisms in American culture. "When you come to a fork in the road, take it." "You can observe a lot by watching." "Ninety percent of the game is half mental." "Nobody goes there anymore, it's too crowded." And, of course: "It ain't over 'til it's over." Quotes like these represent the legacy of Yogi Berra as much as his extraordinary accomplishments on the baseball field.

The museum documents the most important aspects of Yogi's life and career through memorabilia and artifacts, including the catcher's mitt that Berra used to catch Don Larsen's perfect game in the 1956 World Series against the Dodgers. They do much to tell Berra's baseball story. But there are also wonderful displays that go beyond Berra. For instance, upon entering the museum, you see an exhibit on baseball catchers, the most under-appreciated and unglamorous players in baseball, complete with early catcher's masks and mitts. There is also an exhibit on the early history of baseball—as good as any outside of Cooperstown—and the story of how the Yankees grew from the New York Highlanders into the greatest and most successful franchise in all of baseball. Along the way, the museum makes certain to equate the story of baseball, whenever it can, to the story of America in the 20th century.

The Yogi Berra Museum and Learning Center also lives up to the latter part of its name. Museum programs use baseball as a tool to promote literacy, conflict resolution, and human rights. These programs and others regularly take place in the museum and attract kids from around the New York metropolitan area. Visitors to the museum probably won't be able to participate in these programs, but it's nice to know that they exist, and if you become a museum member, some of the membership fee goes to support these programs.

> To find out more about the Yogi Berra Museum and Learning Center, call (973) 655-2378. You can also consult the facility's website at www.yogiberramuseum.org for directions, cost of admission, hours, membership, and educational programs.

WATCH THE MOVIE, *SOUL OF THE GAME* ✦

62

Soul of the Game, an HBO movie that first aired in 1996, tells the story of three Negro League baseball greats, Satchel Paige (Delroy Lindo), Josh Gibson (Mykelti Williamson), and Jackie Robinson (Blair Underwood), and the long-awaited demise of racial segregation in professional baseball. That *Soul of the Game* never made it to movie theaters might be one reason why this wonderful portrait of the Negro Leagues gets overlooked whenever the great baseball films are discussed. That the film lacked big-time African-American actors in starring roles might be another reason. Nevertheless, *Soul of the Game* remains the best cinematic account of this important era in baseball history. Illuminating and entertaining, *Soul of the Game* captures the spirit of black baseball and reminds us that for much of its history, our national pastime was rife with racism, denying great players, like Paige and Gibson, the opportunity to play in the majors and reap its benefits.

Before Jackie Robinson broke baseball's color barrier in 1947, black ballplayers played in the Negro Leagues with clubs like the Kansas City Monarchs, Homestead Grays, Newark Eagles, and Birmingham Black Barons. Baseball's first commissioner, the resolutely racist Judge Kenesaw Mountain Landis, made certain that no black players were signed to major league clubs. But after his death in 1944, the possibility of change surfaced. The more liberal-minded Happy Chandler succeeded Landis as baseball commissioner, enabling the forward-thinking general manager of the Brooklyn Dodgers, Branch Rickey, to sign Robinson to a major league contract. Rickey, though not one of the main figures in *Soul of the Game*, is actually one of its heroes. Played by Ed Hermann, Rickey planned his move to bring black players into the majors with stealth and cunning and in the end, recognized that Jackie Robinson was the right player to take on racism in baseball, and succeed.

Still, there were black ballplayers at the time who were better players than Robinson, and that's what *Soul of the Game* is mostly about. The Negro Leagues' greatest pitcher, Satchel Paige, and its greatest home run hitter, Josh Gibson were both poised to make the jump before Robinson. His unparalleled pitching brilliance made Paige the most obvious choice, but with arm problems and advancing age, he knew his time was running out. Gibson, a ferocious long-ball hitter, would have been a close second choice. But neither player possessed the necessary character traits and emotional muscle to endure the endless taunts, threats, and racist outbursts that would greet the first black ballplayer in the majors on a daily basis. Robinson, a graduate of UCLA and an army veteran who had won a court martial trial for refusing to move to the back of a military bus, knew the stakes and what he would come up against. What Rickey presented to Robinson was less about baseball—though Rickey signed Robinson to help the Dodgers win a World Series—and more about changing American history.

Paige would get his chance to play in the major leagues in 1948, a year after Robinson and another black player, Larry Doby, got major league contracts. Paige signed on with the Cleveland Indians, the same team that signed Doby, and promptly helped Cleveland win the World Series that year. Exactly how old Paige was in 1948 is a matter of debate. Most baseball historians believe he was 41 or 42, making him the oldest rookie ever to play Major League Baseball. Gibson's story is another matter. Suffering from headaches, emotional distress, and alcoholism, Gibson never made it to the big leagues. He died of a brain tumor in 1947 at age 36. Robinson, of course, went on to baseball greatness, helping the Dodgers become one of the National League's dominant teams in the immediate post-war era. He won Rookie of the Year in 1947 and Most Valuable Player in 1949, and helped Brooklyn claim a World Championship in 1955. Robinson, along with Paige and Gibson, became the first black players inducted into the National Baseball Hall of Fame.

As both entertainment and education chronicling one of baseball's most exciting eras, *Soul of the Game* gets it all right—the mood of the country, the baseball style of the Negro Leagues, and the disappointment of Paige and Gibson when they find out they won't be the first black players to be called up to the big leagues. Astutely directed by Kevin Rodney Sullivan, *Soul of the Game* brings back to life a time when baseball was front and center in not just reflecting America, but in changing it, too.

HBO's *Soul of the Game* still plays occasionally on the cable network. Check *www.hbo.com* for its next scheduled airing. DVD copies of the film are also available for rental and purchase from movie stores and online retailers. The film runs 94 minutes and carries a PG-13 rating.

63 SEE THE ROCKIES PLAY AT COORS FIELD

Location has a lot to do with a ballpark's allure. Downtown parks that blend effortlessly into their urban settings—including classics like Fenway and Wrigley along with newer urban gems like Cleveland's Progressive, Seattle's Safeco, San Diego's Petco, and PNC Park in Pittsburgh—are the most admirable. Add Coors Field, home of the National League's Colorado Rockies, to that list. Sitting at the cross-section of 20th and Blake Streets in Denver's lower downtown (or "LoDo" district), Coors Field, with its red brick walls and other architectural references to the classic parks of yesteryear, stands as one of the better retro parks in Major League Baseball.

But while other urban ballpark designs showcase their surrounding cityscapes by offering fans sightlines of downtown buildings, Coors Field showcases a different kind of view. Spectators sitting along the first-base and right-field sections of the ballpark enjoy stunning views of the Rocky Mountains, America's most magnificent mountain range. When the sky is clear, you'll see some of the peaks that help define Denver's special relationship with the mountains and give the Colorado Rockies their name.

Named after the beer company that calls the Denver area home, Coors Field opened in 1995, and quickly emerged as Major League Baseball's most controversial ballpark. Coors' Mile High City location allegedly caused balls to fly further through its thin mountain air. In 1999 alone, 303 home runs soared over the Coors Field fence, making the ballpark the offensive capital of baseball—in both senses of the term "offensive." Because while hitters enjoyed going yard at Coors, opposing pitchers resented serving up so many gopher balls. Leads, even big leads, had a way of quickly evaporating in Coors' mountain air.

Then the scientists got involved. According to their findings, it wasn't Coors' high-altitude that transformed routine fly balls into towering home runs, but Denver's dry air, which made the balls harder and easier to smack out of the park. So the Rockies began to store baseballs in a humidor and, soon after, dingers declined in Denver. Coors Field still hosts a healthy share of home runs, just not the ridiculous quantity of moon shots it served as the launching pad for in the mid-1990s.

With a capacity of just over 50,000, Coors ranks as one of the larger of the new retro parks. The original plan was for some 44,000 seats. But Denver became so taken with the Rockies (the team drew a remarkable 4.5 million fans during its maiden year of 1993 while playing in Mile High Stadium) that the club decided to add more upper deck seats. The Rockies remain one of the better draws in the National League, and when Coors Field is filled, the ballpark looks, sounds, and feels big.

Usually when you go to a ballpark for the first time, you try to sit in the best seats you can afford. One exception is Wrigley Field, where most fans prefer the bleacher experience. The other is Coors Field. When you buy your game tickets, make sure you ask to sit in the 20th row of the upper deck. While all the other seats are dark green, the seats in this row are Colorado Rockies purple. Sit in them and you are officially one mile above sea level. But wait for the summer months for your mile-high baseball experience. In April and May, the weather in Denver can be brutal. The higher you sit, the lower the wind chill.

Debuting in 1991, the Rockies haven't been around long enough to establish much of a baseball tradition. So, you won't find much team history celebrated at Coors Field. But most everything else about the ballpark is impressive and makes for a great Major League Baseball experience.

> For information about tours of Coors Field or tickets to Rockies' games, check the team's website at *www.coloradorockies.com*. To learn more about the Colorado Rockies, read Tony DeMarco's *Tales From the Colorado Rockies* (Sports Publishing LLC, 2008).

64 ATTEND THE TRIPLE-A ALL-STAR GAME

The annual Triple-A All-Star game pits the top players from the International League against those from the Pacific Coast League. (The third Triple-A League affiliated with Major League Baseball—the Mexican League—does not participate.) Held each July around the same time that Major League Baseball holds its Mid-Summer Classic, the Triple-A All-Star game is a celebration of the best Triple-A baseball talent from across the United States.

Many of the players who play will get a call-up to "The Show" before the season ends. Some will go for a cup of coffee and then return to Triple-A for more minor league work. Others will go up to their affiliated big league club and stay there. Among the major league stars that have played in the Triple-A All-Star game are Derek Jeter, Jim Thome, Alfonso Soriano, Todd Helton, Chipper Jones, and Pedro Martinez, to mention but a few.

Although the International League's origins extend all the way back to 1884 and the Pacific Coast League began play in 1903, the first Triple-A All-Star game wasn't held until 1988. For its first ten years, the All-Star game featured the best players from minor league teams affiliated with big league ball clubs from the American League against those with National League affiliations. Most Valuable Player Awards were handed out to the top players from the old American Association, the Pacific Coast League, and the International League. After the American Association merged with the Pacific Coast League in 1997, a true All-Star game that featured the best players from one league against those of the other began. In 1998, All-Stars from the Pacific Coast League played against All-Stars from the International League, and the rivalry began.

Similar to the Major League Baseball All-Star game, the Triple-A game includes a home run derby and a fan fest, plus appearances by former major league greats, autograph signings, and other special programs. Unlike the events that surround the major league classic, which get mobbed by fans that come to the game's festivities from all over the country, the Triple-A events are accessible and easy to navigate. You'll be hard-pressed to get a good ticket for the Major League Baseball All-Star game without corporate connections or spending a lot of money. Tickets for the Triple-A game, on the other hand, are readily attainable, especially if you get them well in advance of the game, and you won't have to take a second mortgage out on your house to pay for them.

Expect to find plenty of families and kids at the game, the way you would at all minor league games. But all those kids in the stands also means mascots aplenty, goofy between-inning competitions, and other gimmicks designed to entertain the young ones. Some serious baseball fans might view all this as a nuisance and a distraction from the game itself, but having families and kids at games helps foster the next generation of baseball fans.

As for the All-Star game itself, chances are you'll see a high brand of minor league baseball, as most players invited to play in it view the game as a prime showcase for their individual talents. Few minor league games get more media scrutiny or more people attending the game, and there are plenty of scouts in the stands. Thus, most of the All-Stars are motivated to play hard.

Keep score. Ten years down the road, you'll be able to look back at your scorecard to determine if any of the players you saw in the Triple-A All-Star game are now major league All-Star. Chances are, a few will have made the jump.

> The Triple-A All-Star game has no permanent location; instead, like the major league game, it moves from one team's host city to another. To find out where this year's Triple-A All-Star game will take place and to get ticket information, see either the website for the Pacific Coast League (www.pacificcoastleague.com) or the International League (www.internationalleague.com).

65 | SEE THE METS PLAY AT CITI FIELD

The argument will continue for decades amongst Big Apple baseball fans: which New York major league ballpark is better: the Mets' Citi Field or the Yankees' new version of "the House that Ruth Built." Both opened in 2009, garnering much attention and acclaim, and both are on the *Baseball Fan's Bucket List*. Of course you need to chart out the parameters of "better" if you really want an answer to the question and avoid understandable emotional loyalty to either the Mets or Yankees. Still, my vote goes to Citi Field.

Located in Queens, on the other side of the subway tracks from the Mets' former home, Shea Stadium, Citi Field rates as one of the most beautiful ballparks in the major leagues. Inspired by the Brooklyn Dodgers' old Ebbets Field, one of the most beloved ballparks in baseball history, Citi Field features a red brick, limestone and granite exterior. Many other retro parks use the same materials. But Citi Field adds numerous, unique touches that make it an especially impressive architectural achievement linking baseball's past with its present.

Aside from the curvy Ebbets Field-like entrance with the large windows and all that brick, the single most memorable aspect of Citi Field is the Jackie Robinson Rotunda. Come into the park through the home plate entrance and you're in the Rotunda, a magnificent gathering place for all baseball fans to contemplate the heroic accomplishments of the Brooklyn Dodger who broke the color barrier in baseball back in 1947. The main entrance to Citi Field, the Jackie Robinson Rotunda feels open and airy, but also conveys an intimacy and stateliness befitting one of America's greatest civil rights heroes.

Inside the rotunda, just above the entry, you'll see one of Robinson's most memorable quotes: "A life is not important except in the impact it has on other lives." Robinson had more impact on other lives than any other major league ballplayer by enduring and then beating racial prejudice and proving that black ballplayers could compete with white ones, forever changing the national pastime and American society. Robinson triumphed by adhering to a series of ideals—excellence, citizenship, commitment, determination, persistence, teamwork, courage, and justice—that are celebrated on the curved rotunda wall. Each ideal is acknowledged and explained on granite blocks. Pause and read them all and you'll appreciate Robinson's greatness, not simply as a player, but more importantly, as a human being.

It was nice of the Mets to create such a tribute to Jackie Robinson, who, after all, played for a different New York team located in a rival city borough and finished his career over a half-decade before the Mets even came into existence in 1962. Perhaps it's an effort to deflect attention from the Mets' early, painful years, including their debut season, when the club lost 120 games, a record of futility that still stands. But the club has gone on to win two World Series, four pennants and field a lot of great players. Mets' history is celebrated at Citi Field by way of player photo banners that hang along the exterior walls. Inside you'll find an interactive mini-museum and Hall of Fame display, plus newer banners celebrating the Mets' best teams on the left-field wall.

With New York ranking as one of the world's great food cities, you'd expect Citi Field to rank among the best in ballpark fare, and it does. But identity confusion is baked into the great food as well. The hamburgers are called Brooklyn Burgers. Nathan's Hot Dogs are a must, but Nathan's made its name at Coney Island, a part of Brooklyn. For more expensive tastes, a trip to either Ebbets Club (dare I say it?) for a five-star ballpark meal is the way to go. But the best place to eat at Citi Field, is the Shake Shack, located in what's called "Taste of the City" just beyond the center-field wall. Order a burger with fries and follow it with a frozen custard and you'll learn why many Mets' fans consider it the best baseball meal in New York.

The New York Mets' gem of a stadium.

But Citi Field offers visitors a lot more than good food, Ebbets Field nostalgia and the Jackie Robinson tribute. The concourse just above the field level has low ceilings, just like the parks of yesteryear, a nice touch. With just under 42,000 seats, Citi Field is considerably smaller than Shea, which held over 57,000. The downsizing leads to cleaner sight lines and a closer view of the playing field. Like Ebbets, the outfield wall is uneven, with nooks and crannies and crazy angles, making balls that carom off the wall a challenge to field. The Mets' old home of Shea Stadium gets a few nods in addition to all the ones directed toward Ebbets. The famous red home run apple that used to pop up just beyond the outfield wall in Shea every time a Met smacked one out of the park has a new home at Citi Field. And the sight and sound of airplanes making their final approach into nearby La Guardia Airport that provided Shea with much of its "ambiance" also add to the look and feel of Citi Field.

For more information about Citi Field and tickets to Mets' games, check the team's website at *www.mets.com*.

66 SUBSCRIBE TO AND READ
BASEBALL AMERICA ✲✲

You know you've turned into a hardcore baseball fan when you start subscribing to *Baseball America*. Read by front office types, coaches and managers, scouts, and serious baseball fans, *Baseball America* is not a consumer-driven publication like *Sports Illustrated* or the *Sporting News*. Coverage of the major leagues moves copies at the newsstand and attracts advertisers. But MLB coverage makes up only a part of *Baseball America*.

The magazine deals with all aspects and levels of baseball, with an emphasis on high school and college players, and all the minor leagues. *Baseball America* also covers Japanese baseball and other international leagues. Columnists such as Peter Gammons and other prominent baseball writers editorialize on different facets of the game and its players, while other scribes detail the business of baseball.

Published bi-weekly, *Baseball America* overflows with statistics, information on prospects and ball clubs. Reading it for a full year will immeasurably broaden your knowledge of contemporary baseball, and give you plenty of insight into its future, too. Such baseball intelligence comes with a price, however. Yearly subscriptions cost in the neighborhood of one hundred bucks, which is why a lot of fans dismiss *Baseball America* as a luxury they can't afford. But the magazine will prove invaluable to fantasy baseball fanatics and fans looking to learn about young ballplayers before they make their major league debuts. An annual subscription also enables you to visit *www.baseballamerica.com*, the magazine's highly regarded website. Enjoy all that for a year and you'll probably consider the *Baseball America* subscription price a bargain.

Baseball America began in 1981 under its original name, *All-America Baseball News*. From the beginning, the magazine presented a Minor League Player of the Year Award, thus creating a reputation for coverage of the minor leagues. *Baseball America*'s credibility increased further when it began publishing baseball books that weren't available in bookstores, yet contained information and insights that made them essential reading for scouts and amateur baseball fans.

Baseball America's *Draft Almanac* covers the baseball draft in detail, with information on draftees, previous drafts, team needs and other pertinent information. The magazine also publishes the *Baseball America Directory*, which contains contact information for every pro team's personnel, plus schedules, league information, ballpark directions, and other assorted tidbits. Then there's the *Baseball America Prospect Handbook*, which includes essential information for the top thirty prospects for every ball club in professional baseball. *Baseball America* also publishes extras like a calendar and an encyclopedia of minor league baseball.

Certain issues of *Baseball America* are more important than others. The amateur draft issues—the one that previews the draft and the one that analyzes it—should be required reading. Same goes for the College Preview and College World Series issues, with their comprehensive and enlightening coverage.

Be advised: the *Baseball America* website can be addictive; you could find yourself habitually visiting it for up-to-the-minute baseball reports and player development progress on all levels. The website, along with all the *Baseball America* publications live up to the magazine's motto: "Baseball news you can't find anywhere else."

For more information on *Baseball America* and how to subscribe, go to *www.baseballamerica.com.*

67 SEE THE YANKEES PLAY AT YANKEE STADIUM

The old Yankee Stadium was known as "The House That Ruth Built." The new Yankee Stadium ought to be called, "The House That A Billion Dollars Built." Actually, more like a billion-and-a-half. Opened in 2009, the extravagant new home of the New York Yankees is massive (500,000 square feet bigger than the old Yankee Stadium), often mall-like, and yet, in many ways, magnificent. It is a temple to baseball's greatest and most successful franchise. No other ballpark on the planet boasts such a stately and majestic design, or such a price tag.

Yankee Stadium is constructed of tons upon tons of concrete, steel and granite. Elegant is the first word that comes to mind when describing it. Expensive is a close second, and that cost has been passed on to the fans. The top ticket at the Bronx stadium resembles a car payment for moderate-income Yankee fans living in the suburbs. Food, a cheap souvenir, a program, and a couple of cold ones can set you back another hundred bucks. Then there's the transportation expenses you incur just getting there. (Note: Do not drive to Yankee Stadium; take the "D" train from midtown Manhattan. You'll save serious money on parking, tolls, etc. and get to experience the arrogance of hardcore Yankee fans up close in the subway tunnels.)

The new Yankee Stadium is actually the third Yankee Stadium. The first two stood across 161st Street on the stadium's south side, on what is now Heritage Field. The Yankees, originally known as the Highlanders, began their baseball lives playing in the old Polo Grounds, the home of the New York Giants. When the rivalry between the two clubs got too hot, the Giants told the Yankees to play their home games elsewhere. Team officials quickly drew up plans to build the Yankees a ballpark of their own. The original Yankee Stadium opened in 1923, the same year the team won its first World Series. Babe Ruth was in pinstripes and banging bombs over the right-field fence.

A half century later, in 1973, Yankee Stadium was all but torn down during a renovation that grew into, essentially, the construction of a new Yankee Stadium. For two years, the Yankees played at Shea Stadium when the Mets were on the road. In 1976, Yankee Stadium #2 opened. The team played there until 2008.

There's plenty to see at Yankee Stadium #3 besides a baseball game. First, admire the beautiful cream-colored granite and the Roman Coliseum-like arches that make up the external wall of the park. Read about the great Yankee gladiator, Babe Ruth, in Babe Ruth Plaza, where small kiosks tell his remarkable baseball story. Walk the Great Hall, that expansive outer ring of the stadium where huge banners of Yankee greats hang. See the amazing Yankee photos hung atop the seemingly endless row of concession stands in the main concourse. Nearly all of the photos are previously unseen rarities mined from the old *Daily News* archives. They are a joy to look at, and attractively tell the story of the Yankees' unequaled haul of world championships (27, at *Baseball Fan's Bucket List* press time) during their century-long existence as an American League team.

You should also visit the Yankee Museum on the stadium's second level. It's free to fans that paid admission into the ballpark. Exhibits include great moments, memories, and memorabilia of the Yankee dynasties. Look for the bat Ruth used to hit his very first home run in Yankee Stadium in 1923. Check out the jerseys of Lou Gehrig, Mickey Mantle, Reggie Jackson and other Yankee legends. Spend time at the exhibit called "Top of the Heap" that recalls the five great Yankee eras: the Babe Ruth era, the Joe DiMaggio era, Mickey Mantle's, Reggie Jackson's, and most recently, Derek Jeter's. The most surprising exhibit in the museum is not about the Yankees, but about the Black Yankees, the Negro League team that wore cast-off jerseys from the other Yankees and

Banners of the past Yankee greats decorate the inside perimeter of Yankees Stadium in New York City.

played at Yankee Stadium on Sundays when the major league Yankees were on the road.

Finally, no visit to Yankee Stadium would be complete without spending some time in Monument Park, located just beyond center field. It showcases monuments to Yankee owners, players and managers, as well as plaques that commemorate Yankees who have had their numbers retired—a remarkable 16 in all, plus Brooklyn Dodger great Jackie Robinson.

Expect a long line to get into both Monument Park and the Yankee Museum. Your best bet is to arrive at the stadium three hours prior to the first pitch, which is the earliest you can enter the ballpark. It makes for a long day, but a great day at Yankee Stadium.

> To find out about tours of Yankee Stadium and tickets to Yankees games, check the team's website, *www.yankees.com*. The Yankees home has inspired numerous books, including Al Santasiere's *Yankee Stadium: The Official Retrospective* (Pocket, 2008) and DVDs, including 2008's *Yankee Stadium: Baseball's Cathedral*, directed by David Check. Both can be purchased through online retailers.

68 CATCH A CAPE COD LEAGUE GAME

A lot of baseball people consider the Cape Cod League the best amateur summer league in America. The league's glowing reputation is backed up by the fact that about one-out-of-every-six major leaguers played "on the Cape," as they say, during their college years. Thurman Munson, Todd Helton, Nomar Garciaparra, Mo Vaughn, Lance Berkman, Jeff Bagwell, Craig Biggio, Jeff Kent, Frank Thomas, Barry Zito, Tim Salmon, Jason Varitek, Darin Erstad, Tim Lincecum, and Evan Longoria are just a few of the players with Cape Cod on their baseball resumé.

What makes this Northeast vacation playground such a baseball hotspot during the summer? Tradition is one thing; they've been playing organized baseball on the Cape since 1885. Then there's the league's special, close-knit, community feel; it's a non-profit, volunteer-run organization that recruits Cape Cod families to provide housing for players from the league's ten teams. And, perhaps most importantly, the Cape Cod League uses only wood bats.

Most amateur baseball leagues still mandate the use of aluminum bats, if for no other reason than cost. Aluminum bats are generally cheaper than wood bats and don't break. Besides, college players are used to aluminum bats since they use them in NCAA play. They are lighter than wood bats, which means a hitter will enjoy a quicker swing and a higher batting average. Out on the Cape, it takes a while for players to get used to swinging wood bats, many of which are made locally at the Barnstable Bat Company (see *Bucket List* item #141). For some players, playing in the Cape Cod League marks the first time that they've used a wood bat in a real game. It's the reason why batting averages are generally lower in the Cape Cod League, despite the presence of many of the best college players in the country. But major league scouts love the idea of wood bats because they make it easier to judge a prospect's true bat speed. And at any given Cape Cod League game, you're bound to see multiple MLB scouts in the stands.

The teams that make up the Cape Cod League are: the Chatham Anglers, the Harwich Mariners, the Brewster Whitecaps, the Orleans Firebirds, the Hyannis Mets, the Bourne Braves, the Yarmouth-Dennis Red Sox, the Cotuit Kettleers, the Falmouth Commodores, and the Wareham Gatemen. Beginning in June, they play a seven-week, 44-game schedule, plus playoffs. Players must be invited to play in the Cape Cod League; many of them are college All-Americans on the verge of being drafted. They come from all over America and they stay with host families. Many players have day jobs, but in the evening, it's all baseball. Nearly all of them will recall their summer on Cape Cod as one of the most memorable in their lives.

The games are free, though the league does pass the hat. The Cape Cod League survives by courting donations and corporate sponsorships and by selling hot dogs and souvenirs. Many people organize their vacations to catch as many games as possible. The Cape Cod League features a different brand of amateur baseball. Rarely will you see high-scoring affairs. You're more apt to see 1-0 and 2-1 games, especially early in the season. The wood bats take their toll, but the pitching on the Cape is

For more information on the Cape Cod Baseball League, including team schedules, visit the league's website at *www.capecodbaseball.org*. You can also read *The Last Best League* by Jim Collins (DaCapo, 2004), a wonderful account of the league, and watch *Touching the Game (The Story of the Cape Cod Baseball League)*, released on DVD by Warner Bros. in 2005.

reputed to be the best in America outside the minor and major leagues. Fans of "small ball," where a successful bunt is as appreciated as much as a long bomb home run, will love the Cape Cod League. Make certain to buy a scorecard and keep score; at least some of the players you see play will make it to the major leagues. You'll be able to say you watched them play before they were stars—before they were even professionals—and have proof.

In 2008, the league opened the Cape Cod League Hall of Fame and Museum in Hyannis in "The Dugout" on the lower level of the John F. Kennedy Hyannis Museum. It comprises two rooms in the museum's basement and features memorabilia, photos, autographs, and plaques of Hall of Fame inductees. Make certain to allot some time while on the Cape to visit it as well as take in a few games of Cape Cod League baseball.

69 CREATE A BASEBALL REFERENCE LIBRARY ✮✮✮✮

Novels, biographies, and histories aside, every serious fan needs a library of good baseball reference books. Okay, maybe not a library's worth of reference books, but at least a short shelf filled with the right ones.

Start with *The Dickson Baseball Dictionary*, 3rd edition (Norton, 2009). This nearly 1,000-page book by longtime baseball writer and researcher Paul Dickson contains a synopsis of pretty much everything you need to know or ever wanted to know about baseball. The first edition of *The Dickson Baseball Dictionary* came out in 1989, the second in 1999, and the third followed in 2009. Each succeeding edition added numerous entries, so the third edition is double the size of the first. You can't really call any baseball book "definitive," but Dickson's dictionary comes awfully close.

Dickson shows his passion for the language of baseball—its meanings, its slang, and how it's impacted American vernacular. Incredibly, Dickson's dictionary entries stretch back to the early years of baseball. He includes terms like "bounder" ("a high bouncing, easy to field ball") first used in baseball in 1868. The dictionary will introduce you to plenty of baseball terms that you probably never even knew existed. For instance, how many baseball fans know that an "ivory nut" is "a minor league player available for the major leagues" or can define a "Snodgrass muff" ("a muff or boner named for the hapless New York Giants outfielder Fred Snodgrass, who dropped an easy fly ball hit by Boston Red Sox pinch hitter Clyde Eagle in the 10th inning of the final game of the 1912 World Series").

Dickson also includes baseball words and phrases with more modern relevancy, of course. You get definitions of terms you may have heard, without knowing exactly what they mean, such as "punch out" (a strikeout) and "bush shaker" (a baseball scout) and "downer" ("an overhand curve ball that drops close to the batter's ankles") and the "I-70 Series" (the 1985 World Series between the St. Louis Cardinals and the Kansas City Royals, named for Highway I-70, which connects the two Missouri cities). Nearly all the entries are written in easy-to-understand language and thoroughly researched by Dickson and his research aides. As one reviewer wrote, *The Dickson Baseball Dictionary* is "a staggering piece of scholarship."

Paul Dickson also wrote some other fine baseball reference books: *The Hidden Language of Baseball: How Signs and Sign Stealing Have Influenced the Course of Our National Pastime* (2003), and *Baseball's Greatest Quotations* (1991), and *The Joy of Keeping Score* (1996), and *The Unwritten Rules of Baseball* (2009). Add all four to your baseball reference library. The books reflect Dickson's deep commitment to researching aspects of the game that, on the surface, might not appear all that fruitful or interesting. But he turns them into good reading the way a classic baseball novelist does—by revealing their underlying stories and all the hidden, essential information they contain.

The Total Baseball Catalog: Unique Baseball Stuff & How to Buy It (Total Sports Publishing, 1998) might be tougher to find for your reference collection than Dickson's dictionary, but it is well worth the effort. Editors David Pietrusza, Lloyd Johnson and Bob Carroll cast a wide net to haul in relevant—and what can, at times, seem irrelevant—baseball information. For instance, the book contains a major section on baseball music, followed by a section called "Lights, Turf, Tarp: The Stadium." It covers baseball backstops and batting cages and all the items found inside a trainer's room, followed by sections on baseball cards

Every true baseball fan needs a library full of all the important baseball books.

and collectibles, radio and TV, baseball books, baseball abroad, amateur baseball, and pretty much whatever other topic interests the editors. Still, *The Total Baseball Catalog: Unique Baseball Stuff & How to Buy It* often comes in handy, especially when you're looking for detailed information on aspects of the game that get short shift in other books.

Finally, every baseball reference library needs a copy of the game's rules, and you won't find a better rendering of them than *Baseball Field Guide* by Dan Formosa and Paul Hamberger. Published by Thunder's Mouth Press in 2006, this excellent guide to the rules of baseball is nicely illustrated and easy to grasp— a great relief to anyone who's become more confused by some other baseball rule book's explanation of "the infield fly rule" and other baseball rules you thought you knew until you read an official explanation of them.

Plenty of other books would make for nice additions to your baseball reference library, particularly those focused on the teams and topics that interest you most. But the seven described above will set you up with the essentials.

> You can purchase *The Dickson Baseball Dictionary* and *The Hidden Language of Baseball: How Signs and Sign Stealing Have Influenced the Course of Our National Pastime* and *Baseball's Greatest Quotations* and *The Joy of Keeping Score* and *The Unwritten Rules of Baseball* and *Baseball Field Guide* from most bookstores and online booksellers. *The Total Baseball Catalog: Unique Baseball Stuff & How to Buy It* can be purchased from used bookstores and online merchants.

 ## 70 VISIT GREEN-WOOD CEMETERY

No cemetery holds as much baseball history or as many of the game's early legends as Brooklyn's Green-Wood. Located in south Brooklyn close to Prospect Park, Green-Wood provides a final resting place for nearly two hundred baseball players, many of them pioneers of the game. Strolling around Green-Wood's grounds and pausing by the gravesites of baseball legends makes for a great way to connect with the game's origins and pay your respects to many of the people who made baseball into a great American institution.

With nearly 500 acres of monuments and memorials; plaques, crypts, and statues; hills and winding paths, Green-Wood might seem daunting. But it's relatively easy to navigate, with many of the baseball landmarks marked with bat-and-ball ornaments and diamond-shaped written tributes signifying that the person buried there played a role in the evolution of the nation's pastime.

If you're more than casually interested in baseball's early days and stars, plan to spend an afternoon at Green-Wood. Start your visit at the main entrance at Fifth Avenue and 25th Street in Brooklyn. At the small gift shop next to the entrance, pick up a free map of Green-Wood Cemetery, or, better yet, purchase a copy of Peter Nash's wonderful guidebook, *Baseball Legends of Brooklyn's Green-Wood Cemetery*. Not so much a marker-by-marker guide, Nash's book instead serves as a primer on the early history of baseball, using the cemetery as an historical platform. According to Nash, "nearly all the important baseball heroes of the nineteenth century found their final rest amongst the half million or so men and women who now inhabit Green-Wood."

Not long into your tour of Green-Wood, it becomes obvious that New York City, not the village of Cooperstown, is where baseball laid down its earliest and most enduring roots. As Nash tells it, Green-Wood "has become a living history of 19th century baseball..." You can make your trip back in baseball time complete with a visit to the old site of Elysian Fields (see *Bucket List* item #162) just across the Hudson River in Hoboken, New Jersey, where many ballplayers buried in Green-Wood regularly played games.

Green-Wood opened in 1838 and during your tour you're apt to run into other cemetery visitors who are less interested in baseball than the site's history and the other American luminaries buried there. On Battle Hill, the highest point in the cemetery and all of Brooklyn, British and American revolutionary forces waged the Battle of Brooklyn in 1776. Famous, non-baseball playing Americans buried at Green-Wood include: 19th-century New York journalist, Horace Greeley; telegraph inventor, Samuel F.B. Morse; painter George Catlin; silent movie star, William S. Hart; the great classical music composer and ambassador, Leonard Bernstein; and New York statesman and governor DeWitt Clinton. The site also hosts memorials to such famous American families as Steinway (piano), Tiffany (glass and jewelry), and Currier and Ives (illustrators). Even one of New York's more infamous corrupt politicians, William "Boss" Tweed of Tammany Hall, is buried at Green-Wood, though it's doubtful he rests in peace.

Just the baseball gravesites are enough to keep you occupied for hours during your pilgrimage to Green-Wood. No visit to the cemetery would be complete without a stop at the monument that celebrates Henry Chadwick's legacy and gravesite, which features a large granite baseball atop the monument. Chadwick did much to promote the game of baseball in the mid-1800s. It was Chadwick, for instance, who created baseball's statistics, giving rise to the batting average and the box score. Chadwick also chronicled the evolution of baseball as America's game by editing annual baseball guidebooks. He wrote down baseball's rules and rigorously fought corruption within the game, and he penned one of the first books on baseball, *The American Game of Baseball*, published in 1868.

If you're a Brooklyn Dodger fan, then the Charles Ebbets site beckons. If baseball and the Civil War are interests of yours, then walk to the graves of John B. Woodward, a Union general who was a member of the Excelsior baseball club; and General Nelson Shaurman, manager of the Brooklyn Charter Oak team. Include in your visit the resting place of James Creighton, Jr. and the obelisk dedicated to him. Back in the late 1850s and early 1860s, Creighton played for the local Brooklyn club, the Excelsiors, where he established himself as the best pitcher of his day and baseball's first true star. Creighton's baseball career was just beginning when he died from unknown causes in 1862 at the age of 21.

Green-Wood Cemetery covers the early history of baseball in a way that the National Baseball Hall of Fame in Cooperstown largely ignores. Chadwick, Ebbets, and a few others aside, many of the players, managers, and baseball businessmen buried in Green-Wood Cemetery are not recognized in Cooperstown, mostly because their singular achievements don't warrant such attention. But collectively, they played a major role in defining the game of baseball and setting it on the path to becoming America's game.

> Green-Wood Cemetery is open daily from 8 a.m. to 5 p.m. It is located at 500 25th Street in Brooklyn, New York. In the spring and fall, the facility offers guided tours that deal with the cemetery's baseball legacy. For more information, call (718) 768-7300, or check the cemetery's website at *www.green-wood.com.*

71 VISIT THE BABE RUTH BIRTHPLACE AND MUSEUM ✷✷

Located a couple of blocks from Oriole Park at Camden Yards in downtown Baltimore, the Babe Ruth Birthplace and Museum celebrates the life and legacy of America's first international sports celebrity and the man many consider baseball's greatest player. From Camden Yards, follow the painted baseballs on the pavement; they lead directly to 216 Emory Street, the one-time Baltimore row home of Pius Schamberger, father of Babe's mother Katherine Ruth, who gave birth there to her son on February 6, 1895.

Katherine and her husband George Herman Ruth, Sr. lived a few blocks away at 622 Frederick Avenue in an apartment atop George's saloon (located right about where center field now sits in Camden Yards). Katherine was visiting her parents when she went into labor. Rather than risk going home in the terrible freeze that swept over Baltimore that early February, Katherine was helped to a second floor bedroom where she delivered her son, George Herman Ruth, Jr., later known to the world as simply "The Babe."

In addition to viewing the bedroom, which includes the original bed and other period furnishings from the family, visitors to the Babe Ruth Birthplace and Museum can view a number of significant baseball artifacts, including a Babe Ruth rookie baseball card from his first professional baseball club (the Baltimore Orioles of the International League), some of Ruth's 1920s Yankees uniforms, and a bat from 1927—the year he hit 60 home runs.

Using mostly photos, the museum presents a biographical overview of Ruth's life and baseball career. The most interesting—and relevant—part of the story, however, deals with his early years in Baltimore. Ruth, an incorrigible child, was sent to St. Mary's Industrial School by his parents, who feared his life would be ruined without the stern and regular discipline dished

The Babe Ruth Birthplace and Museum in Baltimore, MD.

out by Catholic brothers. Ruth spent much of his youth there, where his behavior improved and he learned to play baseball. Many of the most impressive artifacts at the Babe Ruth Birthplace and Museum come from his St. Mary days. On display is his first glove, a catcher's mitt; an early St. Mary's uniform that the young Ruth wore; a bat that he used as a youth; and several rare photographs of the young ballplayer.

In 1919, Ruth was discovered by Jack Dunn, owner of the International League Orioles. Ruth signed his first professional baseball contract with Dunn a few days after his 19th birthday, with the stipulation that Dunn serve as Ruth's guardian until he turned 21. The local media called Ruth, "Jack Dunn's Baby." Later, they shortened it to "Babe." The nickname stuck.

In addition to presenting Babe Ruth memorabilia, the museum celebrates his legacy as one of the game's greatest home run hitters. Ruth smashed 714 round-trippers in all, and each one is memorialized on a museum wall. One of Ruth's most celebrated home runs—hit in Game Three of the 1932 World Series against the Chicago Cubs—gets special attention. Fans and historians alike argue whether or not Ruth actually "called" his home run by "pointing" to center field before he clubbed the ball over the center-field wall. The museum shows footage of the home run and Ruth allegedly calling it before hitting it. In the footage you see Ruth motion with his arm. Whether he's showing where he intends to hit the ball, or whether he's using his arm to emphasize some trash talk directed at the Cubs dugout...we'll never know for sure, since the film includes no sound. Some fans watching the film will swear the home run is "called." Others will walk away skeptical at best. Still, it makes for great fun to register your opinion in one of baseball history's great debates.

Plan to spend about 45 minutes at the Babe Ruth Birthplace and Museum. Needless to say, the museum gets crowded before Orioles' games since it's such a short walk from Camden Yards. Expect the small row house to be jammed when the Yankees are in town—or the Red Sox, since the selling of Babe Ruth's contract by the Red Sox to the Yankees began the long and agonizing "Curse of the Bambino" that was finally broken in 2004 when the Red Sox won the World Series. For Red Sox fans, the Babe Ruth Museum serves as a reminder of "what could have been." For others, it serves as a celebration of "what was"—the life and deeds of maybe the greatest baseball player ever.

> For more information, visit the museum's website at *www.baberuthmuseum.org*. To find out more about catching a game at Camden Yards after your visit to the museum, go to *www.orioles.com* or check out *Bucket List* item #28.

72 OWN AN AUTOGRAPHED BASEBALL COLLECTION ✰✰✰

A baseball fan can own few, if any, things more impressive and more coveted than a great collection of autographed baseballs. You can own just one autographed baseball and check off this *Bucket List* entry. But chances are, one won't be enough. You'll see it sitting there on your bookshelf and hear it calling out for company. In time, you'll amass a collection of autographed balls, each one as fun to get and to own as the other. Call it an investment, if you like. After all, autographed baseballs have become big business. But that's not really the reason why you build an autographed baseball collection. The autographed baseball is a prized possession. Own one and you own a tiny sliver of baseball history. Ask Hall of Fame Cleveland Indians' pitcher Bob Feller to name his favorite baseball possession. Without hesitation, Feller will tell you it's the baseball he got autographed by both Babe Ruth and Lou Gehrig back when he was an Iowa farm boy.

A ball signed by one of the game's legends in legible blue ink is something to savor. For many fans, it's a piece of art to be held in high regard and passed from generation to generation. If you actually got the autograph yourself, instead of buying it, the ball holds even greater value. After all, you saw the autograph being written. You shook the player's hand. You told him how much he's meant to the game and to you. These are things baseball memories are built from, and you'll recall them every time you show someone the ball.

There are plenty of ways to secure balls autographed by major league players, present and past. The easiest place, and the cheapest, is at spring training. During the spring training season, players are more relaxed and accessible and they know it's a tradition to sign baseballs there. But two problems can arise when seeking ball signings at spring training. First, it seems as if everyone at the ballpark or at the batting cages is looking for an autograph, so you'll have competition, and kids usually get preference over adults. Second, because players are swamped, they sign balls quickly, and that often means a signature that is barely legible, and thus, almost worthless.

Fan Fests are another place to secure autographs. Active players will usually sign for free, but the lines for their signatures are almost always long. On occasion, major league teams will bring in former players, so you can wind up with a number of signatures at Fan Fest, if you're lucky and arrive early.

At card conventions, retired and active players will sign balls for fans—for a price. Bring your credit card because the cost of securing a legible autograph from a big time Baseball Hall of Famer could set you back one hundred bucks. Card stores and hobby shops that specialize in sports memorabilia often sell autographed baseballs; but you can't be certain that what you buy isn't a fraud (though more and more such balls come with statements of authenticity) and you didn't meet the player who signed your ball. For some fans, that's a deal breaker. Others are willing to settle for a signed ball simply because the ball fills a void in an autographed ball collection. Then there's *eBay*, which presents the same problems just outlined, but offers a selection of autographed balls that is unmatched.

Still, Cooperstown remains perhaps the best place to get autographed baseballs. Baseball memorabilia shops along Main Street in the village regularly feature signings by retired players during the peak summer months, often at a nominal price. During special events in Cooperstown, like the Hall of Fame inductions and the Hall of Fame Classic weekend, plenty of players that sign baseballs come to town. Whether or not you'll get charged for the signature depends on the player and the setting. And there's something special about getting an autographed ball in the town that holds the Hall of Fame. If you haven't begun collecting autographed baseballs, Cooperstown rates as the best place to start.

One more thing to remember when collecting autographed baseballs: keep the signatures out of the sun. Like most anything else, autographs will fade over time. They'll fade quicker if the sun beats down on your ball day in and day out. To protect your autographed balls, consider purchasing UV-protected ball cases, available at most card conventions and hobby shops. An autographed baseball is a prized possession, so treat it like one.

> For more information, you can scour used bookstores and online used booksellers for a copy of Mark Allen Baker's *Team Baseball's: A Comprehensive Guide to the Identification, Authentication and Value of Autographed Baseballs* (Krause). Published in 1992, the book's valuations are dated, but much of its other information about autographed baseballs remains relevant.

73 | WATCH THE MOVIE, *MAJOR LEAGUE* ⚾

Major League is one of the funniest films ever made about baseball. Its offbeat jokes, clubhouse humor, rough language and quirky baseball bits made it an immediate hit at a time when other baseball films like *The Natural*, *Bull Durham*, *Field of Dreams*, *A League of Their Own*, and *Eight Men Out* took completely different paths to explore the national pastime. So popular did *Major League* become that not one, but two sequels followed it—*Major League II* (1994) and *Major League: Back to the Minors* (1998), though neither film was as funny or as commercially successful as the original.

There is nothing particularly innovative about *Major League*'s story: the Cleveland Indians' new owner—a former Las Vegas exotic dancer (Rachel Phelps) who inherited the franchise from her husband when he died on their honeymoon—wants to move the club to sunny, warm Miami. So she puts together a rag-tag team of has-beens and never-beens to stink up the field and drive down attendance so she can break the team's stadium lease in Cleveland. But instead of losing, the Indians win, enabling the team to remain in Cleveland.

Though the cast is impressive, the acting really isn't. The film stars Tom Berenger as Jake Taylor, an aging catcher with bad knees who's hoping to get one more year in baseball; Charlie Sheen as fastball pitcher Rickie Vaughn, better known as "Wild Thing"; and Rene Russo as Berenger's former babe who falls back into the catcher's arms after the Tribe beats the Yankees. Add in appearances by Wesley Snipes (Willie Mays Hayes), James Gammon (manager Lou Brown), Dennis Haysbert (as Pedro Cerrano, a voodoo-obsessed Cuban power hitter), and Bob Uecker (as Harry Doyle, Cleveland's hard drinking play-by-play man) and you have enough talent to make the film fun, even if there were no Academy Award efforts.

And fun it is, despite its shortfalls. The predictable script, the mediocre acting and the loony antics somehow added up to a wildly funny baseball movie. Directed by David Ward, *Major League* was released in 1989, well before the Indians finally regained long overdue respectability after years and years of forgettable seasons. The film also came out at a time when Indians' home games were still being played in cavernous Cleveland Municipal Stadium and the team was one of the worst in the majors when it came to attendance. Back then, the real Cleveland Indians were funny, if not pathetic, on the field; *Major League* continued the joke on camera.

The star of the film turned out to be Charlie Sheen. His character, Ricky Vaughn, is in prison for stealing a car when he gets the call from the Indians to help fill out their pitching staff. Vaughn throws a wicked, upper nineties fastball, but he can't control it. He picks up the nickname "Wild Thing" and Indians' fans get behind him. Sporting one of the great Hollywood haircuts of all time, a sort of zig-zag mullet Mohawk, Vaughn gets a pair of horn-rimmed glasses and suddenly he's able to find the strike zone. With the guidance of his veteran catcher Berenger, Sheen becomes the Indians' closer and goes on to strike out the final Yankee as the Indians win the pennant.

Major League became required viewing, not just for baseball fans, but for players, too. Pitcher Jonathan Papelbon, the Red Sox closer, actually got himself a Ricky Vaughn haircut to start the 2006 season and, for a time, used the song "Wild Thing" when he entered a ballgame from the bullpen. Over the years, numerous other references to *Major League* found their way into baseball culture.

But what did the film do for the Cleveland Indians? After *Major League* became a hit, sales of their jerseys and caps and other Tribe gear spiked, as did the team's fortunes. Rumored to be on their way out of Cleveland, the Indians stayed in the city, moved into Jacobs Field, and became one of the best teams in baseball. The Indians went to the World Series in 1995 and then again in '97, but lost both times. But just getting there meant a lot to fans of a club that hadn't celebrated a World Series appearance since 1954.

The idea that *Major League* had anything to do with the Indians' success in the 90s is, of course, preposterous. But that doesn't stop the occasional Tribe fan from thinking that the team's turn-around was brought about by Charlie Sheen, Tom Berenger, and the rest of the cast. Still, it's understandable that some fans buy into the myth. After all, a couple of the Indians' on their World Series teams, Manny Ramirez and Albert Belle, both could have been characters in *Major League*.

> *Major League* is available in VHS and DVD format from most movie retailers and rental stores. It continues to play on TV movie channels, especially around spring training and MLB playoff time. The film runs 107 minutes. Cleveland home games were actually filmed in the old Milwaukee's County Stadium.

WATCH THE DOCUMENTARY, *THE LIFE AND TIMES OF HANK GREENBERG*

74

Before Jackie Robinson braved taunts and threats, insults and acts of overt racism to establish himself as the first black ballplayer in the major leagues in 1947, Hank Greenberg persevered through similar social and cultural challenges almost a generation earlier. Greenberg was baseball's first great Jewish star, playing at a time when discrimination towards Jews was nearly as rampant in

America as it was towards blacks. The documentary film, *The Life and Times of Hank Greenberg*, written and directed by Aviva Kempner, is not only a fine biography of one of one baseball's best hitters, but it's also an uplifting account of what Greenberg's success meant to anyone Jewish, then and now.

Greenberg broke in with the Tigers in 1933 and for the rest of the decade proved to be one of the American League's most feared hitters. Although Greenberg could hit for average, ending his career with a lifetime .313 batting average, he was more known as a home run hitter. Nicknamed "Hammerin' Hank," he smashed 58 home runs in 1938, nearly matching the then-major league record of 60, established by Babe Ruth in 1927, and equaling Jimmy Foxx's 1932 mark for most homers by a right-handed batter. Greenberg helped the Tigers get to the World Series in 1934 and '35, and win the latter one. That year, Greenberg also earned the first of his two American League Most Valuable Player Awards.

Where Jackie Robinson used his speed to succeed in the majors, Greenberg used his power. Standing 6'4" and weighing over 200 pounds, Greenberg was an intimidating figure. Many of the Jewish insults that came his way were less barbed only because of Greenberg's size and his potential for retaliation. Like Robinson, Greenberg quickly realized that his role on life's stage was more than that of a big league ballplayer. For Jews all across America, Greenberg became a larger-than-life hero, a representative of his religion and a mentor to every Jewish kid who dreamed of one day playing baseball or taking up any other activity or profession in which Jews were discriminated against.

In 1934, Greenberg stunned baseball by refusing to take the field with the Tigers (who were fighting for the American League pennant) on Yom Kippur, the Jewish Day of Atonement. Not especially religious, Greenberg nonetheless knew the significance of his actions, which only served to make him more heroic in the Jewish community.

The best non-baseball parts of *The Life and Times of Hank Greenberg* feature the recollections of rabbis and personalities, such as actor Walter Matthau, on how important Greenberg was to Jews across America during a time when Jews were so often victimized by discrimination and religious bigotry. Although the film only touches on the looming Holocaust in Europe, the 1930s was one of the most difficult decades in modern Jewish history. That Hank Greenberg provided respite at a time when Jews were nearly wiped out, was more meaningful and important than many baseball fans know.

Like so many other great ballplayers of his time, including Bob Feller, Joe DiMaggio, and Ted Williams, Greenberg had his career interrupted by World War II. Actually, he had been drafted into the army in May, 1940, but honorably discharged a few months later after the U.S. Congress passed a bill preventing men over 28 years of age from being drafted. But when the Japanese attacked Pearl Harbor on December 7, 1941, forcing America into World War II, Greenberg enlisted and served in the army until the war ended in 1945. Greenberg then returned to the Tigers that summer, homering in his first game back and helping Detroit capture another world championship. He was 34 years old.

Greenberg played another few years, all but his last with Detroit. His final season, 1947, was the first for Jackie Robinson, who credited Greenberg with helping mentor him on how to cope with the biases and abuse he would encounter. "Class tells," said Robinson. "It sticks out all over Mr. Greenberg."

Despite missing a large chunk of his prime while serving in the military, Greenberg finished his career with 331 home runs and averaged close to an RBI per game. The five-time All Star and two-time American League Most Valuable Player was inducted into the National Baseball Hall of Fame in 1956, gaining an honor he richly deserved for all his baseball accomplishments. But as *The Life and Times of Hank Greenberg* shows, Greenberg also deserves to be remembered for all his courageous contributions to the fight against religious intolerance.

Released by 20th Century Fox in 1998, *The Life and Times of Hank Greenberg* is rated PG and runs 95 minutes. It is available in VHS and DVD formats. The film features interviews with a number of prominent Americans, including Walter Matthau, attorney Alan Dershowitz, Senator Carl Levin, Ralph Kiner and Bob Feller. The film also offers archive footage of Franklin Delano Roosevelt, Henry Ford, Babe Ruth, Dizzy Dean and Joe DiMaggio, among others. It won "Best Documentary" awards from numerous organizations, including the National Society of Film Critics and the National Board of Review, and also claimed a prestigious Peabody Award.

SEE THE BREWERS PLAY AT MILLER PARK

75

Home of the National League Brewers, Miller Park in Milwaukee stands as one of the most architecturally innovative ballparks in Major League Baseball. Its design is so unique, that, from a distance, Miller Park might be confused with a museum or a public art project. Miller Park offers both a tribute to ballparks of old and a dazzling study of stadium modernity. Known for its fan-shaped retractable roof and its beautiful giant glass windows, Miller Park ranks as a better place to watch baseball than most of the other big league parks with retractable roofs (only the Seattle Mariners' Safeco Field gets a better grade). It provides fans the chance to enjoy baseball no matter what the Wisconsin weather might be doing outside.

Named for the Miller Brewing Company, one of Milwaukee's best-known beer makers, Miller Park opened in 2001. It replaced Milwaukee County Stadium, which served as the home of the Milwaukee Braves, starting in 1953 after the Braves re-located from Boston. The Braves bolted for Atlanta in 1966. But the Brewers moved into Milwaukee County Stadium four years later when the expansion franchise fled the Pacific Northwest after only one season as the Seattle Pilots.

The lack of luxury boxes and other contemporary baseball amenities doomed County Stadium as the luxury-loving 1990s wore on. Club officials and architects drew up plans for Miller Park during the retro rage. With its dark green steel beams and the red brick walls found in so many of baseball's retro ballparks, Miller Park salutes baseball's architectural past. It also adds unique touches, like the old-style clock out in right field with baseball bats for hands and the external clock tower that acts as one of Miller Park's most identifiable marks. But you never get the impression that the retro idea is overdone.

Miller Park blends tasteful nostalgia with some impressive contemporary flourishes. Its high-tech roof opens and closes like a fan, a truly modern piece of machinery. Giant heating ducts surround the stands, pumping in warm air so that you can watch a game in April wearing just a sweatshirt while it's snowing outside. These 21st century conveniences make Miller Park a delightful place to watch a baseball game, good weather or bad.

Still, the best time, to catch a game at Miller Park is during the day in the middle of the summer when the roof is open, the sky is clear and blue, and natural light pours through the giant windows located behind the upper decks on the first- and third-base lines and on each side of the outfield scoreboard. These huge, beautiful windows make Miller Park seem as much like a cathedral as a ballpark.

Miller Park has another unique characteristic: fans regularly tailgate in the parking lots, and I'm not talking the sporadic keg or grill cooking Milwaukee's famous bratwursts on them. Take a quick glance around the lots before Brewers games and you'd swear you were at a Green Bay Packers football game. Tailgating is a baseball tradition in Milwaukee, so when you visit Miller Park, drive and get there early so you can enjoy doing what the locals do before the game: eat brats, drink brew, and talk baseball.

Speaking of brats, catching a game at Miller Park also means watching the ballpark's famous between-inning Sausage Race between a giant hot dog, Italian sausage, bratwurst, and chorizo. These big-headed, meaty mascots run from third base around home and to first base in a race that's cheered on by fans almost as loudly as a Brewers' home run. Nowadays, most major league parks have some sort of mascot race, but few are as fun to watch as the Miller Park Sausage Race.

What's missing at Miller Park? Championship banners. There is only one, from 1982 when the Brewers won the American League pennant but lost to the St. Louis Cardinals in the World Series. It took another 26 years for the Brewers to return to post-season play. Winning ways in Milwaukee is what Miller Park craves. It is simply too wonderful a ballpark to continue to suffer through decades more of on-field mediocrity.

> For information on Brewers tickets and Miller Park tours, check out the team's website at www.brewers.com. To find out more about the club, you can read *Brewers Essential: Everything You Need to Know to Be a Real Fan* (Triumph, 2008) by Tom Haudricourt, with a foreword by Gorman Thomas, a key member of the Brewers 1982 pennant-winning team.

76 | WATCH THE MOVIE, *THE PRIDE OF THE YANKEES* ✯✯

The Pride of the Yankees was the first great baseball film. It hit movie houses in 1942, the darkest year of World War II, when America searched its soul for courage and called out for heroes. *The Pride of the Yankees* was as much a patriotic gesture by Hollywood as a biopic about Yankee slugger Lou Gehrig, a beloved baseball player who faced up to a monumental challenge—death in the prime of his life—and did so with rare dignity and grace. The parallel between Gehrig's story and those of millions of young Americans facing down death to further their country's war effort was unmistakable, and deeply felt.

Gehrig was stricken with amyotrophic lateral sclerosis (ALS), a mean, neuromuscular disease that first sapped his strength, then the use of his limbs, voice, lungs, and, ultimately, his life. After his death at age 36, the disease would become known as Lou Gehrig's Disease. Although he would have undoubtedly played longer had he not gotten terminally ill, Gehrig nonetheless made his mark as a baseball great. The seven-time All-Star and six-time World Series winner played in 2,130 consecutive games, a record that would stand until the Baltimore Orioles' Cal Ripken, Jr. surpassed it in 1995. Nicknamed "The Iron Horse" because of his stamina, Gehrig also hit 436 home runs, batted .333, won the Triple Crown in 1934, a pair of American League MVP awards and played beside Babe Ruth for much of his career. Together they created one of the most feared one-two punches in all of baseball and were the true strength of the Yankee's awesome "Murderer's Row" line-up of the mid-1920s.

Gehrig, a shy, reserved man who avoided the spotlight Ruth craved, is also remembered for delivering one of the most famous and emotionally intense speeches in baseball history. Made at Yankee Stadium on July 4, 1939, a couple of months after he had given up his position at first base, Gehrig's "Farewell Speech," as it has become known, is the ultimate baseball statement of humility (see *Bucket List* item #110). Weak and dying, Gehrig stepped up to the microphone in front of more than 60,000, mostly teary-eyed fans and told them, "Today, I consider myself the luckiest man on the face of the earth." Although in the movie, the classic line got moved from the opening to the end of the speech for greater emotional impact, Gary Cooper, who played Gehrig, so captured the triumph and tragedy of the moment that the scene continues to be considered one of the greatest, if not the greatest, in baseball movie history.

The Pride of the Yankees almost didn't even get made. Samuel Goldwyn, head of MGM, the studio that released the film, knew nothing about baseball and believed that the public wouldn't be interested in a movie about the game. "It's box office poison," Goldwyn is reputed to have said. "If people want baseball, they go to the ballpark." Fortunately Goldwyn got behind the picture after viewing a newsreel copy of Gehrig's speech, and hired Cooper to play the Yankee great. Fresh from his acclaimed title role as America's greatest World War I hero in *Sergeant York*, Cooper didn't have a passion for baseball, either. Other than his matinee idol status, he was the wrong actor for the part. At 40 years old, he was asked by Director Sam Wood (*Goodbye, Mr. Chips*), not just to play Gehrig as an aging and sick ballplayer, but also as a college student at Columbia University, which Gehrig had attended before signing with the Yankees. And then there was the fact that Gehrig batted and caught left-handed, while Cooper was right-handed. Cleverly, Wood had Gehrig's number four sewn backwards on Cooper's Yankee jersey and had him run to third base instead of first when he hit the ball right-handed. Wood then applied a bit of Hollywood trickery by reversing the film in the darkroom, giving the appearance of authenticity.

It didn't hurt that *The Pride of the Yankees* was as much a love story as it was a baseball biopic. Gehrig's deep affection for and courtship of Eleanor Twitchell, played by Teresa Wright, competed with the film's baseball scenes. Occasionally sentimental and sweet, the story of their love for each other was nonetheless sincere and well told. To make doubly certain that women related to the film as much as men, the hugely popular Irving Berlin song "Always" was added as a musical summary of their love. The song was a favorite of Lou and Eleanor Gehrig as well as Goldwyn. To help keep male audience members engaged, director Wood hired Babe Ruth to play himself and gave cameo roles to other Yankee teammates of Gehrig, including Hall of Fame catcher Bill Dickey.

The Pride of the Yankees was nominated for 11 Academy Awards, including Best Picture, Best Actress (Wright), and Best Actor (Cooper). Surprisingly, it won only one Oscar—for Best Film Editing. Today, *The Pride of the Yankees* is, admittedly, quite dated. But you can't say you've seen the first landmark baseball film without seeing it.

> *The Pride of the Yankees* airs numerous times each year on Turner Classic Movies. It is available for purchase or rental from most video stores in VHS and DVD in its original black-and-white or in a colorized version. Released less than a-year-and-a-half after Gehrig passed away, the film runs 128 minutes.

77 | VISIT THE *FIELD OF DREAMS* MOVIE SITE ✮✮✮✮

Even if Hollywood hadn't made *Field of Dreams* (see *Bucket List* item #21), this baseball diamond cut out of an Iowa cornfield, smack in the middle of America, would still be worth a visit. But as the prime filming location of one of the greatest—and certainly the most spiritual—baseball movies, the field in Dyersville, Iowa serves as the shrine of baseball dreams and myths, a place to commune with the inner soul of the sport. Each year, more than 50,000 baseball fans come to Dyersville, nearly all of them in the summer months, to stand on the field where Kevin Costner, Ray Liotta, James Earl Jones, and Burt Lancaster made a movie that was part fantasy and part a romanticized yearn for baseball's past.

Located in the eastern section of Iowa, near where Wisconsin and Illinois press up against her, Dyersville is a small town with a population of just over 4,000. Once you get there, anyone will be able to point you to the *Field of Dreams* movie site out on Lansing Road, named in honor of the Lansing family that owns the property where the *Field of Dreams* movie site sits.

"Build it and he will come" endures as *Field of Dreams*'s most memorable line, one now embedded in American vernacular. In the summer of 1988, set designers built the baseball diamond in four days. It includes a backstop, some bleachers, and as one visitor put it, "an outfield wall whose height varied with the seasons and the success of the year's corn crop." The filming of *Field of Dreams* lasted all summer, with most of the crew and cast staying in Dubuque, 25 miles east of Dyersville. For the most part, the site is the way it was when the film was being made. However, there is a souvenir stand on the premises where you can pick up a *Field of Dreams* memento.

Emerging from the cornfield just like the ghosts of Shoeless Joe and the other Black Sox did in the movie is a popular photo opportunity. One Sunday a month, from June to September, a local group of amateur actors and ballplayers would step out of the cornfields that comprise the outfield boundary and a play a couple of innings of ball, just like in the movie. This doesn't happen anymore, so you're left to wander the grounds, play catch on the field, and do a little bit of your own baseball dreaming.

Bring your own glove, ball, and bat; there is no place to rent equipment. The movie site gets crowded on weekends, so if you want to have the diamond largely to yourself, you'll have to arrive early in the morning, or else visit it in the off-season. But don't wait too long. Winter can come early to Iowa, cutting short autumn, and springtime is apt to be wet. Though it's not open for tours, you can also see the farmhouse that served as home to Costner's fictional Kinsella family in the movie, set a few hundred feet from the diamond.

The only way to get to the *Field of Dreams* movie site is to drive.

The *Field of Dreams* movie site is open from April to November. For more specific directions and more information about the *Field of Dreams* movie site, go to *www.fieldofdreamsmoviesite.com* or call 1-888-875-8404. You can also learn more about the site from the book, *Is This Heaven? (The Magic of the Field of Dreams)* by Brett Mandel (Diamond Communications, 2002).

Dyersville sits about 200 miles west of Chicago on Highway 136. The *Field of Dreams* movie site is located at 28995 Lansing Road.

History shows that baseball took root in urban fields and empty lots in New York and New Jersey. But baseball's romanticized past still thrives in rural

America in places like Cooperstown and Dyersville. The simplicity of life in small town America suggests something more pure and authentic, two things nearly every baseball fan treasures. In baseball, the mythologized past often seems better than the present, and dreams feel more embracing than reality. You'll get a healthy dose of both myth and dreams in Dyersville and at the *Field of Dreams* movie site.

78 ATTEND A THEATRICAL PRODUCTION OF *BLEACHER BUMS*

You don't have to be a Chicago Cubs fan to enjoy the play *Bleacher Bums*. Although it's set in the bleachers of Wrigley Field and its characters are all diehard Cubs' fans, *Bleacher Bums* deals with bigger themes than the just the frustrations of rooting for the Cubbies, year in and year out. The play cheers the fan in the cheap seats, the one who lives and dies with his favorite team and who can't fathom the idea of separating himself from baseball, even when following it brings more hurt than happiness.

Exploring such themes, *Bleacher Bums* could only work as a comedy, and it's a wonderful one at that, as well as one of the best baseball plays ever staged. *Damn Yankees* is more significant than *Bleacher Bums* because of its great soundtrack, remarkably long stay on Broadway back in the 1950s and the successful film interpretations that Hollywood has given us over the years. But *Bleacher Bums* is a better play; it touches the "fan" in all of us in a setting we know. We've all sat in the bleachers at one point in our lives and experienced bleacher culture, lively, even animated fan dedication flowing just like the beer that's sold there. It's where the soul of the baseball fan resides, especially at Wrigley Field (see *Bucket List* item #5). You need to watch a Cubs game from the Wrigley bleachers at least once in your life, and *Bleacher Bums* offers a great preview of the experiences awaiting you there.

The characters in *Bleacher Bums* have come to Wrigley Field on a summer day to cheer for the Cubs against their National League rival, the St. Louis Cardinals (see *Bucket List* item #33). Conceived by actor and Cubs' fan Joe Mantegna and written by members of Chicago's Organic Theatre in 1977, *Bleacher Bums* takes the audience through nine innings of the game, where the action in the Wrigley Field bleachers is as good and as interesting as the action on the field. The audience never gets to see any of the game being played; you hear the cheering and the crack of the bat, and one of the bleacher bums, a blind fan at that, gives play-by-play analysis, for what will inevitably be another Cubs' loss.

It's a motley group of fans, these bleacher bums, but underneath their love of the Cubs, we experience their flaws and hopes and their quest to find not just baseball joy, but also more contentment in their daily lives. We meet a pair of heavy gamblers, a hen-pecked husband, a heckler, and a bombshell looking for a bit more than a Cubs' win. Together, these and the other members of the cast create a perfect platform to re-interpret a familiar theme: baseball as a metaphor for life, except this time, it's less about the players and more about those who watch and cheer for them.

Like *Damn Yankees*, *Bleacher Bums* made it to Hollywood. A film version was released in 2002, but lacked the play's vitality, in part because Major League Baseball refused to grant film-makers permission to use the Cubs as the team the bleacher bums cheer for. In the film, the Cubs are the Bruins and it's all downhill from there. See the film only if you must. The play is the way to go.

> You're much more likely to find a production of *Bleacher Bums* in Chicago than anywhere else. Although Cubs fans are spread across America and the play enjoyed successful runs in New York and Los Angeles and a number of other cities, it is rarely staged outside the Cubs' hometown these days. For performance dates and locations, check the Windy City's arts calendar at *www.chicago.timeout.com*.

79 | READ THE BOOK, *VEECK AS IN WRECK*

One of baseball most colorful characters, Bill Veeck was a team owner with a healthy dose of P.T. Barnum running through his veins. Ever the entrepreneur, Veeck, (whose name rhymed with "wreck") revolutionized baseball. Practically nothing was off-limits when it came to promotional stunts, including giving away live pigs or hiring Max Patkin, the "Clown Prince of Baseball" as a coach. Veeck thought baseball was synonymous with entertainment, and though he respected the game, he had no use for convention when it came to promoting it.

Veeck grew up in baseball. His father, Bill Veeck, Sr., was a baseball scribe turned team president who took over the Chicago Cubs in the late 1920s. After his father died in 1933, Veeck became treasurer of the Cubs. But handling the club's books didn't stop him from planting the ivy on Wrigley Field's outfield walls, creating one of the great ballpark's most significant landmarks.

In 1941, he bought the Milwaukee Brewers franchise in the American Association, a minor league. But World War II temporarily interrupted his steady progress in the baseball world. Fighting in the Pacific Theater, Veeck was seriously wounded, requiring the eventual amputation of his leg. Veeck returned home, sold the Brewers for a tidy profit, and bought the Cleveland Indians in 1946.

And then the real fun began. In 1947, Veeck moved the Indians to Cleveland Municipal Stadium. He signed the American Leagues' first black player, Larry Doby, then brought in the great Negro Leagues pitcher Satchel Paige. The following year, the Indians won their first World Series since 1920. Things were going fine in Cleveland until he tried to trade the popular Lou Boudreau and Veeck's wife walked out on him. Needing a fresh start and money, Veeck sold the Indians and in 1951 bought the St. Louis Browns, a hapless club that drew few fans and played bad baseball in the shadow of the wildly popular Cardinals.

In 1951, Veeck signed 3'7" midget Eddie Gaedel and sent him up to bat, knowing Gaedel's tiny strike zone ensured him of a four-pitch walk. It was Gaedel's only MLB at-bat, as infuriated league officials forced Veeck to release him the next day. Veeck pulled plenty of other crazy stunts in St. Louis, including allowing grandstand fans to manage the Browns by signaling their preferences with placards and posters. Veeck's antics made him unpopular with fellow owners and American League officials, some of whom considered Veeck a madman out to ruin the national pastime. Frustrated in his efforts to relocate the Browns and faced with the threat of having the franchise discontinued, Veeck sold the Browns to owners who moved the club to Baltimore and renamed them the Orioles.

Veeck tried desperately to get back into Major League Baseball, but nothing worked until 1959 when he headed a group that bought the Chicago White Sox, who won the American League pennant in Veeck's first season with the club. Veeck, ever the innovator, unveiled an "exploding scoreboard," complete with flashing lights and sound effects. He had his players' names sewn on the back of their jerseys to help fans identify them. (Veeck was ahead of his time in more than just in his taste for outrageous promotional stunts.) Who knows what else might have been up his sleeve had the ailing Veeck not been forced to sell his share in the Chicago White Sox on doctor's orders in 1961. A heavy smoker, Veeck actually carved an ashtray into his wooden leg.

With his health failing, Veeck wrote, with the help of Ed Linn, his autobiography, *Veeck As In Wreck*. Funny and fascinating, the book told it like it was, calling out owners, players, and anyone else who ever tried to derail his stay in the big leagues. Though originally published in 1961, *Veeck As In Wreck* has easily withstood the test of time. Like Jim Bouton's *Ball Four* (see *Bucket List* item #17), *Veeck As In Wreck* strips away the game's sugar-coating to reveal the flaws of a number of respected baseball men, and of the game itself.

Veeck came back to baseball in 1975, assuming the reins of the Chicago White Sox for a second time. Despite being in his sixties, Veeck remained the game's most outrageous character. He had the Sox play in shorts and signed Minnie Minoso when the outfielder was 51 so he could say he played professional baseball in four different decades, then reactivated him four years later in 1980 so Minoso could play in his fifth decade. For America's bicentennial celebration, Veeck dressed up as the peg-legged, flute-playing patriot in the "Spirit of '76," and marched in Chicago's Opening Day parade. Finally, in 1979, Veeck uncorked his most infamous promotional stunt, "Disco Demolition Night," during which piles of disco records were blown up before a game at Comiskey Park, resulting in a riot and a forfeit to the Detroit Tigers.

Financial pressures forced Veeck to sell the White Sox in 1981. He died of emphysema three years later, leaving a void the game has not dared try to fill.

> The University of Chicago Press released a new edition of *Veeck As In Wreck* in 2001. It remains available from most bookstores and online booksellers. Veeck wrote another memoir with Ed Linn called *The Hustler's Handbook*; it was reissued in 2009 by Ivan R. Dee Publishing.

80 SEE THE PHILLIES PLAY AT CITIZENS BANK PARK

Citizens Bank Park opened in 2004, succeeding Veteran's Stadium, as the home of the Philadelphia Phillies. At the time, Phillies fans had little to cheer about—not that they've ever had too much to cheer about. One of the least successful teams in Major League Baseball history, the Phils were closing in on their 10,000[th] loss as a franchise and hadn't won a world championship since 1980. And, incredibly, 1980 remained the only time they had won the big prize, despite being in existence since 1883.

The Phillies had laid a solid foundation over the previous few seasons for a sustained run at another championship. But Philadelphia's fans had learned pessimism the hard way—they'd earned it through enduring an almost endless series of heartbreaks and disappointments and humiliations. And they gave as bad as they got, showering visiting players with abuse, and even debris when they were feeling particularly foul. Phillies players often got treated just as badly. Phils Hall of Famer Mike Schmidt, probably the greatest third baseman to ever play the game, was booed by Phillies fans almost every time he came to the plate, even when he'd hit a home run the previous at-bat. City officials installed a jail and courthouse in the bowels of Veterans Stadium to process all the fans arrested for criminal behavior during home games of the Philadelphia Eagles, the NFL franchise in the "City of Brotherly Love." Full of potholed turf, crumbling concrete and foul smells that never seemed to go away, Veterans Stadium served as a symbol of the Phillies' history and fortunes.

It's funny what a new ballpark can do for a team and its fans. After moving into Citizen's Bank Park, the Phillies notched three consecutive second-place finishes in the National League East, then claimed the division in 2007, reaching the playoffs for the first time in 14 years. The following season, they won it all, dismissing Tampa Bay in five games in the World Series. That's not to say that the 2008 World Series champs Phillies won a World Series title simply

Citizens Bank Park in Philadelphia, home of the Phillies.

because they were playing in new digs, but it's safe to say that it didn't hurt. Playing in Citizens Bank Park inspired a fresh start for the Phillies and its loyal, long-suffering fans. It fostered a belief that a new tradition—a winning tradition—could begin at Citizens Bank Park. And that's what happened.

So, what kind of ballpark is Citizens Bank? For starters, it's located in South Philly in a kind of sports fans' paradise. Across from Citizens Bank Park sits Lincoln Financial Field, home of the NFL's Philadelphia Eagles. Nearby stands the Wachovia Center, where the NHL Flyers and the NBA Sixers play. Professional baseball, football, hockey and basketball—all on the same large urban campus just minutes by mass transit from downtown Philadelphia.

Citizens Bank Park boasts a number of perks beyond its location. Like many retro-style parks, it's constructed of brick and steel. But whereas most parks paint their steel green, Citizens Bank Park features steel beams of maroon, a color connected to the Phillies' past. It also features a grandstand sunroof and neon Liberty Bell atop right-center field that rings after Phillies' home runs. Bronze statues of former Phillies greats (Richie Ashburn, Mike Schmidt, Robin Roberts, and Steve Carlton) stand at the entrances to the park. Adjacent to the home plate entrance of Citizens Bank Park by the parking area, you'll find a tribute to Connie Mack, the Hall of Fame player, manager, and owner of the old American League Philadelphia Athletics.

These nods to the past are complemented by plenty of modern amenities and some interesting touches that make the park a pleasure in which to watch baseball. The bullpens are stacked atop each other in center field, with the visitor's pen closest to Phillies fans looking down at the pitchers warming up, which makes for some interesting commentary, especially when the game is on the line. The center-field wall, which in many ballparks is simply painted black to aid batters in picking up a pitched ball, is red brick wall draped with ivy. It turns what is usually the dreariest place in a major league ballpark into one of the nicest looking at Citizen's Bank Park. Speaking of the outfield, HOK, the architectural firm that designed Citizens Bank Park, missed the mark by not creating more emphasis on the Philadelphia skyline between the large scoreboard and the edge of the outfield grandstand seats. Granted, the skyline is a bit far off unlike in other cities, such as Pittsburgh and Cleveland, which offer a wonderful close-up silhouette of the city—but you see almost nothing but sky at Citizens Bank Park.

A missed design opportunity, it's true. But Citizens Bank Park misses no opportunities when it comes to food. In a word, it's the best place to eat in the National League, ranking with Boston's Fenway Park in the "Best Ballpark Food" category. A Philly cheesesteak is the obvious choice for any out-of-town visitor. But don't ignore the chance to chow down boardwalk fries, grilled hot dogs with all the trimmings, or a sandwich from the Bull's Barbeque in the outfield concourse. Phillies great Greg Luzinski, who was known as "The Bull" to local fans, owns this concession stand and oversees the making of some great-tasting barbecue. Wash it down with a specialty micro-brew between innings and you've got the makings of great day or night of baseball, Philly style.

> For information on ballpark tours and tickets to Phillies games, check the team's website at *www.phillies.com*.

81 READ THE BOOK, *A FALSE SPRING*

A False Spring, Pat Jordan's memoir about his time spent playing in the minor leagues, often shows up on lists of the best books about baseball and sports in general. *Sports Illustrated* in its now-widely known list of the "Top 100 Sports Books of All Time" ranked *A False Spring* at #37. *Time* magazine called *A False Spring* "one of the best and truest books about baseball," while the great baseball writer Roger Kahn, the author of his own classic, *Boys of Summer* (#2 on the *Sports Illustrated* list), selected *A False Spring* as one of his all-time favorite baseball books.

Originally published in 1973, Jordan's story actually begins in 1959 when he is signed as a promising young pitcher by the Milwaukee Braves. Over the years, critics and historians have praised *A False Spring* for its insight into the often brutal world of minor league baseball and for Jordan's achingly honest writing style. Baseball-wise, Jordan's story does not have a happy ending. He spends four seasons in the minors, trying to live up to expectations and, more importantly, trying to find himself amid the baseball dreams and realities that swirl around him.

Prior to signing a contract to play professional baseball, Jordan had known nothing but success. In high school, he was a baseball hero, one of the best pitchers to ever come out of Fairfield, Connecticut. With a torrid fastball and a mature understanding of the subtleties of pitching that belied his youth, he was judged a "can't-miss" prospect by most of the scouts who saw him play. Jordan got offered a contract upon graduation from high school for a then big-time sum of $40,000 and assigned to the McCook Braves, Milwaukee's minor league team in the Nebraska State League. He was 18 years old, on top of the world, and ready to make his mark in professional baseball.

Jordan quickly found out that baseball is a grueling game. It often chews up players oozing with potential and spits them out as emotional wrecks so stressed out by the pressure that no matter how good their baseball skills are, they are damaged goods and never make it to the big leagues. Jordan had the essential skills; what he lacked was consistency and good fortune. *A False Spring* is the story of Jordan's fight to avoid failure in baseball and to become a man capable of handling defeat with the same grace as he handles victory. It is a tough challenge, and in the end, neither the reader nor Jordan is certain of the outcome.

Read *A False Spring* because it's a beautifully written baseball book, not because it's a joyful read. Often, the book is downright depressing. That Jordan's experience in the minors occurred a half-century ago makes little difference. The relentless grind of the minor leagues and the toll it takes on young players like Jordan remains real, and his story remains all too relevant. Baseball breeds false springs and broken dreams.

Pat Jordan never did make it to the major leagues, and although *A False Spring* ends on a disappointing note, Jordan found success as a writer. Since the publication of *A False Spring* and the rave reviews it received, Jordan, who had long ago hung up his cleats and glove, began writing for such magazines as *Sports Illustrated*, *Rolling Stone*, *Men's Journal*, *Playboy*, and *The New Yorker*. He has also authored nearly a dozen other books. Instead of becoming a major league pitcher, Pat Jordan made himself into a major league writer, one who is still turning out wonderful literary reflections on baseball.

In 2005, Bison Books released a paperback version of *A False Spring*. It is available from most bookstores and online retailers. Jordan has written a number of other fine baseball and sports books, as well as numerous journalistic pieces. Persea released a collection of his work, *The Best Sports Writing of Pat Jordan*, in 2008, which, like *A False Spring* and Jordan's other books, can be purchased from most bookstores and online booksellers.

82 ATTEND JACKIE ROBINSON DAY

Jackie Robinson Day takes place every April 15 to honor one of baseball's most memorable moments: the breaking of Major League Baseball's color barrier by the heroic African-American Jackie Robinson. It happened in Brooklyn on April 15, 1947 at Ebbets Field. Robinson, who had been playing baseball for the

Kansas City Monarchs in the Negro Leagues, had signed a contract with the Brooklyn Dodgers' general manager Branch Rickey to play ball for the Dodgers. Robinson spent some time in Montreal playing for the minor league Royals before being called up and taking the field on that historic day.

The day Robinson appeared in a Dodgers' uniform was, say some historians, the day the civil rights movement in America became a reality. Robinson, a graduate of UCLA and an army veteran, knew that becoming a member of the Brooklyn Dodgers meant more than making baseball history. Black players hadn't been allowed to play in the established major leagues in the 20th century, thus robbing them and the game's fans of the highest level of competition. It was clear to many serious baseball observers that blacks such as Satchel Paige, Josh Gibson, Cool Papa Bell, Buck Leonard, and many other ballplayers in the Negro Leagues had the baseball skills and the natural talent to play in the white big leagues. Only the color of their skin prevented them from doing so in segregated America.

Robinson broke down that wall when he stepped out onto the field that wet and cold day in Brooklyn. Though he went hitless, he whacked a symbolic grand slam for black America. According to sports historian Stuart Miller, "the black press covered the game like a new Emancipation Proclamation—the *Baltimore Afro-American* devoted seven articles, seven photographs, an editorial and a cartoon to it." Other black newspapers covered the game and Robinson's participation in similar fashion. Suddenly, black Americans everywhere had a new hero and something many had never known: hope. To them, Robinson signaled the beginning of a new era of possibility, a new America where blacks, long denied essential rights, equality and opportunity, now had a fighting chance to secure their share of the American Dream.

It took a while, but in 2007 on the 60th anniversary of that historic baseball moment, Major League Baseball announced a new, officially sanctioned annual event: Jackie Robinson Day. With Robinson's number 42 officially retired by all major league teams in 1997, players, black and white, now wear Robinson's number on Jackie Robinson Day as a gesture of respect and honor.

With various pre-game events and special programs, teams across both the American and National Leagues honor Robinson's place in baseball history and the game's ongoing quest to preserve racial equality in all facets of the game. Major League Baseball also uses the day to promote one of its pet programs: getting young black kids more involved in baseball and pushing for better baseball fields and facilities in the inner cities. Major League Baseball has become increasingly concerned with its diminishing number of black ballplayers. Currently, less than ten percent of all major league ballplayers are African-American; in the 1970s, blacks made up nearly 30 percent to the league's rosters.

Catching a major league game on Jackie Robinson Day can be an emotional experience, especially for black baseball fans. It brings goose bumps to those who know the challenges Robinson faced that first year in the majors when both opposing players and fans in the stands hurled racial epithets at him, bringing out the worst qualities of an America deeply segregated by race. Things have changed in America, of course. It's a far different country than the one Robinson and other blacks knew in 1947. You need to look no further than the White House for proof of that.

Jackie Robinson Day stands as a reminder that Robinson ranks with other great American heroes, not just because of his formidable baseball skills, but also because of his courage and determination to make a game that for so long had it wrong when it came to race, finally make it right.

> Jackie Robinson Day takes place every year on April 15 at every Major League Baseball park hosting a game. Check Major League Baseball's website at *www.mlb.com* or the website of your favorite team for more information on Jackie Robinson Day.

83 | OWN A COPY OF *THE NEW BILL JAMES HISTORICAL BASEBALL ABSTRACT* ✦✦✦

Notice how this *Bucket List* item starts with the word "Own," not "Read," even though it refers to a book. That's because *The New Bill James Historical Baseball Abstract* (Free Press, 2001) is not the kind of book you read cover-to-cover. It's much too massive for that. Weighing a couple of pounds and coming in at 1,000 pages, it would take practically an entire baseball season to complete. Also, it doesn't read like a conventional book; you flip through it, looking for information, instead of opening to page one and continuing from there. But as an almost peerless reference manual to the national pastime, *The New Bill James Historical Baseball Abstract* rates as an essential on the *Baseball Fan's Bucket List*.

First formally published in 1985 as an offspring of James' annual *Baseball Abstract*, one of the most influential baseball works ever written, *The Historical Baseball Abstract* was different than its predecessor. Living up to its title, *The Historical Baseball Abstract* surveyed the entire history of Major League Baseball. Though he was already highly regarded in baseball circles, the new book also took Bill James up a notch in the publishing world. James had self-published his annual *Baseball Abstract* in the early 1980s. With the publication of *The Historical Baseball Abstract*, James entered the world of professional publishing.

While James does not rank as one of the most eloquent baseball writers, he is an astute observer of the game, and witty to boot. James wrote about what intrigued him about the game and shared his innovative ideas. Hardcore fans found the book a revelation, since James often presented brand new ways of looking at baseball statistics (while at the same time admitting that analyzing baseball with only numbers was limiting). James called the new information he presented "sabermetrics," a nod to the Society of American Baseball Research (SABR, see *Bucket List* item #48), a group of baseball fans that often looked at the game through the eyes of a mathematician or scientist.

The New Bill James Historical Baseball Abstract represents a major revision of *The Historical Baseball Abstract*—make that a near total re-write. The book is divided into three sections: The Game, Players, and Reference. In part one, James covers the history of baseball, decade-by-decade, and states in the book's Introduction that this section "is, in a sense, about that search for equilibrium, about how the game of each decade was different from the game of the years before." James' premise is hardly earth-shattering, but his colloquial style and curious ideas about aspects of the game that ran counter to many previous baseball histories and theories, make for an interesting read.

Section two of *The New Bill James Historical Baseball Abstract* deals with the baseball players. James rates the top one hundred players at each of the nine positions. He offers analysis and commentary on such data as "Runs Created," "Win Shares," "Clutch Performance," and other categories he deems important. James' all-time team? Catcher: Yogi Berra; first base: Lou Gehrig; second base: Joe Morgan; third base: Mike Schmidt; shortstop: Honus Wagner; left field: Ted Williams; center field: Willie Mays; right field: Babe Ruth; pitcher: Walter Johnson. Let the arguments begin.

The final section of *The New Bill James Historical Baseball Abstract* is the Reference section. James deals mostly with his "win shares" theory here as a way of evaluating players. Win shares blends an array of pitching, hitting, and fielding statistics into an overall rating that quantifies individual performance and calculates both offensive and defensive contributions. This is how James has come up with the results of his top players at each position, which makes up the "Players" section of the book. Rather than explain how, exactly, win shares work, I'll leave that to James, since it isn't easy to describe.

James and his sabermetrics instigated a revolution in Major League Baseball. Oakland A's general manager Billy Beane bought into some of James' main concepts and used them to turn his small-market team into regular pennant contenders (see *Bucket List* item #29). In 2003, the Boston Red Sox, intrigued with James' principles of baseball analysis, hired him as a consultant. The following year, the Red Sox won their first World Series in over eight decades. Many traditionalists felt the game had been taken over by number nerds, when in fact, with the rise of the use of the computer in baseball, the evolution to sabermetrics had been underway for years.

Agree or disagree with James and his ideas about baseball, you need to own and read (if not all at once) *The New Bill James Historical Baseball Abstract* to complete this *Bucket List* entry. James' ideas and his sabermetrics have simply become too important to baseball for any serious baseball fan to ignore.

> Free Press published a revised version of *The New Bill James Baseball Historical Abstract* in 2003. It is available from most bookstores and online booksellers, along with numerous other books on baseball by Bill James.

84 OWN A CLASSIC BASEBALL PHOTOGRAPH ✦✦

Owning a classic baseball photograph is similar to owning a piece of baseball art. It's more than something that hangs on your wall. A great baseball photograph defines a moment in baseball time and captures a piece of baseball history. A fine photographic print, nicely matted and framed, can be with you a lifetime.

It used to be that you could only purchase high-quality baseball photographs from photo galleries. Although the photographs were professionally presented, the choices were few and the cost significant. But over time, photo agencies, newspapers and magazines and even museums came to realize that they could make a lot of money selling sports photographs. Now, baseball fans have full access to literally thousands and thousands of photos. The question then is: which photo is the right one for you to buy?

There are the certified classics, like New York Yankees catcher Yogi Berra jumping into the arms of a jubilant Don Larsen after Larsen threw the final pitch of his perfect game in the 1955 World Series against the Brooklyn Dodgers. There's New York Giant Willie Mays running down Vic Wertz's towering shot to straightaway center field and catching it over his shoulder during the 1954 World Series against the Cleveland Indians. Or what about the close up of Texas Ranger pitching great Nolan Ryan on the mound with a bleeding cut on the bridge of his nose, the result of a bench clearing brawl? There are many, many more. Select a historical photograph such as one of these, or simply pick your favorite photo of your favorite player. Spend as much as you can afford for the print, as well as on the frame.

The photo archive of the National Baseball Hall of Fame and Museum in Cooperstown provides one of the best places to purchase a classic baseball print. Available for sale are hundreds of great photographs that span the history of baseball. They're affordably priced, but the prints lack the high quality of what you'll get if you purchase a fine print from a photo gallery. For the economically minded, though, a Hall of Fame photo will do just fine and look great in your den.

Another place to look for good baseball prints is the *New York Times*. Over the past few years, the *Times* has opened up their photo archives and offered a series of choice prints for sale. Many of the photographs have a New York theme, with, not surprisingly, a special emphasis on the Yankees. But they also have photos of Jackie Robinson and the Brooklyn Dodgers, including Jackie's famous steal of home against the Yankees during the 1955 World Series, and selections from the New York Mets. The good news is that newspapers in other cities are now offering photos from their baseball archives.

Finally, you can always take your own baseball picture, get it enlarged, then matted and framed. It probably won't look as good as one taken by a veteran sports photographer, but the fact that you took it should override any downside. You might even be good enough—or lucky enough—to capture a truly great scene or moment. Plus, a baseball photo hanging on your wall that you shot yourself always holds extra meaning.

> To find out more about classic baseball photos available from the National Baseball Hall of Fame, call (607) 547-0375 or go to *www.baseballhalloffame.org*. Contact the newspaper that covers your favorite team for information about how to get photos of the team's greatest players and moments.

85 SEE THE ANGELS PLAY AT ANGEL STADIUM

Home of the American League's Los Angeles Angels of Anaheim, Angel Stadium is the most fan-friendly of all the big league ballparks. You might not root for the Angels or rank their park with Fenway or Camden Yards in terms of tradition or architectural delights. But after catching a game there, you might root for the Angels' front office, as it has created a baseball experience that should be the envy of the majors.

Maybe it's because of the ballpark's close proximity to Disneyland, located just a couple of miles away. Disneyland practically created the art of customer satisfaction; it's where the visitor is endlessly pampered and smiles abound. Whatever the cause, you'll enjoy an equal amount of pleasantries and courtesies from the Angels' stadium staff. It would be nice if some of what fans experience at Angel Stadium could be bottled and shipped off to, say, Yankee Stadium where getting an answer from a staffer to a simple question like "Where's the Men's Room?" or "Can you help me find my seat?" too often is met with apathy, or worse, a sneer.

The kindness starts in the parking lot at Angel Stadium. The price to park is nominal and the people who take your money are unfailingly polite. At the ballpark entrances, more nice people wait to take your tickets. Go to the concession stand and you'll be pleasantly surprised that food and beer are reasonably priced. Want a scorecard to track the game? No problem. Go to Customer Relations and they'll give you one—for free. Ask for a pencil and you'll get one of those too, along with a parting, "Enjoy the ballgame."

The team's history features a jumble of names. From 1962 until 1965, the Los Angeles Angels played their games at Dodger Stadium in Chavez Ravine. The club's home since 1966, Angel Stadium used to be called Anaheim Stadium. The Los Angeles Angels of Anaheim is the team's official name now, but they used to be called the Anaheim Angels, and before that, the California Angels, and before that, the Los Angeles Angels. To make matters even more confusing, there used to be a Pacific Coast League team also called the Los Angeles Angels, before the Brooklyn Dodgers moved to Los Angeles in 1958. The PCL Angels played at Wrigley Field. (No, not the Wrigley Field in Chicago, but another Wrigley Field in L.A. which is now but a memory.) The major league Los Angeles Angels also played at Wrigley Field, but for one year,

1961, the year the club became a member of the American League.

Not surprisingly, all of the name changes created all kinds of identity problems for the team outside of California. The Angels, however, have finally found peace and stability in Angel Stadium, where the team won its first World Series in 2002. And, by the way, the official name of Angel Stadium is Angel Stadium of Anaheim.

A couple of Angel Stadium trademarks are worth noting. Outside the main entrance are huge red batting helmets and bats. They're a bit gimmicky, and not unlike what you might find at a minor league ballpark, but they present nice backgrounds for photos. Once inside, check out the waterfalls beyond the center-field fence where water cascades down a rock formation and sprays high up in the air whenever there's cause for Angels' fans to celebrate a home run or great play in the field. The waterfalls look is more Disney than Major League Baseball, and some visitors to the ballpark might think it hokey. But it has become such an indelible part of Angel Stadium, that the ballpark just wouldn't seem right without it.

Architecturally, Angel Stadium doesn't rate as high as more contemporary ballparks with their retro notions and traditional lines. Angel Stadium is a suburban park, so there is no city skyline to accent its overall look. Surrounding the stadium are, what else, parking lots. But Angel Stadium passes the test when it comes to essentials, like good views of the action on the field, a scoreboard that provides the kind of fan information that details each player, and an overall ambiance that leads the league in the categories of warmth and kindness.

For information on tours of Angel Stadium and tickets to Angels games, check the team's website at *www.angelsbb.com*. Rob Goldman's book *Once They Were Angels* (Sports Publishing, 2006) provides a historical look at the club through the eyes of some of its greatest players, including Rod Carew, Bo Belinsky, Jim Fregosi, Nolan Ryan and Don Baylor.

86 LEARN THE STORY BEHIND "TAKE ME OUT TO THE BALL GAME"

"Take Me Out to the Ball Game" is the national anthem of Baseball Nation. Think about it. It is played at every baseball game of note. It is sung, not at the beginning or end of the game, but in the thick of it, when it's most meaningful. People stand when they sing it. Fans of opposing teams, including even those of the Boston Red Sox and New York Yankees, come together as one to sing it. It is sung with gusto and pride. Parents teach it to kids and one day they'll teach it to their kids. Everyone knows the chorus and the melody.

But hardly anyone knows the story of the song. All true baseball fans need to know the history behind "Take Me Out to the Ball Game." And they need to know all the words, not just the chorus, which is what everyone sings during the Seventh Inning Stretch.

First, some background information. "Take Me Out to the Ball Game" was written more than one hundred years ago. It was not, however, the first song written about baseball. Baseball's maiden songs—"The Baseball Polka" and "Baseball Days"—were both written in 1858, a half-century before "Take Me Out to the Ball Game." But neither song, nor any other song, for that matter, could compete with the universal popularity of "Take Me Out to the Ball Game."

Jack Norworth, a New York vaudeville actor and songwriter, wasn't a baseball fan before writing the lyrics to "Take Me Out to the Ball Game." In fact, he had never even been to a game. But like all good writers, he was observant and clever, and could write about most anything, given the inspiration. Norworth, who also penned the classic "Shine on Harvest Moon," needed a song for a theatrical piece he was working on for the Amphion Theater in Brooklyn.

One day during the summer of 1908, Norworth was riding the New York subway when he gazed upon a sign that read, "Baseball Today—Polo Grounds." The New York Giants played at the Polo Grounds, which were located at the north end of Manhattan. That year, led by their legendary manager, John McGraw, the Giants were locked in a National League struggle with the Pittsburgh Pirates and the Chicago Cubs. The Cubs were the current world champions of baseball and the Pirates had Honus Wagner, one of the greatest shortstops of all time. But the Giants had their ace pitcher, Christy Mathewson, who, like Wagner, would be later inducted in the National Baseball Hall of Fame. It was an exciting summer to be a baseball fan.

As Norworth was reading the Polo Grounds sign, the idea for a song about baseball sprung into his mind. Out of nowhere, he invented the song's lead girl, Katie Casey, a big time baseball fan, and shortly thereafter, before his subway ride was over, he had the song's plot. Katie Casey wanted to go to a baseball game (presumably to see the New York Giants play at the Polo Grounds) and pleads with her boyfriend to "take me out to the ball game." A short time later, Norworth wrote the full lyrics:

Katie Casey was baseball mad,
Had the fever and had it bad,
Just to root for the hometown crew,

Ev'ry sou, Katie blew.
On a Saturday, her young beau
Called to see if she'd like to go,
To see a show
But Miss Kate said "No,
I'll tell what you can do:"
Chorus:
Take me out to the ball game,
Take me out with the crowd.
Buy me some peanuts and Cracker Jack,
I don't care if I never get back.
Let me root, root, root for the home team,
If they don't win, it's a shame.
For it's one, two, three strikes you're out,
At the old ball game.

Norworth gave the lyrics to his friend and fellow songwriter, Albert Von Tilzer, who wrote a simple but irresistibly catchy melody for them. "Take Me Out to the Ball Game" was published that year. It enjoyed limited success, but certainly nothing to suggest the song's eventual importance. Over time, however, "Take Me Out to the Ball Game" would be sung at baseball games around America. Cubs' announcer, Harry Caray, was famous for singing it loudly and badly, which inspired anyone and everyone to sing it during the Seventh Inning Stretch, good voice, or bad.

America's National Anthem, "The Star Spangled Banner," also gets sung at ballparks across America. Usually, one person, a professional singer, even a star, will sing it, and some, not all, in the stands, will sing along, and usually not too loud. It is a difficult song to sing. But "Take Me Out to the Ball Game" is sung by everyone, loudly and happily as if to proclaim our love and devotion to the national pastime. It is baseball's—and America's—most democratic song.

To find out more about the song, check out the book *Baseball's Greatest Hit: Take Me Out to the Ball Game* (Hal Leonard Corporation, 2008) by Robert Thompson, Tim Wiles and Andy Strasberg, with a foreword by Carly Simon. The book includes a CD with numerous recordings of the song by the likes of Harry Caray, George Winston and Dr. John.

87 READ THE BOOK *THE GLORY OF THEIR TIMES* ✫✫✫

When baseball great and infamous misanthrope Ty Cobb died in 1961, not a lot of people mourned his passing. But New York University economics professor and baseball fan Lawrence Ritter recognized a larger tragedy in Cobb's death. Ritter realized Cobb's death symbolized the imminent extinction of Major League Baseball's pioneers, the generation of men who shaped Major League Baseball in its formative years. So Ritter purchased a tape recorder and hit the road for five years to locate aging baseball legends and record their recollections. He completed his task with Macmillan Company's 1966 publication of *The Glory of Their Times: The Story of the Early Days of Baseball Told by the Men Who Played It.*

Ritter edited his interviews to weave the book's 26 individual stories into a compelling, cohesive narrative that made fans embrace *The Glory of Their Times* and the era it so lovingly brought back to life. Nearly all the players Ritter interviewed were contemporaries of Cobb who played in the early decades of the 20th century. His subjects included Sam Crawford, Edd Roush, Paul Waner, Goose Goslin, Harry Hooper, and Rube Marquard, Lefty O'Doul, Fred Snodgrass, Heinie Groh, along with 17 others. In addition to their words, Ritter managed to transcribe his subjects' personalities and their colorful use of language.

He also got some great stories out of them. Highlights include: humorous accounts of base running screw-ups; life on the road; barnstorming in the off-season; reflections on Cobb, Babe Ruth, and other legends; a firsthand description of Bill Wambsganss' unassisted triple play in the 1920 World Series; an account of the death of Cleveland Indian batter Ray Chapman after he was hit by a pitch and of Fred Snodgrass's famous dropped ball in the 1912 World Series. The book also does a wonderful job of conveying a general sense of what it meant to be a ballplayer back then.

Upon its publication, *New York Times* reviewer Wilfrid Sheed hailed *The Glory of Their Times* as "quite simply the best sports book in recent memory." Many other rave reviews followed and almost overnight, *The Glory of Their Times* was accorded the title "baseball classic." In 1977, a film documentary by the same name was released, using many of the photographs from the book. Then in 1984, a new edition of *The Glory of Their Times* was published with additional interviews, including one with Hall of Famer Hank Greenberg.

Perhaps the best way to enjoy *The Glory of Their Times* is not to read it or watch it, but to listen to it. (Ritter released vinyl copies of the actual recorded interviews that were later converted to CD.) You'll get to hear the full interviews with the baseball legends, and be treated to the nuances and inflections of their language that make their stories even richer than the versions that appeared in print.

Oral histories are tricky business. When people are asked to recall long ago events, vital details often go missing and facts get twisted. But sometimes what's most important is the feel of the story. Ritter didn't conduct courtroom depositions. He merely captured classic conversations about early 20th century baseball that reveal much more than Ritter ever anticipated. The interviews remain priceless historical documents of a past era, especially since the passing of every ballplayer interviewed for the book.

Over four decades after its initial publication, *The Glory of Their Times* remains an essential baseball document, a must read for any armchair baseball historian or lover of the game.

> The 1992 Harper Perennial reissue of the expanded book version of Lawrence Ritter's *The Glory of Their Times: The Story of the Early Days of Baseball Told by the Men Who Played It* remains in print and available from most bookstores and online booksellers. A VHS version of the documentary and the four-CD set of the same name are available from used sellers, some of which you can find through *www.amazon.com*.

88 | LISTEN TO *THE GREAT AMERICAN BASEBALL BOX* ✷✷

No sport has captured the fancy of pop music like baseball. Even before Jack Norworth penned the lyrics to baseball's most famous song, "Take Me Out to the Ball Game" in 1908 (see *Bucket List* item #86), the national pastime inspired composers of pop, parlor and even classical music in America. They forged a relationship between music and the game that hums along to this day.

The rise of baseball in American pop culture in the 1920s coincided with the rise of radio, thus creating another important relationship. Before the advent of television in the late 1940s, most Americans followed baseball by listening to games on the radio. Early baseball fans usually recall some of the game's greatest moments as oral descriptions by radio announcers, along with the images their imaginations conjured to coincide with those audio descriptions.

In addition to songs and famous radio calls, baseball boasts its share of great speeches, compelling recorded interviews with the game's legends, plus entertaining radio advertisements and audio from TV ads that used famous ballplayers to pump sales of products like Wheaties and Lifebuoy soap. They add up to an audio treasure chest of magic moments that help fans embrace baseball history in a unique and exciting way.

In 2005, Shout Factory, a Los Angeles-based record company that specializes in pop music compilations, released a four-disc box set that artfully summarized and beautifully celebrated virtually all the aural elements of the national pastime. Rather than put the CDs in a traditional box, Shout Factory created a replica of a white baseball base to house the discs and the booklet that accompanies them. Pricey, but well worth including in your permanent music collection, *The Great American Baseball Box* ranks as a classic, the very best of the many baseball music collections available.

Disc one is all about baseball music. Most of the 16 tracks are post-World War II tunes, the earliest being "Did You See Jackie Robinson Hit That Ball?" by Count Basie & His Orchestra, featuring Taps Miller. Released in 1949 on the RCA label, the song celebrated Robinson's success in the majors at the same time it proudly portrayed Robinson as being as good as any white ballplayer. Teresa Brewer's "I Love Mickey" from 1956 captured the nation's affection for Mickey Mantle the year he won the Triple Crown. Terry Cashman's "Talkin' Baseball (Willie, Mickey & The Duke)" wasn't released until 1981, well after the legends it celebrates had retired. But the song has since become a classic for those who grew up in the 1950s when loyalty to one of New York's great center fielders—the Giants' Willie Mays, the Yankees' Mickey Mantle, or the Dodgers' Duke Snider—defined a fan's sensibilities. And of course there's Creedence Clearwater Revival alum John Fogerty's "Centerfield" from 1985, a song that celebrates Willie Mays and the game in general as infectiously as anything this side of "Take Me Out to the Ballgame."

Disc two presents 30 classic baseball broadcasts. It begins with an account of the final game of the 1936 subway World Series between the New York Giants and triumphant Yankees, and ends with the dramatic crash of the Bambino curse as the Boston Red Sox beat the St. Louis Cardinals in the 2004 World Series. In between are broadcasts steeped in baseball history: Don

Larsen's perfect game in the 1956 World Series, Pete Rose's breaking of Ty Cobb's all-time hits record, Nolan Ryan's seventh no-hitter, Cal Ripken, Jr.'s surpassing of Lou Gehrig's record for consecutive games played, and so much more.

Even with the richness of the first two discs, discs three and four contain much of the set's most invaluable material. Both discs feature rare player interviews and selections of great speeches, as well as other historic recordings you won't find anywhere else. In addition to the requisite Lou Gehrig 1939 retirement speech, one of the most emotional moments in the game's history (see *Bucket List* item #110), you can hear Whitey Ford discuss pitching fundamentals and Babe Ruth talk about his baseball goals and Jackie Robinson reflect on his historic role in breaking baseball's color barrier and Baseball Commissioner Kenesaw Mountain Landis announce the 1939 opening of the National Baseball Hall of Fame and Museum. Disc four also throws some comic relief into the mix, with tracks like "Beisbol Been Good to Me" from Garrett Morris' *Saturday Night Live* character Chico Escuela, plus Abbott and Costello's baseball comedy skit, "Who's on First" (see *Bucket List* item #103).

Many good public libraries own copies of *The Great American Baseball Box*, but this is a set you'll want to own yourself. It's difficult to digest all of its great moments in a single sitting. It's best to listen to it over the course of a season, sampling some of its selections here and there. The experience will make you appreciate baseball in a whole new way.

> **The Great American Baseball Box** is available from record stores and online sellers. For more information on the box set's contents and history, go to **www.shoutfactory.com**

89 START A BASEBALL BOBBLEHEAD COLLECTION ✷✷

Bobbleheads, those big-headed, spring-necked dolls that always seem to be nodding and smiling, have become one of baseball's most popular collectibles. Major league clubs use the dolls as promotional items to attract fans to the ballpark and celebrate certain players. Bobblehead giveaway games rank as some of the most popular of the season and often sell out in advance.

Unlike a lot of baseball memorabilia, bobblehead collections are easy and relatively cheap to get going. To collect the giveaway dolls of your favorite team, all you have to do is purchase tickets at the start of the season to all the club's bobblehead nights and show up early enough to get one. It's important to note that in most cases during bobblehead nights, only a limited number of the dolls are given away; usually only the first ten or twenty thousand fans entering the ballpark get one. Show up late and you're out of luck. Why do clubs only give bobbleheads to fans who come to the game early? Because arriving to the ballpark an hour or two before the start of the game means you're more likely to spend more money at the concession stands and team shop, thus covering the cost of your "complimentary" bobblehead. Major League Baseball rewrites the fundamental rule of economics as, "There is no such thing as a free bobblehead."

Bobblehead dolls began popping up in Russia and Germany in the mid-19th century; made of plaster and depicting animals, they were known as "nodders." The concept didn't make a significant impact on the sports world until the early 1960s, when Japanese manufacturers distributed bobblehead human dolls with generic faces in the uniforms of each MLB club, and of a few superstar individuals, including Willie Mays, Roberto Clemente, Roger Maris and Mickey Mantle. Made of papier-mâché, these early sports bobbleheads tended to crack and fall apart. Few survive, so you should expect to pay hundreds of dollars to acquire one in good condition.

Later in the decade, bobblehead manufacturers replaced papier-mâché with ceramic and produced dolls for popular music, cartoon and football figures, as well as baseball. The sports bobblehead craze, however, faded into oblivion in the mid-1970s. Collectors scooped up bobbleheads at baseball card and memorabilia conventions, but as promotional items or souvenirs for the casual fan, bobbleheads were passé.

Then a quarter century later, with Baby Boomer interest peaking in vintage baseball items and the construction of retro parks, bobbleheads made a grand comeback. The San Francisco Giants promoted a 1999 game by handing out over 30,000 new Willie Mays bobbleheads. Soon every MLB team, as well as clubs from other sports, were using bobblehead giveaways to beef up attendance and selling bobbleheads in their team stores.

Made of plastic, the new generation of bobbleheads are relatively sturdy and cheap to manufacture.

You can start your bobblehead collection with dolls that you pick up for free at games, then easily expand it using other means. Team shops sell bobbleheads, making them good places to get dolls of players that aren't celebrated with their own bobblehead promotion games during the season. And as a bonus, purchased bobbleheads don't come with the corporate logos that often appear on the free, promotional bobbleheads, and they're usually of higher quality. You can also buy bobbleheads at sports memorabilia stores or on *eBay*.

Like all collecting hobbies, this one can get out of hand. Collecting bobbleheads from one team and then another, and then another might eventually mean having to add shelves in your den or taking another job to finance your hobby. But to fulfill this *Bucket List* item, you can acquire just a few at games and add to your collection as you see fit. The bobblehead makes for an amusing addition to a room and offers a good reminder of all the fun and endearing ways serious fans can celebrate the game of baseball and its players.

> For information on your favorite MLB teams' bobblehead giveaways, go to *www.mlb.com* and click through to the club's homepage. To learn more on the history of sports bobbleheads and the value of particular dolls, you can check out Tim Hunter's book *Bobbing Head Dolls: 1960-2000* (Krause Publications, 2000).

90 SEE THE CARDINALS PLAY AT BUSCH STADIUM

Home of the National League's St. Louis Cardinals, the "new" Busch Stadium opened in 2006. It replaced the "old" Busch Stadium multi-purpose bowl where the Cards had played since 1966, sharing it with the NFL's St. Louis Cardinals for 22 years until their move to Arizona in 1988. The baseball Cardinals' original home, Sportsman's Park, was re-named Busch Stadium in 1953 in honor of the team's owner, Gussie Busch. So, technically speaking, this newest ballpark is actually the third one to be called Busch Stadium in St. Louis. The Cardinals celebrated the inaugural year of the new Busch Stadium in the best possible way—by winning their tenth world championship, defeating the Detroit Tigers, four-games-to-one, in the World Series. The last team to win a world championship in a brand new ballpark? The 2009 New York Yankees.

Geographically speaking, the new Busch Stadium overlaps the old one. Part of the new ballpark's bleacher area sits where the outfield of the old Busch Stadium was located. Thanks to architectural ingenuity, the new ballpark was constructed while the Cardinals were still playing in the old Busch Stadium. Then, right after the 2005 season, wrecking crews knocked down the old stadium and construction crews worked to finish the remaining outfield section of the new park in time for the start of the 2006 season.

The new Busch Stadium boasts plenty more character than the old one. Constructed of brownish-red brick and exposed steel painted black, the new ballpark has a throwback charm to it. Like other retro parks, Busch Stadium features an exposed outfield area, allowing views of the St. Louis skyline. However, unlike Pittsburgh's PNC Park or Cleveland's Progressive Field, which offer views of many downtown buildings designed with roughly the same brick aesthetic, the new Busch Stadium opens onto a skyline of mostly contemporary glass office buildings. What the new Busch Stadium doesn't have, of course, are the memories. But winning the world championship the first year the Cards inhabited their new home put them on the right path for a glorious tenure there.

Busch Stadium has some 44,000 seats, all of them colored Cardinal red. Add the red brick to the red seats and all those Cards fans that sit in them wearing bright red jerseys and t-shirts and jackets, and you know you're in Cardinal country. You'll know it even before you get inside, actually, when you pass by

The "new" Busch Stadium in St. Louis opened in 2006.

statues honoring Cardinal greats Rogers Hornsby, Dizzy Dean, Lou Brock, Bob Gibson, Enos Slaughter, Red Schoendienst, Ken Boyer and Ozzie Smith standing just outside the stadium. (Interestingly, there is no Mark McGwire statue.) "Mr. Cardinal" Stan "the Man" Musial is celebrated with not one, but two statues. The second is located about fifty yards from the cluster of Cardinal greats on the west side of the ballpark. The pedestrian bridge inside the stadium that offers fans a view of the Stan "The Man" bronze statue is called Musial Bridge. And there are two bronze busts to see outside the ballpark, one of Joe Buck, the legendary Cards' announcer, the other of the team's early owner, Gussie Busch. To say that the Cardinals are proud of their heritage is an understatement.

As you walk around Busch Stadium, you'll also notice the many Cardinal logos that the team used over the years embedded into the brick façade. A nice touch. Also nice is the old Busch Stadium scoreboard that ceremoniously hangs in the main concourse behind home plate.

St. Louis is regularly regarded as the best baseball city in America. Chicago, New York, and Boston fans like to debate that title. With the old, soul-less Busch bowl, it was difficult for an outsider to think baseball when he came to St. Louis. Now St. Louis has a ballpark everyone can feel good about. And when the team finally creates its ballpark village across the street from new Busch Stadium on the site where the old Busch Stadium stood, it'll be hard to deny St. Louis its baseball culture supremacy.

> For more information about tours of Busch Stadium and tickets to St. Louis Cardinals games, check the team's website *www.stlcardinals.com*. To learn more about the storied Cardinals franchise (and their old crosstown rivals), you can read Peter Goldenbock's *The Spirit of St. Louis: A History of the St. Louis Cardinals and Browns* (Harper Paperbacks, 2001), available from most bookstores and online booksellers.

91 ATTEND THE LITTLE LEAGUE WORLD SERIES ✦✦✦✦

Some springs, we can get so tied up with following our favorite Major League Baseball teams or our fantasy baseball players that we forget where it all began for most of us: in Little League. Each spring, tens of thousands of kids learn the fundamentals of the game and fair play in a relatively relaxed and supportive atmosphere provided by Little Leagues across the U.S. and the world. Catching a couple local Little League games in spring can put you back in touch with your own baseball roots and remind you of the game's innocence, fun and core virtues.

By the middle of summer, it's hard to ignore Little League, though. Because with August, comes the Little League World Series. Held in Williamsport, Pennsylvania, the Little League World Series now garners dozens of hours of TV coverage, including the airing of full games on ESPN, plus interviews with players and managers, nightly highlights and expert analysis. The Little League World Series has become such an international media event that to even to mention the word "innocence" in relation to it might be stretching things these days. Still, the Series is part of the American baseball fabric. And to experience Williamsport, Pennsylvania during the height of Little League World Series mania makes for a worthy *Baseball Fan's Bucket List* journey.

Little League began in Williamsport in 1939 with three local teams. The first Little League World Series took place in 1947 when a team from Williamsport defeated a Lock Haven, Pennsylvania team. It was more a North-Central Pennsylvania Series than a World Series. But the event and tradition had been established. And as Little League spread across America and then the globe, the series began to live up to its name. A team from Monterrey, Mexico became the first non-U.S. team to be crowned champions when it won the tournament in 1957 (then won it again in 1958). Today, Little League exists all over the world and teams from Japan, Taiwan, South Korea, Venezuela, Curacao and the United States have won the series.

Currently, 16 teams compete in the Little League World Series in Williamsport. Eight teams come from regions in the U.S., while the remaining eight come from the International bracket, which is made up of eight divisions: Canada, Mexico, the Caribbean, Latin America, Japan, Asia-Pacific, Europe/Middle East/Africa, and Trans-Atlantic. The U.S. winner meets the International bracket winner in the final to determine the world champion.

For a team, getting to the Little League World Series tournament is nearly as exciting as the tournament itself. According to Little League International, the governing body that oversees foreign play, hopeful teams play 16,000 Little League baseball games in 45 days to determine the finalists for Williamsport. That's a lot of baseball.

Teams competing for the honor of playing in Williamsport consist of 11-13-year-olds. They are all-star teams made up of the top players in their local leagues, as opposed to the individual teams that won their local league titles. Over the years, more than a few future Major League Baseball players have competed in

Williamsport. Little League World Series alumni include: Carney Lansford, Derek Bell, Gary Sheffield, Boog Powell, Rick Wise, Jason Varitek and Dan Wilson.

All Little League World Series games are free and open to the public. But in recent years, thanks to all the television coverage, tickets to games, especially the finals, have become increasingly difficult to obtain. You should also make reservations well in advance for hotels or other accommodations that you'll require while visiting the Williamsport area. Be sure to bring plenty of water to the games, as it can get hot and muggy in Williamsport in August.

When not watching kids play baseball, you can visit the Peter J. McGovern Little League Museum to learn about the history of Little League, all the players who have gone onto the big leagues, the rules, and the Series' most exciting moments, among other displays that deal with athletic nutrition, equipment, and other related baseball topics.

> For more information about the Little League World Series, check the Little League website at *www.littleleague.org*. To find out more about hotels and other amenities in Williamsport, contact the Williamsport Chamber of Commerce at (570) 326-1971 or check their website at *www.williamsport.org*.

92 SEE THE RANGERS PLAY AT RANGERS BALLPARK

Rangers Ballpark in Arlington, Texas opened in 1994 at the dawn of the retro-park movement in Major League Baseball. After the rousing success of Oriole Park at Camden Yards, both the Cleveland Indians and the Texas Rangers—two American League teams badly in need of new homes—built ballparks that celebrated a bit of baseball's past while guaranteeing its future. Fans loved the nod to baseball stadium history and wallowed in the nostalgia that went with it. At the same time, they enjoyed the modern amenities that the new parks offered. It was a classic case of having your cake and eating it, too.

Rangers Ballpark replaced Arlington Stadium, where the Rangers previously played. With a capacity just shy of 50,000, the club's new ballpark pays tribute to the belief that everything in Texas is big—including its ballparks. The park would have scored a higher number on the *Baseball Fan's Bucket List* had it not been stuck out in the suburbs (most of the retro parks are integrated into their cities' downtown areas) and if it wasn't so hot and humid in the Dallas-Fort Worth-Arlington area for much of the baseball season. Some baseball traditionalists prefer day games over night games, but except for the start of the season, when mid-afternoon temperatures in April and May are still bearable in Texas, you won't find many day games at Rangers Ballpark. If visiting the ballpark during the day is important to you, plan to visit to Arlington in the early part of the season.

Those two gripes aside, Rangers Ballpark in Arlington is actually a fine place to watch baseball and celebrate its history. The arched "Sunset Red" granite and brick façade honor the traditional lines and look of baseball's older ballparks. The exposed steel that's painted dark baseball green and the columns that hold up the roof of the Home Run porch in right field offer another nice nod to the past—and to Fenway Park. (Just try to stay out of the seats that suffer obstructed views because of them.) And could any Texas sports edifice fail to include steer heads (there are 35 of them at Rangers Ballpark), plus a lot of Lone Stars? They are located along the upper external arches of the park and contribute to the ballpark's allure and local flavor, as do the murals that celebrate Texas history on the external walls.

But maybe the best thing about Rangers Ballpark in Arlington is that it includes Legends of the Game, the best baseball museum in America that's not called the National Baseball Hall of Fame or the Negro Leagues Baseball Museum. Since Legends of the Game also rates a spot on the *Baseball Fan's Bucket List* (see item #45), come early enough to visit the museum before taking in the game and accomplish two goals in one day. Plan to spend at least an hour in Legends of the Game, more if you're the type of baseball fan who truly relishes the sport's history. The museum holds more major baseball artifacts than any facility outside Cooperstown.

Mass transit isn't really an option, so you'll have to drive to get to Rangers Ballpark in Arlington. But you'll at least find plenty of parking around the ballpark. And you may get a kick out of the name of one of the major thoroughfares near the ballpark: Nolan Ryan Expressway (just don't try to travel it at the speed of a classic Ryan fastball). The greatest Ranger of them all, Nolan Ryan is also celebrated at Rangers Ballpark. A bronze statue of him stands outside the park. Inside, he is honored with a banner, along with other Rangers who have been inducted into the club's and Major League Baseball's Hall of Fame.

For information about ballpark tours and tickets to Rangers' games, check the team's website at *www.texasrangers.com*. To find out more about Legends of the Game museum, see *Bucket List* item #45.

93 VISIT DEDEAUX FIELD AND THE USC BASEBALL HALL OF FAME ✲✲

The University of Southern California's Rod Dedeaux ranks as the greatest collegiate baseball coach in history. Dedeaux won 11 of the Trojans' 12 national baseball championships (by far the most won by any one school; as of 2009, Arizona State was second with five). Dedeaux captured his first national title in 1948 and during one amazing stretch from 1970 to 1974, USC and Dedeaux won five titles in a row, another record that still stands.

Dedeaux died in 2001, but USC certainly didn't forget Dedeaux's contributions to collegiate baseball and to turning USC into the nation's most storied baseball program. In fact, they began honoring him over a quarter-century before his passing. In 1974, when the Trojans finished construction on its new baseball field, they called it Dedeaux Field, an honor usually bestowed on a retired coach or player. And, as if a Hollywood screenwriter had been brought in to script things that season, USC pitcher Russ McQueen threw a no-hitter against the Cal Berkeley Bears on Opening Day at Dedeaux Field. And the Trojans went on to win another national title, Coach Dedeaux's next-to-last (his final one came in 1978). Speaking of Hollywood, Dedeaux Field has served as a set for such baseball movies as *A League of Their Own* (see *Bucket List* item #27), *For Love of the Game* (see *Bucket List* item #43) and *Mr. Baseball*.

The USC campus sits in downtown Los Angeles, just off the Harbor Freeway and across from three of the city's main museums, as well as the Los Angeles Coliseum where the Trojans play football. Dedeaux Field is located on the campus's west side, next to the USC tennis stadium. These days USC gets more acclaim for its football program (currently overseen by another legend-in-his-own-time coach, Pete Carroll) than the school's exploits on the baseball diamond. But it's impossible not to be overwhelmed by USC's baseball glory as you approach Dedeaux Field. Twelve banners that celebrate each of USC's baseball championships lead you up to the ballpark's gates. Adjacent to them wave banners honoring Trojan baseball's greatest players, including Tom Seaver, Mark McGwire, and Randy Johnson. Upon entering Dedeaux Field, you'll see a large baseball to your left. The plaque under it celebrates Rod Dedeaux as collegiate baseball's "Coach of the Century." As a professional player, Rod Dedeaux only made it to the majors for one day with the Brooklyn Dogers in 1935. But as a college coach, he climbed to the top of his profession and stayed there for decades. Wherever you go in Dedeaux Field, you are surrounded by the spirit of Coach Dedeaux and all his accomplishments.

As college ballparks go, Dedeaux Field ranks with the best of them, even if you ignore its glorious history. The park seats over 2500 fans, boasts an MLB-caliber lighting system, has the lines and look of a major league spring training park, and is tastefully trimmed in cardinal and gold. The facility houses the Rod Dedeaux Research for Baseball Institute, which includes high-tech training and video analysis facilities.

Above the seats along the first-base line stands the Trojans' Baseball Hall of Fame. Every other USC sport celebrates its legacy and national championships in Heritage Hall, home to Heisman Awards, Olympic gold medals, and trophies, jerseys, autographed balls, and banners. But Trojan baseball history merits a home all its own. Take time before the game to visit the Hall of Fame. You'll be amazed at how many Trojans honored there went on to became Major League Baseball stars.

> For more information about USC baseball and Dedeaux Field, go to *www.usctrojans.com*. To find out about getting tickets to a Trojans baseball game at Dedeaux Field, call (213) 740-GOSC.

94 READ THE BOOK, *YOU KNOW ME AL* ✶

Ring Lardner established himself as baseball's first great fiction writer. A sports columnist and short story author who was well-schooled in the subtleties of the game, its characters, its idiosyncratic language, and the humor that could be found on the field and in the stands, Lardner loved baseball and loved writing about it.

Lardner's most famous book, *You Know Me Al (A Busher's Letters)* is comprised of correspondence penned by a proud but dimwitted fictional ballplayer Jack Keefe to Al Blanchard, his best friend back home in Indiana. Published as a book in 1916, *You Know Me Al* first appeared two years earlier as a set of short stories in one of the most popular magazines of the day, *The Saturday Evening Post*. The book gets laugh out loud funny in a number of spots. But *You Know Me Al* rates a *Baseball Fan's Bucket List* entry mostly due to all that it reveals about the game and culture of baseball from a century ago.

Keefe is a "bush leaguer" or "busher," (hence the book's sub-title: *A Busher's Letters*). The bush leagues were hardly the major leagues, more like the minor leagues of today. They were called the "bush" leagues because most of the teams hailed from rural areas around America, providing entertainment and baseball to farmers and fans of the game living in small towns, especially in the Midwest. Around the turn of the last century, young ball players looking for a chance to play baseball and to leave the farm in search of adventure and opportunity joined bush league teams and traveled from town to town, making just enough money to get by. Many of the bush league players, like Jack Keefe, weren't all that educated, and their lack of cultural sophistication showed in their speech—which is what Lardner focused on in *You Know Me Al.*

Lardner was a great fan of the Chicago White Sox, and when he has Keefe called up to the majors, it's to the Sox that he goes. Keefe maintains his bush league ways in the big city, providing plenty of opportunities for his teammates to chide him and the club's owner to take advantage of him. In one letter, Jack writes Al to tell him of his call up to the White Sox: "I was out to the ball park early yesterday morning and some of the boys was there allready fanning and kidding each other. They tried to kid me to when I come in but I guess I give them as good as they give me. I was not in no mind for kidding, Al, because I was there on business and I wanted to see Comiskey and get it done with." Infamous cheapskate Charles Comiskey owned the Chicago White Sox. Lardner often used real life baseball people in *You Know Me Al.* In addition to Comiskey, Lardner references Ty Cobb, Walter Johnson, and Tris Speaker, among others.

Lardner's love of baseball was nearly broken by the Black Sox scandal of 1919 when eight White Sox players conspired with gamblers to throw the World Series. Lardner had a number of good friends on the team and was crushed when he found out they had given away the world championship. Lardner serves as a character in *Eight Men Out* (see *Bucket List* item #32), writer/director John Sayles' excellent film about the Black Sox scandal. Sayles himself plays Lardner.

Lardner continued to write about baseball throughout the 1920s, but never with the passion and conviction he displayed in his earlier writings before the Black Sox scandal. Lardner died in 1933, at age 48, of tuberculosis. His four sons all went into writing. One of them, Ring, Jr., won a pair of Oscars for screenplays for *Woman of the Year* (1942) and *M*A*S*H* (1970).

> Several different editions of Ring Lardner's classic baseball novel *You Know Me Al* remain in print and can be purchased from most bookstores and online booksellers. Many public libraries also carry copies of the book available for check out. To get acquainted with all of Lardner's baseball works, pick up a copy of *Ring Around the Bases: The Complete Baseball Stories of Ring Lardner* (Scribner's, 1992).

As an American humorist, Lardner ranks with Mark Twain and Will Rogers. Like his more celebrated literary colleagues, Lardner portrayed people as reflections of an America in transition from rural to urban life. He saw sport not just as entertainment, but also a means by which to judge the good and bad things that life had to offer. Lardner's editor was the famous Max Perkins and he counted both Ernest Hemingway and F. Scott Fitzgerald among his friends. Writer Virginia Woolf and critic H.L. Mencken, a man not generous with his praise, hailed Lardner as a great writer and artist. *You Know Me Al* may have been his finest effort. It's a fast and fun read that you'll return to often.

95 WATCH THE MOVIE, *BANG THE DRUM SLOWLY* ★★★★★

A small, but passionate number of baseball movie buffs rank *Bang the Drum Slowly* among the best of Hollywood's many attempts to capture the baseball life on the big screen. The film was released in 1973, years before the baseball movie boom that produced *The Natural, Bull Durham, A League of Their Own, Eight Men Out, Field of Dreams*, and *Major League*. While not quite up to their standard, *Bang the Drum Slowly* is, nevertheless, a fine baseball film, mostly because of the performance of a relatively unknown who went on to become one of the best actors of his generation.

A young Robert De Niro plays hayseed catcher Bruce Pearson who can't hit, can't carry a conversation, is the constant butt of locker room jokes, and is in danger of being traded or released from the team. It was De Niro's first major role, and it was clear by the end of the film that we'd be seeing him in other films as well. (We did, of course, in classics like *Mean Streets, Taxi Driver, The Deer Hunter* and *GoodFellas*, as well as many others).

At the beginning of *Bang the Drum Slowly*, we find out that Pearson is mortally ill. That he dies at the end of the film is why *Bang the Drum Slowly* is often compared to *Brian's Song*, a football film that also deals with the death of a young athlete. Based on a true story, *Brian's Song* is about Brian Piccolo, a Chicago Bears' running back who dies of cancer. It's a real tearjerker, and because Pearson in *Bang the Drum Slowly* also succumbs to cancer, the two films share a similarity not lost on movie historians and sports fans.

But *Bang the Drum Slowly* is not a notable film because it tugs hard at the heart and causes watery eyes. Rather, its triumph lies in the way director John Hancock created the surprisingly realistic baseball scenes, as well as how actors De Niro and co-star Michael Moriarty, who plays pitcher Henry Wiggen, forge a bond that goes deeper than baseball. As one reviewer put it, *Bang the Drum Slowly* is more about the "story of the friendship between a star pitcher (Moriarty), wise to the world, and a half-wit catcher (De Niro)" than death. When Pearson finally dies, it's more or less taken for granted and almost anti-climatic.

The film *Bang the Drum Slowly* was based on a book by the same name written by Mark Harris, one of the game's better novelists, and published in 1956. That same year, it was produced as a television film starring Paul Newman for *The U.S. Steel Hour.* If you can get your hands on the original screen interpretation of Harris' book, it'll be interesting to compare the television version with the cinema version. It's also a good idea to read the book as well. It's a quick read, and you'll discover that Harris has a lot to say about the national pastime that wasn't included in the film.

Harris also wrote the screenplay for *Bang the Drum Slowly.* The title came from a line in the country & western song, "The Streets of Laredo" that a cowboy pitcher named Piney Woods serenades his teammates with during a scene near the end of the story after everyone has found out that Pearson is dying. That the script stayed fairly close to the novel helped guarantee the film's success. Interestingly, however, Harris not only tells his baseball story through the eyes of Wiggen, but Harris would also make the character a part of other books, most notably *The Southpaw,* another baseball novel worth reading.

Wiggen is a memorable character, not just because he puts his friendship with Pearson, his catcher, above most everything else, but also because he has a way with words and with telling stories. When the team's manager (Vincent Gardenia) grows suspicious of Pearson and Wiggen's off-season road trip to the Midwest (where Pearson went to visit the Mayo Clinic), Wiggen's cover story grows more wild and less believable as the movies progresses, becoming one of the highlights of *Bang the Drum Slowly.*

Despite its many qualities, *Bang the Drum Slowly* certainly seems of another baseball

The 1973 film *Bang the Drum Slowly,* starring Robert DeNiro, Michael Moriarity and Vincent Gardenia, is available for rental or purchase from many movie stores and online merchants in VHS ad DVD formats. The original 1956 television production starring Paul Newman is also available on VHS from some used movie sellers. A revised edition of Mark Harris' 1956 novel *Bang the Drum Slowly* was released in 2003 by Bison Books and remains available from most bookstores and online booksellers.

movie era. In other words, it's a bit dated. Watch it and enjoy it for what it is: the best baseball film that was made in the 1970s.

96 ATTEND THE COOPERSTOWN SYMPOSIUM ON BASEBALL AND AMERICAN CULTURE ✦✦

The casual fan might not think he'd find much to interest him at the Cooperstown Symposium on Baseball and American Culture. The three days in June spent in Cooperstown, home of the National Baseball Hall of Fame and Museum, are filled with academic and quasi-academic papers and presentations on all things baseball. Admittedly, it sounds overly intellectual, but the symposium is actually also fun and engaging. In three days you'll get to what amounts to a compact baseball education, filled with things you never knew about the national game. You'll also meet people who think long and hard about baseball and how it has affected us as Americans. And if it all gets a little too heady, you can always tour the museum, which sponsors the annual event, or go baseball shopping on Main Street in Cooperstown (see *Bucket List* item #123), where you'll find everything from autographs and baseball cards, to caps and jerseys.

One of the highlights of the Cooperstown Symposium is the keynote speaker speech. A number of great baseball writers and historians have made the trek to New York state to speak in front of the symposium crowd. They include novelist W.P. Kinsella, and non-fiction writers Jonathan Eig, George Plimpton, Roger Kahn, Eliot Asinof, Jules Tygiel, and Paul Dickson. The celebrated documentary maker Ken Burns gave the keynote address in 1994, while baseball luminary Marvin Miller, head of the player's union, spoke in 2004. The symposium also features panel discussions that attract distinguished baseball writers and scholars, along with baseball men who've helped determine the course of the game. In recent years, Branch Rickey III (head of the Triple-A Pacific Coast League) and presidents of the National Baseball Hall of Fame and Museum, like Dale Petroskey and Jeff Idelson, have also attended the symposium.

Most of the attendees of the Cooperstown Symposium present papers, but it's not required. If you would like to present a paper, you'll have to first write a proposal, submit it for scrutiny, and do so well enough in advance to be placed in one of the numerous sessions. Just because you've written a paper proposal and met the required deadline, doesn't mean it will be accepted for presentation. Many are accepted, but not all. They're judged by the uniqueness and relevancy of the topic and the scholarship behind them. In order to complete this *Bucket List* entry, all you have to do is attend the conference. Actually presenting a paper would be a plus.

So what, exactly, are these papers all about? All of them deal with some aspect of baseball and its relationship to American culture. Here is a sampling of papers presented at recent symposia: "A Calculus of Color: The Slow Integration of the American League"; "The Plantation Owner and Brother Vida Blue: Charley Finley, Vida and the Politics of Race in Oakland"; "The New York Yankees Cope with the Great Depression"; "Bad Dudes and Baseball: 60s Culture and the Fate of Baseball's National Status" and "Computer, Sabermetrics, and QuesTec: Baseball's Uneasy Relationship with Technology."

In addition to all the paper presentations, there is plenty of time for socializing and informal baseball chats. They occur at the museum, at the hotel, over dinner, and in local bars. Debating baseball and arguing the merits of this player or that game and questioning the many theories about baseball and American culture that surface during the symposium's three days is what makes attendance at one of them such fun.

The Cooperstown Symposium on Baseball and American Culture usually occurs during the first week of June and is co-sponsored by the State University of New York College at Oneonta. There is a fee to attend. For more information on the symposium, visit the National Baseball Hall of Fame and Museum's website at *www.baseballhalloffame.org*.

97 | VISIT THE BOB FELLER MUSEUM

Not many major league ballplayers warrant their own museum. Bob Feller does.

Bob Feller was one of the greatest pitchers of his time. A young, strapping farm boy from Iowa corn country, by age 16, Feller could already throw harder than just about anyone else in Major League Baseball. Skipping the minors, he signed a pro contract in 1936 with the Cleveland Indians while still in high school and was barely shaving when he made his major league debut. With his high-kick wind-up, young Feller could fire a fastball with such speed that, for many batters, facing him was downright scary.

Feller quickly made his mark on Major League Baseball, but history got in the way of a career seemingly without limitation. World War II made baseball and everything else less relevant in December 1941, when the Japanese bombed Pearl Harbor. Feller was among the first Major League Baseball players to volunteer for military service, signing up almost immediately after the U.S. declared war on Japan. Like a number of other Major League Baseball players, Feller spent the better part of four baseball seasons in the military at the absolute prime of his career. Who knows what he might have accomplished on the pitcher's mound had not war interfered? Having served in the navy, Feller came back to baseball in 1946 as a war hero, then promptly picked up where he had left off, winning 26 games that year.

Nicknamed "Rapid Robert," Bob Feller played 18 years of Major League Baseball, all of them with the Cleveland Indians. Despite the four years lost serving his country, he still managed to win 266 games and post a .621 winning percentage. Six times he led the American League in wins; seven times he had more strikeouts than any other pitcher. Over his career, he threw three no-hitters, and even more amazingly, he tallied a dozen one-hitters. Legendary players like Joe DiMaggio, Ted Williams, Lou Gehrig, and Hank Greenberg often called Bob Feller one of the most challenging and intimidating pitchers they had ever faced.

Feller was inducted into the National Baseball Hall of Fame in 1962, the first year he was eligible. In the years following his illustrious baseball career, Feller became an ambassador of baseball and of the Cleveland Indians, a model ballplayer and American who exemplified the highest standards of sportsmanship and patriotism. In countless speeches over the ensuing years, Feller could light up a room with his baseball stories and inspire everyone with his pride of being an American. Even at age 90, Feller could be found on the pitcher's mound, throwing out a ceremonial first pitch or even playing an inning or so, as he did in 2009 at the National Baseball Hall of Fame and Museum's first Hall of Fame Classic in Cooperstown (see *Bucket List* item #57).

The Bob Feller Museum is located on Mill Street in the center of Van Meter, just a few miles from the Iowa farm where he grew up and learned to throw a baseball. Van Meter sits some 12 miles west of Des Moines. A typical Iowa farm town with a rural landscape and plenty of Midwest charm, Van Meter feels as if little has changed since the days when young Bobby Feller, Van Meter's favorite son, helped his father with farm chores and learned how to throw strikes on the family's "field of dreams" diamond that the boy and his father built near the barn.

The Bob Feller Museum opened in 1995. Bob Feller's son, Steve, a local architect, designed the simple brick building. Inside, there are two rooms stocked with artifacts that trace Feller's remarkable life. On display are pieces from Feller's childhood and early years, along with artifacts from his baseball and military careers. You'll get to see Feller's Cleveland uniforms (his number 19 has been retired by the Indians) along with his hat, glove and personal items.

Also on display are awards, photographs, newspaper clippings, and baseballs, including one signed by both Babe Ruth and Lou Gehrig for a young Feller during one of the Yankee greats' barnstorming tours through Iowa in their glory years. In addition, the museum features occasional special exhibits and displays that tell the Feller story, or examine a particular baseball theme. The museum also has a small gift shop and hosts a number of public programs, including autograph signings with major league ballplayers, both past and present.

It won't take long to go through the Bob Feller Museum. You'll see and read everything in an hour or so. But no trip to the museum would be complete without a drive over to the old Feller farm, where Bob's father grew wheat instead of corn (a more demanding crop) so that he could spend more time with his baseball-loving son. Located about three miles or so from the museum, the farm is where the Feller legacy began. You can get directions to the farm from the museum staff.

> To learn more about Bob Feller before you visit the Bob Feller Museum, read *Now Pitching, Bob Feller* (Citadel Press, New York, 1990), written by Feller with Bill Gilbert, and view the documentary *The Bob Feller Story*, available on DVD. For more information on the museum, including directions, admission fees and hours, check its website at *www.bobfellermuseum.org*.

98 | SEE AN INDEPENDENT LEAGUE GAME

One of baseball's more popular non-big league teams isn't even affiliated with Major or Minor League Baseball. An Independent League franchise, the St. Paul Saints is owned by comedian Bill Murray. Independent Leagues exist in major cities and rural areas, in all corners of America. Renegade in spirit and affiliation-free because neither Major nor Minor League Baseball will sanction them, Independent Leagues have been around for much of baseball's history, but it's only been since the 1990s that they've attracted much attention beyond their local fan base.

The surge in popularity of baseball in the past couple of decades has also spurred the growth of Independent Leagues. Most fans can't tell the difference between the quality of play in the Independent Leagues and of that in the lower divisions of Minor League Baseball. Nor do they seem to care. On a warm summer night in the middle of America, baseball is baseball and when you make it fun, people will buy tickets.

Currently there are eight main Independent Leagues: the American Association League, Atlantic League, Can-Am (Canadian-American) League, Continental Baseball League, Frontier League, Golden Baseball League, Northern League, and United League. The players that make up Independent League rosters most likely were not drafted by a major league organization or are minor league cast-offs looking for a second chance. Occasionally, you'll find ex-major leaguers on Independent League rosters. John Rocker, Ricky Henderson, José Canseco, Ruben Sierra, Carlos Baerga, and Darryl Strawberry—all former major league stars—have logged time playing for an Independent League ball club. When highly-touted prospect J.D. Drew didn't like the deal offered to him after being drafted second overall by the Philadelphia Phillies in 1997, he bided his time playing Independent League baseball before becoming eligible for the following year's draft, when he was selected fifth overall by the St. Louis Cardinals.

With only a few exceptions, the Independent Leagues provide baseball to towns and small cities where neither major nor sanctioned minor league ball is played. Expect to see equal parts entertainment and baseball when you attend an Independent League game. They often feature the wackiest pre-game and between-inning entertainment skits and promotion programs their marketing departments can concoct. It's almost as if the spirit of the King of Baseball Schlock, Bill Veeck, the late owner of the St. Louis Browns, Cleveland Indians, and Chicago White Sox (see *Bucket List* item #79) gets summoned at the best Independent League games.

The St. Paul Saints, which began play in 1993, is a charter member of the more recent Northern League (the league actually has roots that extend all the way back to the early part of the 20th century) and has been the role model for many Independent League franchises. Playing in Midway Stadium just outside downtown St. Paul in Minnesota, the Saints have racked up more sell-outs than practically all of the other teams within the Independent League system combined. Spurred by actor Murray, who loves baseball, but also knows how to get a laugh and then another one, the Saints are legendary for their promotions, like enabling fans to talk to a dentist about their teeth between innings, or walking in a "Nerd Pride Parade." You can also get a haircut at a Saints game.

Two good books, *Slouching Toward Fargo* by Neal Karlean and *Rebel Baseball* by Steve Perlstein capture the style and story of Independent League Baseball. If you decide to go to just one Independent League game, making the trek to St. Paul to see the Saints in action is your best choice. But you don't have to travel far to catch an Independent League game, if you don't want to. Independent baseball is alive and well all across America.

> As of 2009, eight Independent Leagues operate in North America. Six of them (American Association of Professional Baseball, Atlantic League, Canadian-American Association, Frontier League, Golden Baseball League and Northern League) make up the Independent Baseball Federation. You can find more information on those six at www.independentprofessionalbaseballfederation.com. The other two (the United League Baseball and the Continental Baseball League) both operate in Texas and Louisiana. You can get information about them at www.unitedleague.org and www.cblproball.com.

99 | READ THE BOOK, *ONLY THE BALL WAS WHITE* ✷✷

The story of the old Negro Leagues remains one of the most interesting and least known chapters of American baseball history (see *Bucket List* item #11). Black professional baseball began in the New York Yankees' first era of dominance, the 1920s, and ended in the 1950s, another golden age for baseball and the Bronx Bombers. With all the attention the Yankees got in those two decades in New York, the media capital of the world, and the continued growth and success of Major League Baseball elsewhere, it's no wonder that it was hard for the Negro Leagues to attract much interest outside the black community.

When Jackie Robinson broke the color barrier in Major League Baseball in 1947, he also unintentionally set the Negro Leagues on a path to extinction. After Robinson, major league teams began raiding Negro Leagues teams and signing their best players to contracts. By the mid-1950s, the Negro Leagues were all but emptied of their best players as Negro Leagues veterans like Don Newcombe and Roy Campanella of the Dodgers, Monte Irvin and Willie Mays of the Giants, Larry Doby and Satchel Paige of the Indians and many others all made certain that the integration of baseball stuck.

The 1970 book *Only the Ball Was White* by Robert Peterson was one of the first full-scale attempts to document the history of the Negro Leagues and describe the culture that surrounded it. The book is drawn from interviews with many of the Negro League greats who were still alive and looking to tell their stories. What we learn is that bubbling under America's fascination and love of mainstream white baseball was a completely different baseball world, a black one, every bit as rich and as vital to its community as its white counterpart was. Begun in 1920 by Rube Foster in Kansas City, the Negro National League gave the best black ball players a chance to compete in an organized league and earn a living in the process. Just as importantly, it provided black fans the chance to follow teams made up of players of their own race.

Only the Ball Was White doesn't just tell the story of black baseball. It is as much a story of Jim Crow America as it is the Negro Leagues and its ballplayers. Peterson outlines a country in the pre-civil rights era where racism was a fact of life and segregation was so embedded in the national psyche that it would take a long hard struggle led by one of the great leaders of the 20th century, Dr. Martin Luther King, Jr., to change things. Baseball was on the cutting edge of this revolution. It could be argued that Robinson's presence in a Brooklyn Dodgers uniform was the real beginning of the civil rights movement that would push a reluctant America toward a more equal and just society.

Since the publication of *Only the Ball Was White*, numerous other histories of the Negro Leagues and black baseball culture have emerged, and many of them are more comprehensive and insightful, thanks to a mother lode of new information and research that surfaced in the ensuing years. But Peterson's book was the first to explore the territory and despite its age, it still holds up. Especially engaging are Peterson's player profiles, most of which reveal a deep-seated desire by black ballplayers like Paige, Judy Johnson, Buck Leonard, and others to compete with whites on the national stage and gain the sense of respect that eluded them playing in black-only leagues. Their stories all make for a great read, and an essential one, if you're to grasp the full, complete meaning of baseball in America.

As a companion to the book, pick up a copy of the documentary by the same name. Directed by Ken Solarz for public television, *Only the Ball Was White* premiered in 1981 and brought to life the story of Negro Leagues baseball on film. Inspired by the work Peterson did in his book, the film is narrated

Robert Peterson's 1970 book, *Only the Ball Was White*, was reissued in 1992 by Oxford Press and remains in print. It is available for purchase from most bookstores and online booksellers. The documentary film based on the book is available from movie sellers in VHS and a 2008 DVD edition.

by Paul Winfield and features interviews with Campanella, Paige, Leonard and other Negro League players, as well as Effa Manley, who, owned the Newark Eagles with her husband Abe and became the first woman elected to the National Baseball Hall of Fame. The documentary, *Only the Ball Was White*, runs just 30 minutes, not nearly long enough to do justice to the important and entertaining history of black baseball. But it makes a good companion piece to the fine book of the same name.

 100 VISIT THE TY COBB MUSEUM

It's a question that can never truly be resolved: who was the greatest baseball player of the classic era—Babe Ruth or Ty Cobb? Both, of course, made huge marks on the game. Both were feared hitters for different reasons, Ruth for power, Cobb for consistency. Both were inducted into baseball's Hall of Fame in Cooperstown as members of its maiden class. Both are baseball giants with legacies so large that only their own museums will suffice in containing and celebrating them. Ruth's is in Baltimore, at his birthplace, a couple of blocks from Oriole Park at Camden Yards. Cobb's stands in his hometown, Royston, Georgia, a couple of hours north of Atlanta. Both are necessary *Baseball Fan's Bucket List* visits.

Where the legacies of Ruth and Cobb diverge is in how we've come to separate the men from the ballplayers. Ruth was beloved, adored by the American public, the savior of baseball after the shocking "Black Sox" scandal of 1919, an athlete bigger than life with an appetite for life (and food) that never was fully realized. Cobb, on the other hand, was not a popular person—on the field or off. Arrogant, aggressive, obnoxious, able to stymie any warmth coming his way with a scowl, Cobb was Ruth's opposite. Yet, as his museum shows, Cobb performed a number of significant charitable acts that probably never even occurred to Ruth.

Ty Cobb established himself as baseball's first great player. Because he played most of his career during the dead ball era—before small ball was eclipsed by the long ball (as in Ruthian home runs)—it's difficult to compare his stats to Ruth's. So we'll let the ongoing argument on who was the better player rest, except to say that, when the votes were tallied for the induction of players into the first class of the Baseball Hall of Fame, Cobb received a greater percentage of votes (98.2 %) than Ruth (95.1%), not by much, but enough to allow him the privilege of being the very first ballplayer to receive the esteemed honor.

The Ty Cobb Museum doesn't get into the Ruth-Cobb debate; it hardly acknowledges its existence. What it does is celebrate Royston's favorite son. The Ty Cobb Museum is a small museum, situated in the Joe A. Adams Professional Building, a physician's complex, of all things. However, there is a logical reason for the location. Cobb, the first player to earn a million dollars and a shrewd investor, became quite wealthy during his lifetime. Rather than waste his money, something his detractors might have expected him to do, Cobb used some of it to establish the Cobb Memorial Hospital in Royston, and a local health care system, part of which is housed in the Joe A. Adams Building.

Though the Ty Cobb Museum celebrates the ballplayer and citizen, it doesn't whitewash the more controversial aspects of the way he played baseball and lived much of his life. He was, as the museum points out, "reviled and respected." Cobb played the game with a no-holds-barred, often belligerent attitude. He used his exceptional speed to steal bases—no one in baseball history stole home more often than Cobb, who pulled off the difficult feat a remarkable 50 times— yet he often went into his slide spikes up, caring not a hoot for the player attempting to get him out. At a whim, he would curse you or fight you. He wasn't social or friendly with fellow teammates. "Win at all costs" was Cobb's mantra and every time he stepped up to the plate to swing a bat with his "spread grip" or raced down a fly ball in the outfield, he carried it to the fullest. Baseball has never known a fiercer competitor. Only Pete Rose comes close.

Cobb's relentless competitive zeal enabled him to reach baseball's zenith. He set nearly one hundred major league records during his career, and still holds

Ty Cobb Museum in Royston, Georgia.

or shares nearly three dozen, including some of the most prestigious: highest career batting average (.367); the American League career mark for most hits (4,189); and the record for most batting titles (11 or 12, depending on the source). You will get a full list of Cobb's records in the museum's Fact Sheet, which gets handed out to all visitors.

The exhibits include rare photographs, artwork, and artifacts, along with audio interview clips, a theater and footage of Cobb in the field. On display are Cobb's Detroit Tigers uniform, his glove, autographed baseballs, bats, personal mementos, awards, and even his false teeth. Displays also examine Cobb's love of the outdoors—he was an avid hunter—and his oft-overlooked work as a humanitarian.

It'll take you less than an hour to peruse the Ty Cobb Museum. When you're done, get directions from the person at the ticket counter to the gravesite of "The Georgia Peach," located just a few minutes drive from the museum, then visit the resting place of Ty Cobb, the greatest baseball player of the pre-Ruth era—nobody can argue that.

> For additional information on the Ty Cobb Museum, visit the museum's website at www.tycobbmuseum.org or call (706) 245-1825.

101 UMPIRE A BASEBALL GAME ✄

Every baseball fan has been an umpire critic, dissecting an ump's performance during a game, sometimes muttering the critique, sometimes screaming it at the TV or the umpire himself from the stands. But have you ever put on the face mask, blue chest protector and shin pads and gotten behind home plate to actually umpire a game of baseball? You can't say you've experienced all aspects of baseball until you have.

The best and easiest place to experience umpiring is in Little League baseball. Umping above the Little League level often requires formal training, and a lot of it. Umpiring schools that train people for umpiring careers usually take at least a couple years to get through.

If you're going to be an umpire, even just for Little League, be a good one. First, learn the rules. Get a baseball rulebook for the league you'll be umping for and memorize it. Second, learn the ground rules of the field you'll be umping on. If a ball thrown by the third baseman flies over the head of the first baseman, hits the side of a building and caroms into right field, what's the

Umpire Bob Shulak at an old-timer Fourth of July baseball game played on Bainbridge Island, Washington.

ruling? The kids will need to know—instantly, so they can continue the play. Third, always be decisive. Call strikes and balls in an authoritative voice. Be firm and fair. Losing the confidence of the players and control of the game spells disaster for a baseball umpire. You're in charge out there on the diamond. Act like it.

Speak with other umpires before you ump your first game. They'll give you pointers on how to handle situations that you might not think of and offer other invaluable advice. For your first game, be a field umpire rather than the one behind the plate. Calling balls and strikes takes time to master, and though it's fun, it's also tedious and demands steady concentration. If you make a mistake, brush it off. All umpires make mistakes even if they don't ever seem to admit it. And if fans get on you for your blunder, well, you'll finally find out what umpire critiquing is like from the other side.

> Contact your local Little League for a rulebook and instructions on how you can umpire a game. *The Umpire's Handbook* by longtime major league ump Ed Brinkman is a good book to read to help prepare you for your first umpiring experience.

102 | JOIN THE BASEBALL RELIQUARY ✝

A colorful alternative to the National Baseball Hall of Fame and Museum in Cooperstown, the Baseball Reliquary preserves the oddities of the sport and the stories and legends that might not be "respectable" enough for more formal quarters. Where else could you find on exhibit a stogie smoked by Babe Ruth at a Philadelphia whorehouse, or the jock strap a midget used when pinch hitting for the St. Louis Browns in 1951? The Reliquary (official definition: a place of storage or container for religious relics) has no permanent museum, but does put exhibits on display, mostly in southern California, where the group's founder, Terry Cannon, resides.

Cannon kicked off the Reliquary in the mid-90s, and in 1999 inducted the first members of its "Shrine of the Eternals," a hall of fame for people like Yankees' pitcher/author Jim Bouton, whose book, *Ball Four*, introduced baseball's seamier, weirder underside to the general public (see *Bucket List* item #17). Bouton called the Reliquary a place where "rebels, radicals, and reprobates" are honored.

The Reliquary holds an induction ceremony each year, usually at the Pasadena Central Library, to honor three legends for "the distinctiveness of play; the uniqueness of character and personality; and the imprint that the individual made on the baseball landscape." Fortunately, the Reliquary has no shortage of candidates; baseball history is spotted with oddballs, eccentrics and innovators not exactly appreciated by baseball's mainstream, along with anti-heroes, comics and maulers of the English language. Past inductees include great on-field characters Satchel Paige, Mark "The Bird" Fidrych, Yogi Berra (see *Bucket List* item #61), Casey Stengel, and Dizzy Dean, along with Bill Veeck—owner of the St. Louis Browns, Cleveland Indians, and Chicago White Sox and one of baseball's great showmen (see *Bucket List* item #79).

To get in on voting for inductees, you need to join the Reliquary, which will cost you a fee but there's no screening process. Despite boasting a membership that includes former MLB players and some top sportswriters, the club refuses to take itself too seriously. And although its members share an absolute love for the history, culture, and tradition of baseball, they don't take them all that seriously, either. Because in the minds of the Baseball Reliquary members, taking baseball too seriously would take the fun out of the sport, and that would be sacrilegious.

> For more information about upcoming exhibits or membership in the Baseball Reliquary, check its website at *www.baseballreliquary.org* or call (626) 791-7647.

103 WATCH THE ABBOTT & COSTELLO SKIT, "WHO'S ON FIRST?"

Baseball's most famous comedy skit, "Who's on First?" is also an integral part of American popular culture. Over the years, professional and amateur performers at baseball games, fairs, fan fests, theaters and community events have acted out countless versions of the routine. In 1999, *Time* magazine named "Who's on First?" the Best Comedy Sketch of the 20th Century, while the American Film Institute included it on its list of the one hundred most memorable movie quotes. A copy of the skit resides in the National Baseball Hall of Fame and Museum in Cooperstown.

The routine was made popular by comedians Bud Abbott and Lou Costello, who took an old burlesque skit built from confusing names and gave it a baseball theme. After perfecting it with nightly performances while on tour with the Hollywood Bandwagon vaudeville revue in 1937, Abbott and Costello performed "Who's on First?" on radio in 1938 after joining *The Kate Smith Hour*. The baseball wordplay drew rave reviews. Two years later, the comedy duo put "Who's on First?" in their first film, *One Night in the Tropics*. Physically acting out the sketch on film infused it with new life and increased its popularity. Abbott and Costello redid "Who's on First?" for the 1945 film, *The Naughty Nineties*. It is considered the duo's finest version, one they also later performed on their own television show.

In the skit, straight man Bud Abbott played a tall and suave baseball manager, while short and plump Lou Costello took the role of an increasingly befuddled baseball fan. Costello asks Abbott the names of the players in his baseball lineup. The laughs start flying when Abbott tells Costello that "Who" is on first base and "What" is on second. The dialogue becomes a hilarious mash of confusion for Costello, who thinks Abbott is asking him questions, instead of answering them. Abbott and Costello's comedic genius is largely responsible for the enduring success of "Who's on First?" With pinpoint timing and inflection honed over years of performing together, the pair created classic set-ups and responses that kept building up the tension and hilarity as the skit progressed. You've probably seen it before, and you'll probably laugh out loud when you see it again.

> You can see Abbott and Costello perform "Who's on First?" in the films *One Night in the Tropics* and *Naughty Nineties*. Their radio performance of the skit is included in *The Great American Baseball Box Set* (see *Bucket List* item #88).

104 SEE A DOUBLE-A GAME

In some ways, Double-A represents the best of what minor league baseball has to offer. Double-A play is more polished than what you'll see in Single-A. And its rosters tend to be more stable than those in Triple-A, which acts as a way station for a lot of players on their way up to—or on their way back down from—the majors. Players also move in and out of Double-A during the season, just not as frequently. The greater roster stability enables fans of Double-A teams to get to know their players, which breeds greater support. Double-A consists of three separate leagues: the Texas League, the Southern League, and the Eastern League.

The Texas League was formed all the way back in 1888. Over the years, it has adopted various configurations, and been forced into a few starts and stops. As with the two other Double-A leagues, its teams occasionally change cities and major league affiliations, but interest in minor league baseball in Texas and nearby states that have Texas League teams has remained high. Currently, the Texas League has two divisions. Its North Division includes teams from Arkansas, Oklahoma and Missouri, while the South Division contains all Texas teams.

The eldest sibling of Double-A, the Southern League formed in 1885. Like the Texas League, over the years it's gone through a number of transformations, as well as name changes. During its long history, it's also been known as the Southern Association and the South Atlantic League (or "Sally League" for short). All of its teams play out of mid-size southern cities in one of the two divisions. Clubs from Alabama, Tennessee, and North Carolina comprise its North Division, while teams hailing from Alabama, Mississippi, and Florida make up the South Division.

Debuting in 1923, the Eastern League originally went by the name, the New York-Pennsylvania League, since all of its teams hailed from these two states. When other clubs from nearby states joined, the league renamed itself the Eastern League in 1938. Its Northern Division includes clubs from New Hampshire, Connecticut, New Jersey, Maine and New York, while the league's Southern Division features teams from Ohio, Maryland and Pennsylvania.

For more information on Double-A history, schedules and ticket information, check the websites of the Texas League (www.texas-league.com), the Southern League (www.southernleague.com) and the Eastern League (www.easternleague.com).

105 SEE THE ROYALS PLAY AT KAUFFMAN STADIUM ✮✮

Home of the Kansas City Royals since 1973, Kauffman Stadium remains the only baseball-specific ballpark of its generation that's still used by a Major League Baseball club. Why? Because unlike so many ballparks built in the 70s, Kauffman Stadium boasts some character, at least inside.

Kauffman's suburban setting and plain exterior—ringed by the circular walkways that homogenized so many of the multi-use sports bowls of its era—does little to excite the visitor. But once you get inside, it's a different story. Kauffman's water walls spout just beyond the center-field fence. Before and after games and when a Royals' player hits a home run, water shoots a hundred or so feet in the air, falling into large pools set in the bleachers. During the game, water cascades down the sides of the bleacher walls. Other ballparks now celebrate water architecture, but Kauffman was one of the first.

Originally known as Royals Stadium before its 1993 rechristening to honor Royals owner Ewing M. Kauffman just before his passing, Kauffman Stadium remains the most kid-friendly park in the majors. This can be a good thing and a bad thing. The Kids Zone beckons young fans from beyond the outfield seats, where they can run bases on a junior baseball diamond, hit in kids' batting cages, play miniature golf and take a ride on a carousel, among other things. A blessing when your children get antsy or bored waiting for the game to start, the Kids Zone becomes a curse when you're trying to impress your son or daughter with the subtler joys of watching a Major League Baseball game.

Three bronze statues in the outfield concourse celebrate the Royals three all-time greats: infielders George Brett and Frank White, plus manager Dick Howser. Each participated in many of the franchise's glory years in the 1970s and 80s, when the club claimed seven division titles and two American League pennants, plus the 1985 world championship. In 2009 the Royals opened a small museum called The Royals Hall of Fame that celebrates these three, along with other Royals greats.

Kauffman Stadium, which has some 38,000 seats, received a major facelift for the start of the 2009 season. Watching a game at the "K" as Royals fans fondly call the ballpark is now on par with watching a game in parks half its age.

> For information about Kauffman Stadium tours or tickets for Royals' games, check the team's website at *www.kcroyals.com*.

106 OWN A PIECE OF BASEBALL ART

Buying a piece of baseball art can be an expensive proposition, especially since prices started spiking over the past couple decades. To complete this *Bucket List* item, you don't need to fork over thousands of dollars for a painting or some other piece of creative expression. What you buy and what you pay for it is up to you. What's important is that you learn about the many kinds of baseball art and their histories, and that you acquire at least one piece that you can afford and which brings you enjoyment.

You can find baseball art in museums and galleries. The museum pieces won't be for sale, but will enable you to see great baseball art up close. The baseball art hanging in galleries will, most likely, be for sale, but will probably be expensive. Many galleries now post their pieces on *eBay*, as well as on their own websites. Though it's difficult to judge art online.

A good print or lithograph of a baseball scene provides a budget-conscious alternative. If you become more knowledgeable about baseball art and more interested in owning other pieces, then you can take the plunge and splurge for an original painting, or other art piece.

Baseball folk art offers another option. It is becoming increasingly popular, which means, of course, that prices are rising. But you can still get good deals on baseball folk art if you spend some time looking. Your best bet is in the South, where the folk art scene flourishes. If you find a folk artist that you like whose work falls within your price range, you could also commission a piece.

Whatever option you choose, the most important thing is to select a piece that you enjoy. For most baseball fans, owning a piece of baseball art that you're crazy about brings a special kind of satisfaction to your baseball world. And finding it is often as much fun as owning it.

> To learn more about baseball art, check out Shelly Mehlman Dinhoffer's book *The Art of Baseball (The Great American Game in Painting, Sculpture, and Folk Art)* (Harmony, 1990), *Baseball (A Treasury of Art and Literature)* (Hugh Lauter Levin, Associates, 1993), edited by Michael Ruscoe, and *Baseball (The National Pastime in Art and Literature)* (Time Life Books, 2000), edited by David Colbert and with a foreword by W.P. Kinsella (see *Bucket List* items #21 and #122).

107 READ THE BOOK, *BASEBALL: A HISTORY OF AMERICA'S FAVORITE GAME* ✦✦

A number of good baseball histories have been published over the years. Many of them are fat with facts and pages, like John Helyar's *Lords of the Realm: The Real History of Baseball* (Villard, 1994), Jules Tygiel's *Baseball as History* (Oxford University Press, 2000), and David Block's *Baseball Before We Knew It: A Search for the Roots of the Game* (University of Nebraska Press). Baseball fans who crave nourishing reads such as these will find any of them entertaining and enlightening and well worth the time it takes to complete them.

For the rest of you—the ones who like their history books short and sweet—there's *Baseball: A History of America's Favorite Game* (Random House, 2008) by George Vecsey. This relatively slim history—it checks in at 222 pages— is exceedingly well-written, reading the way a sports car cruises the freeway in fifth gear. Vecsey realized that if he was going to write a history of baseball using fewer words than most, he'd need to make every one count. He effortlessly and effectively unfolds the game's complicated story, taking just enough time to revise the occasional worn-thin theory about the game.

The veteran *New York Times* sports columnist sweeps through baseball history, from its vague origins in the American colonies to the early 1800s when the game began to come into focus and into its 20th century boom years. Rather than provide reams of convincing detail, Vecsey serves the reader bright observations and overviews that show us where the game came from and where it's heading. Along the way, he discusses seminal baseball figures like Henry Chadwick, Alexander Cartwright Jr., Ty Cobb, Christy Mathewson, Babe Ruth, Branch Rickey, Jackie Robinson, Curt Flood, Barry Bonds and Ichiro Suzuki.

Vecsey also offers and supports a couple of key premises: that baseball was largely shaped by great men taking hold of opportunities and moments and driving them home; and that the fans, not the game itself, give baseball its meaning and sustain it through good times and bad.

To conclude, we'll make a key point as succinctly and directly as George Vecsey does: you'll find no better compact history of baseball than *Baseball: A History of America's Favorite Game.*

> George Vecsey's book *Baseball: A History of America's Favorite Game* is available for purchase from most bookstores and online booksellers, and can be checked out from many public libraries.

108 SEE A DURHAM BULLS GAME

Dozens of minor league and independent league teams dot the American baseball landscape. The vast majority of these teams' fans come from the communities they play in. Why would anyone from California be a fan of, say, the Staten Island Yankees? But one minor league team—the Durham Bulls—might well be considered "America's (Minor League Baseball) Team."

In 1988, the Bulls played in the Class-A Carolina League in Durham Athletic Park, a small, beautiful old-style ballpark celebrating its 50th anniversary. Back then hardly anyone outside of Durham knew about or cared about the Bulls. Then came the release of the movie *Bull Durham* (see *Bucket List* item #14), considered by many the best baseball film of all time. After it became a hit, nearly everyone who followed baseball or movies knew about the team. Fans from outside North Carolina started showing up in Durham to see the Bulls play or just to visit Durham Athletic Park, where much of *Bull Durham* was filmed.

Two year's after the release of *Bull Durham*, the Durham Bulls had grown so popular that they became the first Single-A ball club to draw over 300,000 fans in one season. By 2008, they were drawing over a half-million fans per season. The Durham Bulls became a leader in minor league merchandise sales; their familiar "D" with the charging bull can be found on blue caps sold in baseball shops around the country. Along the way, the Bulls jumped from Single-A, to Triple-A and built a new stadium that holds 10,000. Visit the Durham Bulls' team office and you'll see an old, framed *Bull Durham* movie poster hanging on the wall, a reminder of the film that transformed the franchise.

Over two decades after the film's release, fans still flock to Durham Bulls games and old Durham Athletic Park, still standing despite the Bulls move to a new ballpark. Like Bowman Field in Williamsport, Pennsylvania, another old classic minor league park, Durham Athletic Park sports a small, two-story tower where tickets are sold and old brick walls that remind visitors of Durham's old tobacco warehouses.

Most minor league games don't require that you purchase tickets in advance, but it's a good idea to do so for the Durham Bulls. And make sure to visit old Durham Athletic Park before or after the game.

> For information about tickets to Durham Bulls games, check the team's website at *www.durhambulls.com*.

109 SEE THE TWINS PLAY AT TARGET FIELD ⚾⚾

If you've ever seen the Minnesota Twins in their former home, the Metrodome, you know how badly the team needed a new place to play. "Bland" is a nice way to describe the baseball/football complex. Though "ugly and depressing" is more to the point. "Frustrating" is also accurate, as when players lost high fly balls blending into the white ceiling, or pop-ups that hit the Metrodome's hanging speakers.

Loyal fans that they are, the Twins faithful were rewarded with a brand new place to watch Twins baseball. Set to open in April 2010, Target Field is the first ballpark the Twins won't have to share with the National Football League Minnesota Vikings. Target Field is a contemporary ballpark that eschews the nostalgic yearnings of the old-style ballparks such as Camden Yards, AT&T Park, and Coors Field. Instead, Target Field is a true 21st-century major league ballpark. Made mostly of local limestone, concrete, and lots of glass, Target Field has sharp angles, recessed lighting, and other contemporary features that, at first, glance, make it seem an unlikely place for baseball.

Unfortunately, Target Field is shoehorned in between rail lines, the Hennepin Energy Center, and the Target Center (home of the NBA's Minnesota Timberwolves). So it's practically impossible to walk around Target Field and enjoy the ballpark's innovative, exterior design. But the two adjacent rail lines at least make it easy to get to it via mass transit.

Holding some 40,000 fans, Target is smaller than most other major league ballparks. But its design emphasizes space, with fans occupying its 18,000 infield seats treated to wide-open views of the entire field. It's a wonderful place to watch a baseball game, provided the weather cooperates.

Its lack of a retractable roof (like the one that keeps baseball fans warm and dry in Milwaukee's Miller Park) means you may have to sit through a Minnesota spring snowstorm, or at least freezing temperatures. So shoot for a July or August *Bucket List* visit to Target Field.

It will take some time to truly determine all of Target Field's merits and faults, since it only opened in 2010. Whatever the ultimate verdict, one thing is for certain: at least you're watching baseball played outside, where it's meant to be played.

For information about tours of Target Field and tickets to Twins games, check the team's website at *www.twinsbaseball.com.*

110 LISTEN TO LOU GEHRIG'S FAMOUS FAREWELL SPEECH ✦✦✦

It ranks with the greatest sports speeches of all time. At a mere 277 words, it's also one of the shortest and certainly the most humble. It occurred at Yankee Stadium on "Lou Gehrig Appreciation Day," July 4, 1939. Head bowed, cap in hand, and struggling with his emotions, Yankee slugger and first baseman Lou Gehrig spoke into a microphone set up for him at home plate to the 60,000 fans who had come to pay tribute to his sterling career in pinstripes.

In addition to smacking 493 home runs and retiring with a batting average of .340, Gehrig played in 2,130 straight games, an incredible record some thought would never be matched. It was broken, of course, by Cal Ripken, Jr. in 1995. But it took over a half-century, and if Gehrig hadn't been stricken with Amyotrophic Lateral Sclerosis, an incurable neuromuscular disease that killed him less than two years after his famous speech at age 37, who knows how many more consecutive games he would have played.

Gehrig began the speech with, "Fans, for the past two weeks, you have been reading about the bad break I got. Yet today I consider myself the luckiest man on the face of this earth." Dripping with humility and honesty, these first two sentences set the tone for the rest of the speech and remain two of the most famous sentences in baseball history. Gehrig continued to laud the Yankees and praise his family; he even paid tribute to his mother-in-law. He ended by saying that he had suffered "a tough break, but I have awful lot to live for."

On July 4, 2009, in honor of the 70th anniversary of Lou Gehrig's Farewell Speech, major league ballparks celebrated Gehrig and his words by reading them during the seventh-inning stretch, a poignant reminder of his courage and humility. The ceremony was also a way to raise money and awareness for Lou Gehrig's Disease, which, despite years of research into its causes, is still with us. But so are Lou Gehrig's words from that day, and they will live on long past the disease that killed him.

> The Lou Gehrig website (www.lougehrig.com) contains a full text version of the speech, plus an edited film clip of it you can also find on YouTube. The speech is part of the National Baseball Hall of Fame and Museum archives in Cooperstown, New York.

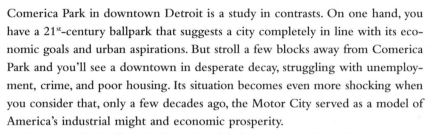

111 SEE THE TIGERS PLAY AT COMERICA PARK

Comerica Park in downtown Detroit is a study in contrasts. On one hand, you have a 21st-century ballpark that suggests a city completely in line with its economic goals and urban aspirations. But stroll a few blocks away from Comerica Park and you'll see a downtown in desperate decay, struggling with unemployment, crime, and poor housing. Its situation becomes even more shocking when you consider that, only a few decades ago, the Motor City served as a model of America's industrial might and economic prosperity.

Comerica Park offers the Tigers' loyal fanbase a respite from the many problems Detroit faces. Perhaps that explains why Comerica Park is a study of mascot excess. As you approach the ballpark you're confronted with the concrete heads of seemingly dozens of tigers attached to every external column of the park's exterior. From the outside, you might confuse the place for a zoo. In the park's Big Cat food court area, you'll find a carousel where kids can ride tigers instead of horses. Nearby stands a Ferris wheel with giant baseballs as seats. When a Tiger player belts a home run, the pair of prowling Tigers above the left-field scoreboard roar with approval. Supersized statues of six of the greatest Tigers—Ty Cobb, Charlie Gehringer, Hank Greenberg, Willie Horton, Al Kaline, and Hal Newhouser—stand along the left-center field wall.

Comerica Park doesn't need so many extras, because it's a great place to see a ballgame. With only 41,000 seats, Comerica is cozy with excellent sightlines. The lack of an upper deck in right field adds to its allure; the open space there celebrates the Detroit skyline. Comerica Park's light towers, long and narrow, represent a throwback to the days when lights for night games were a novelty. Another nice retro touch: the strip of infield dirt that runs from the pitcher's mound to home plate.

In their lucky seventh season in Comerica in 2006, the Tigers under manager Jim Leyland engineered a remarkable turnaround, enjoying their first winning season in over a dozen years and reaching the World Series for the first time since 1984. The unexpectedly great season helped raise hopes amongst Detroiters that some day their region's economy will enjoy a similar turnaround and that much of downtown Detroit will be as beautiful and inviting as Comerica Park.

> For information on Comerica Park tours and Tigers tickets, go to the team's website at www.detroittigers.com.

112 | HIT IN THE BATTING CAGES ✮✮

Everyone loves to hit a baseball. Who can object to the unabashed joy of whacking a ball in the sweet spot of a bat and watching it sail away? And what about the sound? How wonderful is the "thwack!" when the bat hits the ball and sends it soaring? We love to hear it at ballgames. But it sounds even better when you do it yourself. And easy, too. Not to create the sound, mind you. That depends on your hitting ability. What's easy is finding a place where you can attempt to make the sound again and again. All you need to do is visit your local batting cages.

For a few bucks and less than a half-hour of your time, you can smack balls in the cage and get your fill of baseball's most pleasurable activity: hitting. The pitching machines can be set to various speeds and you can choose the one that fits your hitting level. If you're older or haven't swung a bat in a long time, prepare yourself with at least a couple of weeks of stretching out muscles in your waist, arms, and especially your shoulders. Also, practice swinging, gently at first, to get your body used to the idea of it again.

Go easy the first time in the cages. Concentrate on proper stance and swinging a level bat. Get used to keeping your eye on the ball as it comes off the machine. Just try to connect bat with ball, preferably at the fat of the bat.

During baseball season, try to visit the batting cages once a week. Not only will it improve your batting ability, but you'll also feel more physically connected to the game. In baseball's offseason, make it every other week, or once a month. But remember to keep up your stretching regimen during your downtime.

Above all, have fun. Hitting a baseball in the batting cages is something you can do for most of your baseball life. Make it a habit and you'll be surprised at how much you'll improve and how much more you appreciate the game of baseball and the art of hitting.

You can find the batting cage facility nearest you by entering "batting cages" into the "Find" box at www.yellowpages.com and your zip code into the "Location" box. You can also check local phone directories or ask at sporting goods shops.

113 GO TO AN OLD TIMERS' DAY ✗✗✗

A celebration of the greats who once donned a major league team's uniform, Old Timers' Day is a dying tradition in baseball. A number of teams used to bring back former players once every season to be honored in front of fans and then play a short game prior to a regular season game, usually on a Saturday or Sunday afternoon in mid-summer. But these days, with scheduling growing more complicated due to television contracts, excess promotions and costs, only a few teams regularly stage the event. For most clubs, Old Timers' Day is, like the players who play in them, running out of steam.

The exception is the New York Yankees, who started the tradition just after World War II and have kept it going strong ever since. The roots of Old Timers' Days go back to the retirements of Babe Ruth and Lou Gehrig. These two legends were so popular with Yankee fans that the team's front office created special ceremonies at Yankee Stadium to honor them with tributes and gifts of appreciation. A number of their already retired teammates were brought back to the stadium to honor first Ruth, then Gehrig. Fans so enjoyed seeing the old Yankees at the stadium again that team officials created the concept of Old Timers' Day in 1946 to honor numerous former Yankee greats every season.

The Old Timers' game usually lasts just a couple of innings. None of the players go all out, and winning is not what the game is about. The point is for fans to see these retired greats on the field once more and relive memories of former glory. Before the Old Timers' game begins, each player is formally introduced and their baseball accomplishments are rehashed so the fans can cheer them. The players wear their old uniforms and numbers and seem to enjoy Old Timers' Day as much as the fans do.

There is no special ticket or additional cost to see the game. However, since the Old Timers' game takes place before the regular game occurs, you'll have to arrive at the stadium a couple of hours early to see it.

> Check the website of your favorite team to find out if the club will be hosting an Old Timers' Day in the near future. You can find links to MLB teams' websites at *www.mlb.com.*

114 WATCH THE MOVIE, *SUGAR*

The first great feature film made about Latin baseball, *Sugar* drew raves from critics upon its 2009 release. *The New York Times* called it "undeniably noble and beautiful." *Sports Illustrated* hailed its "masterly storytelling" and said, "the film's greatest strength is its authenticity." *The Los Angeles Times* claimed that "the best films about sports, and the baseball-themed Sugar is surely one, understand that when a character says 'it's just a game, right?' the answer is both yes and no."

Sugar begins in the Dominican Republic, a place where baseball is a religion and a possible bridge to a better life in the United States for young ballplayers like Miguel "Sugar" Santos, played by Algenis Perez Soto. When cast to play the film's lead, Soto wasn't even an actor, but an ex-infielder with a local Dominican team. His performance gives the film its emotional intensity.

Sugar gets bittersweet when the 20 year-old Santos leaves the Dominican Republic, goes to spring training in Arizona, and then reports to the Class-A Bridgetown Swing in Iowa, a farm team for the fictional Kansas City Knights. As Santos quickly learns, Iowa is a long way from the Caribbean, geographically and culturally.

Though *Sugar* is fiction, it could, at times, be mistaken as a Latin baseball documentary. Much of its dialogue is in Spanish, adding to the authenticity of the film. It shows the struggles many Caribbean players face in the U.S. Often scared, confused, homesick, and not confident about anything they do or say, they also face the daily pressure of trying to climb the rungs of the minor league baseball ladder to the big leagues.

Written and directed by Anna Boden and Ryan Fleck, *Sugar* is beautifully shot and presents its story without sentimentality while still tipping its cap to baseball dreams and tradition. The filmmakers understand the nuances of the game and, more importantly, the complexity of human emotion. Santos doesn't play baseball for just himself. Back home, his family's hopes and economic future depend on him.

Santos learns much about himself during *Sugar*, and we learn a lot about Latin baseball culture and about failure and triumph in baseball when the game is so much more than a game for those playing it.

> *Sugar* is available for rental or purchase from most movie stores and online movie merchants. The film runs 120 minutes and is rated R, though you can find a PG-13 version in DVD.

115 VISIT THE IVAN ALLEN JR. BRAVES MUSEUM AND HALL OF FAME ✦

Located at Turner Field (see *Bucket List* item #120), the Ivan Allen Jr. Braves Museum and Hall of Fame celebrates the Atlanta Braves baseball club, the oldest continuously running franchise in the game. Begun in 1871, the club used numerous names—Red Stockings, Beaneaters, Doves, and Rustlers before settling on the Braves in 1912 (sort of, anyway—the club temporarily abandoned the name Braves from 1936 to 1940 when it switched to the Bees). The team took up residence in Boston, then Milwaukee, and then Atlanta. As for Ivan Allen Jr., he was the Atlanta mayor who, in the early 1960s, began a campaign to bring the Braves from Milwaukee to Atlanta—an effort that finally paid off in 1966.

Most people come to the museum to relive the 1991-2005 Braves golden age when the team won an unmatched 14 straight division titles, a few pennants, and the World Series in 1995. No team, not even the Yankees, can boast a similar streak of divisional dominance. The Braves museum shows a locker for each title year filled with jerseys, mementos, and baseball equipment from many of the Braves players who contributed to the club's astounding run.

As one might expect and hope, the museum offers a lot on Hank Aaron, undoubtedly the Braves'—and arguably Major League Baseball's greatest player. Gloves and bats, historic baseballs, uniforms, plenty of photographs, newspapers clippings and a video loop celebrate other Braves legends, including pitchers Lou Burdette, Phil Niekro, Tom Glavine, Greg Maddux, John Smoltz and Warren Spahn, plus hitters like Eddie Mathews and Dale Murphy. The museum reminds visitors that Babe Ruth was also a Brave for a short while before retiring in 1936. And you can see the ball Hank Aaron hit into the left-field seats at Atlanta-Fulton County Stadium on April 8, 1974 to break Ruth's record of 714 career home runs, on his way to an amazing 755 career dingers.

The museum includes another interesting exhibit featuring an authentic Pullman railroad car to recall the era when teams traveled by train from one city to the next. And plan to spend some time in Monument Grove, the large public area that leads up to the Turner Field ticket booths and the museum, admiring the bronze statues of Aaron and others.

For more information about the Ivan Allen Jr. Braves Museum and Hall of Fame and tickets to Atlanta Braves games, go to *www.braves.com*.

116 SEE THE WHITE SOX PLAY AT U.S. CELLULAR FIELD

When baseball fans talk about Chicago ballparks, the conversation almost always focuses on the Cubs' Wrigley Field (see *Bucket List* item #5). But we shouldn't forget about a park on the south side of the Windy City where the Chicago White Sox play. U.S. Cellular Field might not possess the storied history and grand legacy of Wrigley, but as contemporary ballparks go, it's a good one and well worth a visit.

Opened in 1991 as Comiskey Park, it became U.S. Cellular Field in 2003. Most White Sox fans bemoaned the name change; after all, the name Comiskey (as in longtime Sox owner Charles Comiskey) had been synonymous with White Sox history since the early 20th century. But U.S. Cellular's involvement was about more than just naming-rights money. The arrival of U.S. Cellular led to numerous changes that brought the park more in line with other retro-parks going up in major league cities at the time. The Sox' hideous blue seats changed to a traditional dark green and the ugly blue awning that ran most of the length of the grandstands got replaced.

The club left intact some features that contributed to the park's inherent charm, including the unique, strawberry blonde sandstone that makes up the external walls and the windows ringing the upper deck just below the roof. Afternoon light pouring through those windows create a spacious, airy ambiance that makes U.S. Cellular Field seem larger than its 40,000+ capacity. Only the Milwaukee Brewers' Miller Park (see *Bucket List* item #75) makes better use of windows.

Before you enter U.S. Cellular Field, go to the Gate Five entrance; just beyond it, embedded into the ground, is a home plate at the exact spot that the old Comiskey Park home plate sat for so many years. Once inside, check out the ballpark's two remaining blue seats. One sits beyond the left field wall where Paul Konerko's grand slam ball landed in the second game of the 2005 World Series; the other sits in right-center in the area known as The Patio where Scott Podsednik's walk-off home run from the same game came to rest. Sox fans cherish both homers as key moments leading to the team's first world championship since 1917.

> For information regarding tours of U.S. Cellular Field and for White Sox tickets, check the team's website at *www.whitesox.com*.

117 PLAY APBA ✶✶

For baseball fans that love the idea of Fantasy Baseball, but loathe the fact that, aside from drafting and trading players, you really have no control over the game itself, APBA provides an alternative. The first baseball board game, APBA makes you the manager, controlling when a player bunts, steals, and even when he plays. You can skipper the 1961 New York Yankees, the 1909 Pittsburgh Pirates, or pretty much any team you wish. APBA has them all.

APBA (pronounced Ap-bah) stands for the American Professional Baseball Association. Created in the 1930s by Dick Seitz, the game came to market in 1951. Essentially, it's a dice game. A manager picks his lineup, then, as each game situation arises, rolls the dice. Whatever number comes up determines the outcome of the particular situation in reference to the probabilities set by the card of the player involved. The cards feature ratings that reflect how a player performed the previous season in different areas of play. After each baseball season, APBA, using complicated mathematical formulas, creates new cards for every major league player. As with being a real MLB manager, you can get lucky. But your long-term success depends on how smart and informed you are in making decisions.

If you're a Baby Boomer and a longtime baseball fan, you might have run into APBA in your youth. The game grew steadily in popularity from the 1960s to the early 1980s, its sales fueled mostly by baseball stat junkies and hardcore fans. If it wasn't APBA, you might have played Strat-O-Matic (see *Bucket List* item #125).

If you get hooked on the game, you can join an APBA league. APBA draws players from all over America for its annual convention and tournament, often staged near its headquarters in Lancaster, PA, but sometimes in other locations like Las Vegas.

In the age of video and computer games, and, of course, Fantasy Baseball, APBA is old-school and an acquired taste. But it has endured all these years because it is, fundamentally, a great baseball board game that didn't need to change much to stay relevant for serious baseball fans looking for some serious fun.

> For information about where you can purchase APBA, check its website at *www.apbagames.com*. The website also has information about the annual APBA Convention and Tournament. You can also call (800) 334-2722.

118 SEE THE REDS PLAY AT GREAT AMERICAN BALL PARK ★★

Opened in 2003, the Cincinnati Reds' Great American Ball Park foregoes red brick walls and arches and large swaths of classic ballpark dark green—all pretty much standard décor for Major League Baseball parks built in the retro craze era beginning in the early 1990s. Instead, Great American Ball Park adorns itself in bright red and white, the Reds' colors, and features lines and visuals that identify it as distinctly modern.

Unlike many other new urban ballparks that accent their cities' urban skyline, the Reds' chose to look away from their city and instead celebrate the area's river legacy. Nestled on the northern bank of the Ohio River in downtown Cincinnati, Great American Ball Park replaced old Riverfront Stadium. If you sit in the middle or upper decks, you get a wide-angle view of the Ohio River and Kentucky, just across it. A replica riverboat in straight away center field called the "Cincinnati Bell" reinforces the theme; its pilothouse serves as

The Great American Ball Park, home of the Cincinnati Reds Ball Club.

a concession stand and its deck allows you to take in the long view of Great American. Nearby a pair of riverboat smoke stacks blow smoke and launch fireworks whenever a Reds' player smacks a home run. Admittedly, the center-field landscape at Great American leans a bit toward minor league kitsch, but Reds' fans don't seem to mind.

It seems odd that of all the major league teams, the Cincinnati Reds, the very first professional baseball club to begin play back in 1869, chose to create a more contemporary kind of ballpark. That's not to say, Great American fails to pay any tribute to the Reds' long history. A group of life-sized bronze statues outside its entrance depicts a baseball scene featuring Reds greats Ted Kluszewski, Ernie Lombardi, Joe Nuxhall and Frank Robinson. The first-rate Reds Hall of Fame (see *Bucket List* item #49) lies within the Great American Ball Park complex.

Despite the open views of the river and red seats that shout at you when they're not filled with fans, Great American feels smaller than its 42,000 capacity. The ballpark's intimate feel comes courtesy of the shortened sections of seats behind home plate and along the baselines. It makes for a cozy, friendly place to watch a game in a city that loves its baseball and major league franchise as much as any other in the major leagues.

> For information on tours of Great American Ball Park and tickets to Reds' games, check the team's website at *www.cincinnatireds.com*.

119 PLAY IN A VINTAGE BASE BALL LEAGUE

Before the Civil War, baseball was known as "base ball" and teams played using rules and uniforms quite different from the ones that became standard by the 20th century. In the 1980s, some baseball purists began turning back the clock to that era, playing vintage base ball games on holidays, especially the Fourth of July. Players wore funny uniforms and fake mustaches and fans showed up in the fashions of yesteryear. Barbershop quartets sang and ladies used umbrellas to shield themselves from the sun.

In 1996 a group of base ball fans in Columbus, Ohio formalized the base ball hobby by creating the Vintage Base Ball Association (VBBA). The league applies rules collected by Henry Chadwick (often called the "Father of Base Ball") in his 1860 text "Beadle's Dime Base-Ball Player." The VBBA added

Co-author Robert Santelli (second from left) playing the game he loves, wearing traditional wool baseball attire and a four-fingured glove.

teams and "ballists" (that's what players were often called back then) dedicated to playing base ball, true to the earliest rules.

Then in 2007, the base ball revival received a jolt of fanfare and innovation when former Yankees pitcher Jim Bouton announced the creation of the Vintage Base Ball Federation (VBBF). Author of the irreverent baseball classic *Ball Four* (see *Bucket List* item #17), Bouton created a league that adheres to most 1880s base ball rules, but adds humor and theatrics that outrage some base ball purists. Bouton and his VBBF cohorts (who include the celebrated *Sports Illustrated* writer Frank Deford and former big league pitcher Bill "Space Man" Lee) claim their league captures "the spirit" of base ball, if not all its details. Bouton also announced plans to build a 19th-century replica base ball park in Westfield, Massachusetts, a sort of old style "field of dreams" to eventually serve as the hub of all things vintage base ball.

Today, more than 250 base ball clubs play in over two dozen U.S. states. Most of the games feature players in traditional uniforms catching bare-handed (as ballists did early on). There is no pitcher's mound and the original rules of the game mandate that you need six balls to gain a base on balls, not four. And you don't ever argue balls or strikes or any other call with the umpire. Because 19th-century "base ball" was—and is—a gentleman's game.

> For more information on the Vintage Base Ball Association and Vintage Base Ball Federation, go to their websites www.vbba.org and www.vintagebbf.com.

SEE THE BRAVES PLAY AT TURNER FIELD

Turner Field had an unusual beginning. Originally built as Centennial Olympic Stadium to stage track-and-field events for the 1996 Summer Olympics in Atlanta, it was re-fitted and renamed after longtime Atlanta Braves owner Ted Turner to serve as the Braves' new home for the start of the 1997 baseball season.

Constructed in the heat of baseball's retro ballpark mania, Turner Field features a neo-classic baseball design (though it did retain the Greek columns and famous rings from its neo-classic Olympic design origins). Built with red brick and steel painted dark green, it is a delight to look at from the parking lots or the mass transit train station nearby. Located less than ten miles from Atlanta's downtown in a residential neighborhood not far from the freeway, Turner Field still feels urban.

Approach Turner Field by way of Monument Grove to see its by bronze statues (transplanted from the Atlanta Braves' original home, Fulton County Stadium) honoring Braves greats Hank Aaron, Warren Spahn and Phil Niekro, plus Georgia native Ty Cobb, one of baseball's three or four greatest ever players (see *Bucket List* item #100). Monument Grove's Walk of Fame celebrates many other local baseball legends and leads you into the Ivan Allen, Jr. Braves Hall of Fame and Museum (see *Bucket List* item #115). Look for lines of Fulton County Stadium's infield super-imposed on its parking area, then a large baseball painted on the still-standing north wall of Fulton to mark where Hank Aaron's 715th homer landed. Aaron's historic dinger in 1974 broke Babe Ruth's long-standing career home-run mark.

Once inside Turner Field, you'll notice a great view of the Atlanta skyline, plus a plethora of advertisements, including a giant Chick-fil-A cow and a towering Coke bottle dressed up with baseball equipment. Just below sits a baseball-themed playground. Spray showers in the outfield bleacher area known as Sky Field cool fans during the humid Georgia summers. In short, Turner Field has created the ultimate experience for young fans and families—but at the expense of the game happening on the field. And despite all its family-friendly efforts, Turner Field's 50,000 seats and massive scoreboard (the major leagues' largest) deprive Turner Field of any sense of intimacy.

Turner Field might not rank with the best of the modern ballparks, but you'll find few ballparks that are more family and kid-friendly.

> For information about tours of Turner Field and tickets to Braves games, check the team's website at *www.braves.com*.

121 | OWN A BASEBALL ANTIQUE ✦✦

Owning a baseball antique is like owning a piece of baseball history. All kinds of baseball antiques are available for a wide range of prices. You can purchase something from the 19th century for thousands of dollars, or you can pick up something from the 1950s for less than a hundred bucks. Just know: you'll pay a premium for anything directly connected to a seminal baseball moment, player, or event. If you're thinking of an item attached to Babe Ruth, the 1919 World Series or Bobby Thomson's homer to win the 1951 National League pennant, know that you'll have to pay top dollar.

Generic antiques—ones not connected to any specific player or historical event—are the best way to go for the budget-minded. Antique baseball gloves (particularly ones from before the 1930s) remain especially reasonable. Other types of old baseball equipment, as in catcher's masks and chest protectors, are also usually affordable and look good hanging in your den. Old baseball board games, plates and prints of 19th-century baseball scenes, old photographs, pennants, programs, press pins, awards, uniforms and caps offer more options. Antique baseball bats and balls are usually more pricey, but a regular check of *eBay* should eventually land you a bargain.

Look into items from the Negro Leagues. Antiques from the former are rising in price, thanks to increasing attention paid to the history of the Negro Leagues. You won't be able to touch anything from Jackie Robinson, Satchel Paige or Josh Gibson without spending a lot of money, but more generic Negro League pieces can still be had at bargain prices. Minor league items are also worth looking into. They usually won't have the prestige level of antiques from the majors or the Negro Leagues, but the right piece can bring lots of personal enjoyment.

There are numerous websites dedicated to sports antiques where you're sure to find a fine piece in your price and interest ranges. Baseball memorabilia auctions are another avenue to explore, or you could make the rounds of garage and estate sales and find a hidden gem on your own. In the end, unless you make collecting baseball antiques a serious hobby, buy what you like and what you can afford.

For more information on baseball antiques, check the websites for Memory Lane, Inc (*www.memorylaneinc.com*), Heroes of the Past (*www.heroesofthepast.com*), Limited Editions of New York (*www.limitededitionsports.com*), Left Field Collectibles (*www.leftfieldcollectibles.com*) and Sports Heritage Auctions (*www.sports.heritageauctions.com*).

122 READ THE BOOK, *SHOELESS JOE* ✦✦✦✦

There aren't many ballplayers in baseball history like Shoeless Joe Jackson. Despite being one of the best players of his era, Jackson rarely gets recalled for his exploits on the field, because of what he allegedly did off the field: agree to throw the World Series in 1919 along with other members of the Chicago White Sox.

Jackson always maintained his innocence, and plenty of fans today believe him. Although he was acquitted of the conspiracy charges in court, baseball's first commissioner, Judge Kenesaw Mountain Landis, banned Jackson and the rest of the White Sox allegedly involved in the ploy from ever playing Major League Baseball again.

To get the full story of what has become known as the "Black Sox" Scandal of 1919, read Eliot Asinof's fine book, *Eight Men Out*, or see the movie by the same name (see *Bucket List* item #32). For a wonderfully nostalgic, romanticized version of Jackson, turn to W.P. Kinsella's book *Shoeless Joe*. One of the finest baseball novels ever written, it also inspired one of the best baseball films, *Field of Dreams* (see *Bucket List* item #21). A fantasy, the book gave Shoeless Joe's reputation a second chance while creating an imagined baseball world in rural Iowa—far away from the madness of the city and the temptations that swirled in its underbelly.

Kinsella, a Canadian, had fallen in love with baseball and books as a boy. Showing enough promise as a writer to be accepted into the University of Iowa's Writer's Workshop, perhaps the most prestigious writing program in America, Kinsella used what he learned about writing and what he saw around him in Iowa to develop his classic baseball novel. Focused on Shoeless Joe Jackson, the book also deals with weightier issues like yearning for things lost and the need to reconcile the past with the present. Published in 1982 to great acclaim, *Shoeless Joe* won reviewers' praise for its compelling, unconventional story and avoidance of the many baseball book clichés and worn-out plots that could have easily trapped the writer and buried his book. Instead *Shoeless Joe* was rich with originality and a love of baseball. If you've seen *Field of Dreams*, you know the plot. If you haven't, see the movie and read the book. They're both very much worth it.

> W.P. Kinsella's *Shoeless Joe* remains in print and is available from most bookstores and online booksellers.

123 SHOP FOR BASEBALL MEMORABILIA IN COOPERSTOWN ✦✦✦

While Cooperstown is not the real birthplace of baseball, the upstate New York village still serves as a Mecca for baseball fans. Spending a day at its National Baseball Hall of Fame and Museum goes without saying. But reading this book, you'll come across nearly a half-dozen other "musts" that have a Cooperstown address. And Cooperstown also offers baseball buffs something else: great shopping. Nowhere else will you find a more concentrated set of shops selling the best of baseball memorabilia.

Main Street in Cooperstown features nearly two dozen shops worth exploring. Some of them attract the casual visitor just looking for generic tourist t-shirts and general baseball merchandise. But others cater to the more sophisticated baseball enthusiast, the kind of fan who sets out on a bucket list quest.

Willis Monie (139 Main St., (607) 547-8363, *www.wilmonie.com*) sells old and rare baseball books. Yastrzemski Sports (134 Main St., (607) 547-7150, *www.yazsports.com*) is a good place to shop for autographs and items to fill the holes in your baseball card collection. On Deck Circle (139 Main St., (607) 547-6208) sells lots of goodies for baseball card collectors, as well as an impressive set of autographed baseballs and photographs.

What about baseball caps? Mickey's Place (74 Main St., (800) 528-5775, *www.mickeysplace.com*) offers dozens of minor league caps, retro caps from the Cooperstown Collection, and more variations of Red Sox and Yankee hats (due to the relative proximity of Boston and New York, Cooperstown is always thick with Red Sox and Yankee fans) than you've probably ever seen. Other recommended places to shop for baseball mementos, apparel, and collectibles include, America's Game (75 Main Street; 607-547-2559), Legends Are Forever (133 Main Street; 607-547-7165), Extra Innings (54 Main Street; 607-547-0100), and Safe at Home (91 Main Street; 607-547-1317). For souvenir baseball bats, try Cooperstown Bat Company

For more information about shopping for baseball memorabilia in Cooperstown, check the shops' websites listed above. You can also go to the website for the National Baseball Hall of Fame and Museum website (*www.baseballhalloffame.org*) or the Cooperstown Chamber of Commerce (*www.cooperstownchamber.org*).

(118 Main Street; 607–547–2415. And finally, don't forget to save some time and money for a thorough browse of the shop in the National Baseball Hall of Fame and Museum. Become a member of the museum and you'll receive a 10% discount on what you buy, not to mention free entry into the museum.

124 READ THE BOOK, *THE SUMMER GAME* ✖✖✖

Roger Angell rates as one of baseball's finest writers and most astute observers. Angell came from good writing stock. Both his mother, Katharine White, and stepfather, E. B. White, were acclaimed *New Yorker* editors. One of the deans of American essayists, E.B. White also co-authored the classic writing manual *The Elements of Style*, which is still used today by many teachers, editors, and writers.

Surrounded by writers at home as a child, Angell preferred the company of regular folks at ballgames as an adult when he worked as an editor, essayist and critic for the *New Yorker* magazine. He considered himself a baseball fan who happened to be a writer, and watched games from the stands instead of the press box. The baseball company he kept may have helped keep Angell's observations so fresh and remarkably thoughtful. And working for a monthly magazine allowed him the luxury of rewrites and contemplation not enjoyed by reporters for daily newspapers. But you get the impression that even if Angell hadn't had a place to publish his baseball essays, he would have written them anyway, just because he loved the game and loved writing about it so much.

Most of Angell's baseball books present compilations of his work for the *New Yorker*. His best, *The Summer Game*, collects his baseball-related *New Yorker* essays from 1962-72, a period of great upheaval for baseball and American society. While *The Summer Game* consists of essays nearly a half-century old, the book's exceptional prose and insights into baseball, its fans and the soul of the game, will keep it relevant and enjoyable as long as baseball is played.

Since *The Summer Game*, Angell has gone on to publish other collections of baseball essays; the best is *Once More Around the Park: A Baseball Reader* and *Game Time*. Only one of his baseball books, *A Pitcher's Story* (about New York Yankees' pitcher David Cone), isn't a compilation, and it may be his least interesting book.

Humble yet knowledgeable, literary yet able to reach the common fan, Roger Angell elevated the art of the baseball writing to heights frequented by the other famous baseball writing Roger—Roger Kahn. His work offers extraordinary observations on the national game, all built into beautifully written essays that glow with insight and passion.

In 2004, Bison Books published a new edition of Roger Angell's *The Summer Game*. Most of Angell's other books remain in print and are available from bookstores and online booksellers.

125 PLAY STRAT-O-MATIC BASEBALL ✦✦✦✦

As with Fantasy Baseball and APBA, Strat-O-Matic Baseball appeals to the baseball fan who wants to engage the game at a deeper level without taking the field. It's armchair baseball, pure and simple. But it's wonderful fun, and it takes skill and knowledge of the game to win.

While Fantasy Baseball (see *Bucket List* item #9) speaks to the general manager in all of us, Strat-O-Matic, like APBA (see *Bucket List* item #117), put us in the dugout. Players assume the role of the manager, deciding on batting orders, pinch hitters, relief pitchers, hit-and-runs, etc.

Strat-O-Matic Baseball came out in 1961, a few years after APBA reinvigorated the hobby of tabletop baseball. (The earliest of the popular tabletop baseball games, All-Star Baseball, was created by Cadaco-Ellis and came out in 1941.) Strat-O-Matic's originator, Hal Richman, was a baseball and mathematics nerd, which probably explains why his game tends to attract similar types.

Strat-O-Matic issues a card every year for each MLB player covered with scenarios and situational outcomes for all the possible numbers in dice rolls. The numbers on the card correspond to the player's previous year's performance. Numbers for a power hitter make him more likely to hit a home run, numbers for fast runners make them more likely to succeed in a steal attempt. Strat-O-Matic, like baseball itself, is a game of statistics.

The game comes in different levels. The more advanced levels present

For more information about where to purchase Strat-O-Matic Baseball or how to join a league, check the company's website at *www.strat-o-matic.com*.

more strategic options and card numbers gleaned from more detailed statistical analyses. The "Super-Advanced" level even accounts for a player's success rates at different major league ballparks.

You can get carried away with Strat-O-Matic in same way that Fantasy

Baseball can take over your life. As far as the *Bucket List* is concerned, you need to experience Strat-O-Matic just once to check it off. If you find you like it, try joining a Strat-O-Matic League on the Web or in your community and playing a full season. You can also play solo, though it's not nearly as much fun as when you go up against fellow Stat-O-Matic enthusiasts in a structured league.

126 SEE THE NATIONALS PLAY AT NATIONALS PARK ✹✹

After a 32-year absence, Major League Baseball returned to Washington D.C. in 2003 when the Montreal Expos defected to the U.S., renamed themselves the Washington Nationals and moved into RFK Stadium, former home of the NFL's Washington Redskins and the old American League Senators. But the club wanted a new ballpark of its own, and after a long battle with city officials, the Nationals secured funding and a suitable piece of land on the banks of the Anacostia River.

HOK (Hellmuth Obata & Kassabaum), the noted architectural firm that ignited the retro craze with the opening of Oriole Park at Camden Yards just up I-95 in Baltimore, won the design contract. But whereas most HOK ballparks emphasize tradition and reference baseball's past, the firm's architects took inspiration for Nationals Park from D.C.'s many monuments. The design of Nationals Park celebrates simplicity and majesty. Its light stone and concrete external walls reflect the color and feel of the Washington Monument and other D.C. landmarks.

Unlike the city's monuments, though, Nationals Park doesn't reference much past glory. Probably, because despite a baseball history dating back to the original Washington Nationals' 1859 debut, Washington D.C. doesn't have much past baseball glory to reference. The city's great black baseball team, the Homestead Grays, won nine Negro National League titles. But the city's two Nationals franchises and three different versions of the Washington Senators have managed only one World Series win (1924) and an awful lot of last-place finishes.

With nearly 42,000 seats, Nationals Park isn't especially large, yet like so many other HOK ballparks, it seems larger. Its balance of steel and glass give it an open, airy ambiance. Not surprisingly, red, white, and blue—the official color chord of both the Nationals and the nation's capital—appear throughout the ballpark.

Since it's positioned near a station stop of Washington, D.C.'s subway system, nearly three-quarters of the team's fans arrive at the park by train. But, curiously, the stadium's layout guides fans through its center–field gate, not the park's official entrance at home plate, which has a wonderful walkway to the turnstiles. If you arrive at Nationals Park by Metro, take the time to walk around the outside of the park and enter through the home plate entrance, a more meaningful way to enjoy your visit.

> For information about tours of Nationals Park or tickets to Nationals games, check the team's website at www.nationals.com.

127 OWN A COPY OF *THE BARRY HALPER COLLECTION OF BASEBALL MEMORABILIA* ✄ ✄ ✄ ✄

The bug that bites every collector of baseball memorabilia bit Barry Halper, except Halper's collecting fever proved incurable. Arguably history's greatest baseball collector, Barry Halper began amassing memorabilia in 1968. Over the next 20 years, Halper went on a baseball buying binge. His suburban New Jersey home became the unofficial repository of baseball history. Boxes upon boxes of gloves, uniforms, letters, autographs, jewelry, posters, pins, cards, balls, bats, caps, photos, trophies, paintings, pennants, and so much more, packed nearly every room in his home from floor to ceiling. Magazines like the *Smithsonian* and *Sports Illustrated* wrote extensive profiles on Halper. Curators from the National Baseball Hall of Fame and Museum and other baseball institutions came knocking when they needed an object to borrow for an exhibit.

In 1999, Halper put his collection on sale. Charged with selling off the most impressive baseball collection of memorabilia anywhere, the famous auction house Sotheby's, published not one, but two volumes—"The Early Years" and "The Modern Era"—of a catalogue for the auction, which took a full week to complete.

Titled *The Barry Halper Collection of Baseball Memorabilia*, the auction catalogue presents some of the most precious objects in the history of the game, all eloquently presented in striking photographs and detailed descriptions. So many baseball fans that had no intention of ever bidding on a single item bought the catalogue, that bookstores requested extra copies and started selling it. Enclosed in a box, the *The Barry Halper Collection of Baseball Memorabilia* includes the two auction catalogues, plus a third book with essays by writer Peter Golenbock and baseball legends Yogi Berra and Ted Williams, along with a baseball timeline and information about the auction (dates, conditions of sale, etc.). Reading through the catalogue is like reading through the history of baseball.

It will be difficult to find *The Barry Halper Collection of Baseball Memorabilia*; most of them wound up in the hands of collectors. But it's worth the time, effort and cash to secure one. Use it as a historical reference, or as a catalyst to your own quest to become a baseball memorabilia collector. Few publications of baseball history or culture are as interesting as these, or as enjoyable to thumb through.

> Your best bets to find a copy of *The Barry Halper Collection of Baseball Memorabilia* are estate sales, sellers of rare books, baseball memorabilia shops and online auction sites like *eBay*.

128 HOST A MINOR LEAGUE BALLPLAYER

Hosting a young minor league ballplayer in your home rates as one of the most personal and enduring aspects of being a baseball fan. You not only give him free room and board, you share in the highs and lows of his season and help him deal with the many challenges he faces in his quest to someday play in the majors. For players from other countries, the host family experience is even more important. Language and cultural differences and homesickness can make a player's life off the field difficult, and diminish his on-field performance.

A good host family can step to the plate to give the player the emotional support and security he'll need to realize his baseball dreams. Over the weeks, a host family's emotional stake in their player's team and his day-to-day achievements grows. You'll find yourself going to more games than usual and gaining a new understanding and appreciation of baseball from the perspective of a player. It's not uncommon for host families to establish long-term friendships with the adopted player, following them throughout their careers and even getting invited to weddings and their major league debuts.

There can be a down side to hosting a player. What seemed like a good match between a player and family can go sideways. If that happens, the host family has the option to end the relationship. Fortunately, according to most minor league host family representatives, such problems rarely occur because of the team's screening process before a match is made.

Not all minor league teams have host family programs. But they remain common in the lower levels, especially in the short season leagues, where the players are young and often living away from home for the first time. Teams establish requirements for host families to determine if they can afford to comfortably host a player and if their home is close enough to the ballpark. Contact your local minor league team before the season to get all the requirements from the team before the season begins and fill out the necessary applications to become a host family. It is a memorable experience; host families often stay in the program for years.

> For more information about minor league host family programs, contact your local minor league franchise. You can get a complete list of minor league franchises and how to get in touch with them by going to *www.minorleaguebaseball.com* and clicking on "Team Affiliates."

129 SEE THE DIAMONDBACKS PLAY AT CHASE FIELD ✹✹

The most comforting sound heard at Chase Field, home of the National League Arizona Diamondbacks, is not the cheers of the fans or a home run crack of the bat. Rather, it's the steady hum of its giant air conditioners. Without a cooling system, playing Major League Baseball in Phoenix in summer—when temperatures routinely jump the century mark—would be unimaginable. Chase Field's chief architect, Ellerbe Becket, topped the ballpark with the nation's first modern retractable roof to keep the cool in and heat out.

Originally known as Bank One Ballpark, Chase opened for the expansion Diamondbacks maiden season in 1998. Less than four years later, it hosted history, with the Diamondbacks becoming the first franchise to win an MLB title in just its fourth season when the team bettered the Yankees in a thrilling World Series Game 7.

From the outside, Chase Field doesn't look like a place destined to host something that special. Essentially a rectangular box, it more resembles an airport hangar than a baseball park. It incorporates a downtown Phoenix warehouse to serve as the ballpark's commissary for the concession stands, but most visitors don't even notice it.

Inside, Chase Field gets more attractive. It holds over 48,000 seats, yet feels far smaller. Baseball traditionalists love the old-school strip of dirt running from the pitcher's mound to home plate. A state-of-the-art scoreboard stands behind center field, dominating an interior that avoids the clutter of excess billboards and special screens. Its gimmicky swimming pool originally drew a lot of unfortunate attention and use. (How can anyone call himself a baseball fan if he spends part of the game floating on his back in a pool?) But it's positioned discreetly enough to keep it from being too bothersome.

If you can, visit Chase Field in the beginning of the baseball season, when your chances of catching a night game with the roof open, are better than they are in the torrid summer months. The star-speckled desert sky, coupled with the lights from the ballpark and a cool spring breeze make watching a game at Chase Field a delightful experience.

> For information about Chase Field tours and tickets to Diamondbacks' games, check the team's website at www.dbacks.com.

130 TAKE IN A LOCAL MUSEUM BASEBALL EXHIBIT

With baseball being such an important part of American popular culture, museums listed in this book often create exhibits on the game for local museums. Usually, they focus on a regional theme or a particular aspect of baseball's history. They often include public and education programs that are informative and surprisingly fun to attend. Many of the objects displayed at these exhibits come from a local baseball collectors or the host museum's own permanent baseball collection.

Presentations in local history museums might not approach what you'll see in Cooperstown or the Negro Leagues Baseball Museum. But they usually tell a compelling and locally relevant story through artifacts, photos and other memorabilia. Recent examples of baseball exhibits presented in non-baseball museums include "Black Baseball in Washington, D.C." in the City Museum, "Take Me Out: Baseball Rocks!" at the Rock and Roll Hall of Fame and Museum in Cleveland, and "Baseball Beyond the Mississippi" at the Jefferson Center for Westward Expansion in St. Louis.

The National Baseball Hall of Fame and Museum and the Negro Leagues Baseball Museum also, on occasion, create traveling exhibits for special events such as Fan Fests, and the Major League Baseball All-Star Game or World Series. More displays than full-blown exhibits, they usually require less than a half-hour to take in. The exception was the Hall of Fame's excellent traveling exhibition, "Baseball As America," the first major traveling exhibition to explore the connection between American culture and baseball, starting with the game's origins in the mid-19th century. Most museums where "Baseball As America" appeared also featured robust public programs where some of baseball's best historians and cultural observers gave talks and did book signings. Many institutions also showed baseball films and brought in baseball legends for panel discussions. Unfortunately, "Baseball As America" is no longer touring. If you saw it, you saw something special, not apt to be repeated anytime soon.

But if you're lucky and pay attention, especially during the baseball season, you should eventually find a baseball exhibit at a museum near your home or in a city you plan on visiting.

To find a baseball exhibit at a local museum, check museum websites and newspaper arts calendars in your area. Since the National Baseball Hall of Fame and Museum often lends objects to such exhibits, it can help you find out about new baseball exhibitions in museums around the country. For more information, call the National Baseball Hall of Fame and Museum at (888) HALL-OF-FAME.

131 READ THE BOOK, *THE TEAMMATES*

Author David Halberstam first made a name for himself as a war correspondent and writing books about the Vietnam War and the men back in Washington D.C. who crafted its tragic blueprint. But Halberstam, who died in a car crash in 2007, also found sports, particularly baseball, equally compelling. His first two baseball books—*The Summer of '49* and *October 1964*—demonstrated his love and knowledge of the game, as well as his wonderful sense of story. Put these two books on your baseball reading list. But first enjoy *The Teammates: A Portrait of Friendship*, Halberstam's heartwarming book about baseball camaraderie.

Published in 2005, *The Teammates* focuses on four friends—Dominic DiMaggio, Johnny Pesky, Bobby Doerr, and Ted Williams, all players on the Boston Red Sox in the late 40s. The book chronicles how, despite the stellar play of Pesky, Williams, Doerr, and DiMaggio, Boston was never crowned world champion in that era, though the team came close in 1946, losing to the St. Louis Cardinals in the World Series. But *The Teammates* is as much about the four men who wore Red Sox uniforms and forged a bond that went beyond baseball, and was unbreakable.

Halberstam built his book from two journeys: a trip back in time when all four friends were teammates on the Red Sox, fighting the Yankees to win a pennant and living out their individual baseball dreams; the other a classic baseball road trip that DiMaggio and Pesky took to visit their old friend Ted Williams in Florida. Doerr wanted to be part of the trip, but was caring for his sick wife in Oregon. Yet, Halberstam artfully works Doerr into the narrative, so that "my guys" as Williams referred to his friends, were all there, at least, spiritually.

Of the four, Williams was undeniably the best ballplayer and the team leader. Loud and contentious, Williams had little patience with most people. But he was a great friend, even in his final years, when he and everyone else around him knew that he was dying. Like many great books about baseball, *The Teammates* deals with bigger themes than just the game, namely friendship, loyalty, growing old, and ultimately, facing death.

> David Halberstam's *The Teammates: A Portrait of Friendship* remains in print and is available from most bookstores and online booksellers, along with his books *The Summer of '49* and *October 1964*.

132 DELVE INTO SOME BASEBALL SCHOLARSHIP ✷✷✷

You can increase your understanding of baseball in many ways. But an often overlooked way to broaden your baseball knowledge is to regularly read the handful of scholarly baseball journals found in better libraries, and available by subscription. Some of the pieces that fill these journals are academic in design and complexity and deal with esoteric issues that won't interest the average fan. But if you're serious about your baseball education, you'll find many of their articles both informative and rewarding.

McFarland Publications produces a pair of baseball journals worth investigating. One of them, *Base Ball: A Journal of the Early Game* deals with just that—baseball back when it was still referred to with two words in the 19th century. Twice a year, *Base Ball* gives you a big dose of fresh scholarship that reveals all kinds of new information and theories about baseball's origins and early years that only find their way into books over time. McFarland's biannual *Black Ball* explores the history and culture of black baseball in America. Many of the articles deal with the Negro Leagues that flourished during the first half of the 20th century, but others go back to the 19th century, before the Jim Crow era, when blacks did play baseball with whites.

The University of Nebraska Press publishes the biannual *Nine: A Journal of Baseball History and Culture*. Unlike the more specialized McFarland baseball journals, *Nine* covers virtually anything about baseball history and culture. *Nine* also hosts an annual spring training conference in Florida or Arizona where papers on the historical and sociological impact of baseball are read and discussed.

It's not necessary to subscribe to all three journals to complete this *Bucket List* entry. One will do. To save money (the cost of an annual subscription can run in the neighborhood of $50), you can ask your local library to purchase a subscription. Also, there's plenty of similar, though far less academic-oriented information, in the magazine *Memories and Dreams*, published quarterly by the National Baseball Hall of Fame and Museum. Sign up as a museum member and you'll get *Memories and Dreams* for free.

> For more information about *Base Ball: A Journal of the Early Game or Black Ball*, check www.mcfarland.com. More information about subscribing to *Nine* and announcements about future *Nine* conferences can be found at www.nebraskapress.uni.edu. For more information about *Memories and Dreams*, visit www.baseballhall.org or call (888) 425-5633.

133 SEE A SINGLE-A GAME

Single-A or Class-A, as it's also called, is one of five minor league classifications sanctioned by Major League Baseball. It falls between the Double-A and the Short Season A levels. Single-A ball is then divided into two levels of its own: Class A-Advanced, often known as "High A," and Class-A, or "Low A."

When you add into the equation the lowest level of minor league ball, the Rookie level, which also has two classifications, it's easy to see why ballplayers spend so much of their early careers in the minors. A player does not have to play on all seven levels before making it to the majors, but he'll usually play on most of them on his road to the bigs.

Not surprisingly, the quality of baseball played in the Single-A levels is not as good as Double-A or Triple-A, but usually better than the classifications below it. Baseball fundamentals can still be a problem for players on this level, but because they show much promise, managerial and front-office patience is practiced more in A-level ball than levels above it. Where you really see a difference, though, is in the pitching. Single-A pitchers often have problems with control or consistency, which can make for long games.

Minor leagues in the Single-A Advanced category include the Carolina League, the California League, and the Florida State League. If you're looking to go to a Single-A Advanced game where the ballpark is historic, look into a game in Daytona, Florida. Jackie Robinson Ballpark, where the Daytona Cubs play, was built in 1914 and reputedly was the ballpark where the first racially integrated non-Major League game in baseball history took place.

Minor leagues in the standard Single-A category include the Midwest League and the South Atlantic League. Catching an Asheville Tourists game in beautiful Asheville, North Carolina is recommended; if for no other reason than the city is located in the midst of the mountains and the ballpark—McCormick Field, which opened in 1924—is nearly as old as Jackie Robinson Ballpark.

Nearly all the High A and Low A minor league teams are located in small cities and towns, making them often difficult and costly to travel to. Yet, there is something magnetic that draws serious baseball fans to out-of-the-way minor league teams and ballparks, where the traditional spirit of baseball lives, minus the overt commercialism of the game in big major league cities.

> For more information about Single-A leagues and clubs, go to www.minorleaguebaseball.com

134 WATCH THE MOVIE, *FEVER PITCH* **

It didn't take long for Hollywood to make a movie that capitalized on the triumphant end of the "Curse of the Bambino." In October 2004, after an 86-year drought that began, many Boston fans swore, when the Red Sox foolishly sold a young Babe Ruth to the Yankees way back in 1920, the team finally won a World Series, sweeping the St. Louis Cardinals. The Red Sox survived an incredibly dramatic baseball battle against the hated Yankees to get there in the first place.

Actually, the directors of *Fever Pitch*, Peter and Bobby Farrelly (already famous for wild comedies such as *There's Something About Mary*, *Kingpin* and *Dumb and Dumber*) began work on the film during the 2004 season, before Boston's World Series heroics. The original ending of the film had the Red Sox failing in their bid to get to the World Series. When the Sox won it all, the script had to be quickly re-written and new scenes shot.

A romantic comedy as much about relationships and falling in love as about baseball, *Fever Pitch* nonetheless delightfully captured a magic moment in modern baseball history. Jimmy Fallon does a masterful job as Ben Wrightman, the ultimate Red Sox fan. Everything about him revolves around the Red Sox. Hardcore baseball fans know how intense feelings can get when following your favorite team. *Fever Pitch* demonstrates that, and more.

Barrymore is equally effective as the intensely focused executive who finds Fallon cute, but can't quite understand how he could be so passionate over a baseball team. Clearly, she knows nothing about the cultural significance of the Red Sox in Boston, nor does she care, at least initially. But over time both Fallon and the Red Sox grow on her—at least until Fallon misses one of the greatest comebacks in Red Sox and baseball history, and blames her. They break up, only to reconcile at Fenway Park in grand fashion at the end of the movie.

Fever Pitch is a feel-good baseball film, and there is nothing wrong with that, especially if you're a Red Sox fan. And if you're a Yankee fan, you won't switch allegiances (an impossible thought), but you might empathize with Wrightman and his unrequited love for the Red Sox. Then again, maybe not.

> *Fever Pitch* is available for purchase or rental from most movie stores and online movie merchants. It is rated PG-13.

135 ATTEND THE ANNUAL CIVIL RIGHTS GAME

Started in Memphis in 2007, the 60th anniversary of Jackie Robinson's successful crusade to end segregation in Major League Baseball, the annual Civil Rights Game commemorates one of the game's most significant events and reaffirms baseball's ongoing commitment to racial equality. That Major League Baseball chose Memphis as the site of its first Civil Rights Game seemed only natural. The site of the game, Autozone Park, sits but a few blocks away from the National Civil Rights Museum and perhaps the most sacred ground of America's Civil Rights movement: the Lorraine Motel, where Dr. Martin Luther King, Jr. was assassinated on April 4, 1968.

The day before the game, the museum sponsored a free forum on baseball and civil rights that included such panelists as ESPN commentator Peter Gammons, baseball Hall of Famers Dave Winfield and Bill White and a charity luncheon. Finally, ceremonies on the field prior to the game celebrated the courage and legacy of Jackie Robinson and brought attention to baseball's ongoing commitment to honor the early plight of baseball's black pioneers.

The inaugural Civil Rights Game took on additional meaning as time and again it was mentioned how the number of African-Americans playing Major League Baseball has dramatically declined, so now blacks make up less than ten percent of all major league ballplayers. The game and the events that surrounded it served as both a call-to-action to reverse this disturbing trend and a tribute to Robinson for breaking the color barrier in baseball. Many of the events that occurred in Memphis have been repeated by other cities hosting the Civil Rights Game.

The Civil Rights Game is an admirable way for baseball to honor Robinson's heroic accomplishment and to portray the sport as sensitive to social issues that continue to plague society. For baseball history buffs the game is yet another way to remember the past and celebrate its heroes. Now an annual tradition, the Civil Rights Game moves from city to city and from team to team, but retains its theme of celebrating baseball's role in the Civil Rights struggle.

To find out when and where the next Civil Rights Game will be played, go to *www.mlb.com/mlb/events*, then click on the "Civil Rights Game" link.

136 SEE THE ASTROS PLAY AT MINUTE MAID PARK

The new home of the Houston Astros opened in 2000 and went through three name changes in three years before settling into life as Minute Maid Park. Another of the new major league ballparks with a retractable roof, Minute Maid Park can protect fans from Houston's oppressive heat and the swift moving storms that frequent the Gulf region during baseball season. And thanks to the ballpark's broad line of large windows above left and center fields, Minute Maid Park is frequently bathed in natural light, even when the roof is closed. For Astros fans, Minute Maid Park represents a big improvement over the club's previous home, the dark, cavernous Houston Astrodome, which set off the unfortunate Astroturfed, multi-use bowl craze of the 1970s.

Minute Maid Park holds about 41,000 fans and boasts some unique features. Since Houston's history is linked to the railroad and the ballpark is connected to Union Station, above left field and center field runs a line of track, complete with a locomotive that carries a load of not coal, but oranges. The deepest part of center field features a grass incline, a tribute to old ballparks like Cincinnati's Crosley Field. Most players dislike it. Still, these idiosyncrasies make for nice throwback touches.

Minute Maid Park does disappoint a bit on the outside. The majority of the structure's look is pleasantly retro, with brick walls and other classic touches. But a large exterior section of the park resembles more a jai alai stadium than a baseball park. Its retractable roof sports a hideous steel frame colored a washed-out turquoise (why not the standard dark green?). It's almost as if the designers ran out of retro ideas for Minute Maid's exterior and created some-thing that had absolutely nothing to do with the brick and concrete that make up the rest of the ballpark's walls. Fortunately, the designers invested Minute Maid Park with fine sight lines, pleasant lighting, and, of course, air conditioning for those sultry summer days, making it a good place to visit and watch a baseball game.

For information on tours of Minute Maid Park, check out the Astros web-site at *www.houstonastros.com*. If you want to attend an Astros home game at Minute Maid Park, you can also find the team's schedule, seating map and ticket purchasing instruc-tions on the club's website.

137 CATCH AN ARIZONA FALL LEAGUE GAME

Most baseball fans take a respite from the game in the fall after the World Series concludes. The weather is chilly in most parts of the country. Major League Baseball's season is over. Football is in full swing, not to mention basketball and hockey. So what's an incurable baseball fan to do if he or she needs a strong baseball fix during these down months?

Head to the sunny and warm Southwest, where the Arizona Fall League kicks into action in early October. Other leagues begin at nearly the same time in Mexico, the Dominican Republic, Venezuela, and Puerto Rico. But the Arizona League attracts the best ballplayers. It's also easier to follow and more accessible for most U.S. fans.

Arizona Fall League rosters come together in August. Each Major League Baseball team gets to assign six players to the league, meaning 180 MLB players are invited to play in the league, 30 to a team. Mostly, they are Double-A and Triple-A prospects that their teams want to see working on their skill sets in a place that they can be easily monitored. Arizona Fall League managers and coaches, as well as umpires, are, in a way, prospects in their own right. The men in blue come from Major League Baseball's Umpire Development Program, while the league offers aspiring managers and coaches the chance for their first pro experience.

Six teams comprise the Arizona Fall League, with team names that mirror the state's desert geography: the Phoenix Desert Dogs, Surprise Rafters, Peoria Javelinas, Mesa Solar Sox, Peoria Saguaros, and the Scottsdale Scorpions. The teams play and train in Major League Baseball spring training complexes.

The quality of Arizona Fall League baseball varies from season to season, but generally you can expect it to resemble that of Triple-A minor league baseball. You're likely to see a few future MLB stars there. League graduates include: Derek Jeter, Nomar Garciaparra, Albert Pujols, Roy Halladay, David Wright, Grady Sizemore, Chase Utley, Torii Hunter, Jimmy Rollins, and Ryan Howard.

The Arizona Fall League remains one of baseball's best-kept secrets. A game ticket costs less than ten dollars and fans are laid back and scarce. And the weather tends to be near perfect. Arizona Fall League baseball makes for a great baseball experience at a time of the year when baseball experiences are hard to come by.

> For more information on the Arizona Fall League, go to *www.mlbfallball.com.*

138 | WATCH THE MOVIE, *THE SANDLOT* ✦✦✦

The Sandlot may not pack the comic punch of *Bull Durham* or the dark mystery of *The Natural*. But it's a delightful baseball comedy that seeks only to entertain and recall simpler times; call it a kid's film for adults. Released in 1993, *The Sandlot* received enthusiastic reviews from nearly everyone who saw it, thanks to its charm and warmth and a cast of loveable characters to go with a sunny storyline. Now considered a classic in family film entertainment, *The Sandlot* is about growing up and playing baseball, and how, back in the early 60s, the two were often one and the same.

Directed by David Mickey Evans, the film tells the story of Scotty Smalls (Tom Guiry) a kid who's just moved to Los Angeles with his parents, (Karen Allen and Denis Leary). His new neighborhood is full of baseball-crazy kids who play ball on a sandlot field. But Smalls can hardly throw and catch a baseball, which makes it difficult for him to fit in with his new friends. Fortunately for Smalls, he is befriended by the best player on the sandlot—Benny "The Jet" Rodriguez—who teaches Smalls the fundamentals of baseball.

Still, playing baseball on this sandlot comes with a price, especially when one of the kids hits a home run over the left-field fence, on the other side of which awaits "the beast"—a ferocious dog that devours baseballs—and would probably devour a kid, if it could only get its teeth into one. Equally feared is the irascible owner of the property, played by James Earl Jones.

One day, Benny hits a ball so hard that he tears the leather off it. Smalls comes to the aid of his friend by taking a ball from his father's collection—one signed by Babe Ruth—so that the sandlot kids can finish their game. When Smalls hits the autographed ball over the left-field fence for his first-ever home run, he realizes the valuable ball is as good as gone once the Beast starts chewing on it. The movie culminates with Benny saving the ball—and Smalls' hide—and the sandlot kids finding out that the beast and his owner aren't so bad after all.

> *The Sandlot* is available for rental or purchase from most movie stores and online movie merchants. Its success led to two sequels, though neither was as good as the original.

139 THROW OUT THE FIRST PITCH ✗✗✗✗

Though throwing out the ceremonial "first pitch" before a baseball game is traditionally performed by Presidents, war heroes, baseball legends, Hollywood stars and other prominent figures, it's an honor regular baseball fans actually have a better chance of gaining than they probably think.

According to baseball historians, the first dignitary to throw out a first pitch was popular Japanese statesman ?Kuma Shigenobu in 1908. The tradition took hold on American soil two years later when U.S. President William Howard Taft did the honors on Opening Day at the Washington Senators' Griffith Stadium. Since then, virtually every U.S. President has followed suit. Early on, a person threw out the first pitch from his or her box seat to a catcher standing a few feet away on the edge of the field. Today, the first pitch usually gets thrown from the pitcher's mound to a catcher crouched behind the plate, making it a far tougher task.

You might never throw out the first pitch at a major league game, but many minor league clubs award first pitch honors to people who have made a positive difference in their communities. And some club's promotion departments stage contests with throwing out a first pitch as top prize. Contact the community relations department of your local minor league team to learn about their first pitch opportunities.

Throwing out the first pitch means you'll likely get to keep the ball and get it autographed by the catcher. It makes a nice keepsake, along with a photo snapped to capture the moment. If you've done something really important, you might also get a team jersey or dugout jacket; that usually only happens in the majors, though, due to costs.

If you get the chance, make it count. Firing a strike is probably asking too much. But you should get the ball to the catcher without it bouncing. So in the week leading up to the game, practice throwing from the pitcher's mound at a local field. If you have trouble reaching home plate, stand at the base of the mound. On the night of the game, wear clothes that allow you to execute your pitching motion. Throwing out the first pitch is an honor, and you don't want to embarrass yourself while doing it.

> You can get a complete list of minor league franchises and how to get in touch with them by going to www.minorleaguebaseball.com.

140 EAT AT A FAMOUS BALLPLAYER'S RESTAURANT

Popular ballplayers own restaurants in many major league cities. Most are theme restaurants, filled with memorabilia and photographs recalling the owner's greatest moments, along with autographed balls and bats of teammates and other pieces of baseball history.

Hamburgers and pub fare are the staples at most ballplayers' restaurants. Occasionally, the menu offers more sophisticated fare. One of the best ballplayer restaurants is also one of the classiest and oldest. Joe DiMaggio's Italian Chophouse (*www.joedimaggiosrestaurant.com*) in San Francisco has featured fine dining in the Yankee Clipper's hometown for years. Though it's changed locations, Joe DiMaggio's continues to offer steak and seafood entries that rank with the offerings of many of San Francisco's top restaurants. Unlike most ballplayers' places, Joe DiMaggio's is not a sports bar, so save your visit for a more formal affair.

Less formal but more popular is Mickey Mantle's Restaurant and Sports Bar (*www.mickeymantles.com*) just off Central Park in New York City. Because of all the Mantle and Yankees memorabilia on the walls and the sports bar ambiance, Mickey Mantle's is a tourist draw. The food here is pedestrian; do lunch instead of dinner. But if you're a Baby Boomer who grew up idolizing the Mick, a stop at the restaurant that bears his name is a must.

St. Louis features more ballplayer eateries than any other major league city. Mike Shannon's Steaks and Seafood (*www.shannonssteak.com*) sits a block or two from Busch Stadium and is a popular hangout for Cardinals' fans. Hall of Fame shortstop Ozzie Smith has Ozzie's Restaurant and Sports Bar (*www.ozziesrestaurantandsportsbar.com*), which offers above-average fare; but the real reason to visit is to check out the great Cards' memorabilia on its walls. Albert Pujols' Pujols 5 Westport Grill (*www.pujols5grill.com*) is located in the suburb of Westport and features nearly fifty high-definition screens to watch baseball on, along with a menu dominated by sports bar fare. Pujols 5 goes out of its way to cater to families and young children. Cards bullpen legend Al Hrabosky has Al Hrabosky's Ballpark Saloon (*www.alsballparksaloon.com*) in St. Louis and the broadcasting family of Jack and Joe Buck have J. Buck's Restaurant (*www.jbucks.com*). Drink at Hrabosky's and eat at Buck's, and check out the photos and memorabilia at both.

> For more information about ballplayers' restaurants in your town or a city you will be visiting, check the local eatery guides. You can also contact the public relations departments of the city's major league team.

141 VISIT THE BARNSTABLE BAT COMPANY

Baseball fans who vacation on Cape Cod or catch a Cape Cod Baseball League game (see *Bucket List* item #68) ought to make time for a stop at the Barnstable Bat Company in nearby Centerville. Located in a Cape Cod–style cedar shake building in a picture postcard Cape setting, the Barnstable bat-making operation is both homegrown and personal. Barnstable bats are, in short, a labor of love.

Here's how it goes: After a new batch of wood is delivered, it gets dried over the course of nearly a month. Then the wood is rounded and trimmed to vaguely resemble a baseball bat. There are about a dozen popular baseball length and weight bat patterns with variations for components like barrel size. (The best bats, says Barnstable, weigh an ounce per inch, as in, say, 32 ounces and 32 inches.) But the weight and length is ultimately the decision of the player who places the order. After the bat dimensions are set, the wood is shaped on a lathe, then finished. You see all of this in the company's shop during an informal tour. Don't be afraid to ask questions; the people here care about their craft, and are happy to talk about it.

Started in 1992 by woodworking baseball fan Tom Jones, the Barnstable Bat Company produces over 10,000 bats a year, a tiny percentage of the hundreds of thousands produced by Louisville Slugger (see *Bucket List* item #34). Although many of their bats are still made with ash or maple, the company was instrumental in introducing birch bats to baseball a few years ago. According to Jones, birch is lighter than maple and tougher than ash. With good wood bats approaching the $100 price tag, baseball players, especially amateurs, want a bat that's a good investment. That's why many players in the Cape Cod League now swing birch bats made by the Barnstable Bat Company.

You can buy more than baseball bats from Barnstable, which also sell fungo, softball, youth and T-ball bats, and even stickball bats. All of them can have your name engraved on them. Unlike the Louisville bat factory where baseball bats are big business, the Barnstable Bat Company is a small but precious operation. Like the league it supplies, there is a small-town, throwback quality to Barnstable that baseball purists will undoubtedly savor.

> For more information about the Barnstable Bat Company, refer to its website at *www.barnstablebat.com*.

142 TAKE A BASEBALL TOUR OF JAPAN

Experiencing Japanese baseball culture requires time and money. You'll need at least a week to fly there, recover from jet lag, attend two or three games at different ballparks, pick up some souvenirs and visit the Japanese Baseball Hall of Fame and Museum. That will cost you at least a couple thousand dollars. But it's worth it. The experience will give you insights into Japanese baseball and help you see American baseball in new ways.

If you've never been to Japan, your best bet is to go with a baseball tour group like Japan Ball (*www.japanball.com*). They'll handle all the logistics and let you just enjoy baseball. You'll also be with other Americans who speak English and who are as excited and as interested in experiencing Japanese baseball as you are.

Going to a Japanese baseball game may throw you off at first. Strategies are different. Ballpark food is different. The ballparks themselves look and feel different. And Japanese baseball fans have very different ways of cheering, more like what you'd see and hear from American football fans than our baseball ones. In short, you'll be amazed at how cultural differences can change the overall feel of a baseball game. But after a few games under your belt, the Japanese approach to baseball becomes something you'll appreciate, even admire.

If at all possible, catch at least one Yomiuri Giants game. The Giants are the oldest Japanese professional baseball team, the most popular, and also the most successful. Sadaharu Oh, Japan's greatest home run hitter, played for the Giants. Also, at the Tokyo Dome, the Giants' home, you'll find the Japanese Baseball Hall of Fame and Museum, a must stop on your Japanese baseball tour.

Prepare for your Japanese baseball experience by reading Robert Whiting's *You Gotta Have Wa!*, a great overview of Japanese baseball written for American baseball fans. You'll also want to learn a few Japanese words, basic terms like "hello" and "thank you" and familiarize yourself with essential Japanese customs, such as bowing to avoid insulting anyone or looking foolish. Finally, make sure to pick up some baseball souvenirs while in Japan. Most baseball tourists purchase Japanese team baseball caps and/or jerseys, but there are plenty of other options.

> For more information about taking a baseball tour of Japan, visit the website of Japan Ball (*www.japanball.com*) or read the book, *You Gotta Have Wa!*, which is available from online booksellers.

143 READ THE BOOK, *THE SCIENCE OF HITTING*

Widely regarded as one of the greatest hitters in baseball history, Ted Williams is the last major leaguer to hit over .400 for a season (he hit .406 in 1941). Williams also whacked 521 home career runs and wound up with a lifetime .344 average. Another great hitter, Joe DiMaggio, called Williams "absolutely the best hitter I ever saw." Had Williams not fought in Word War II and the Korean War—losing a total of five prime baseball years in service to his country—his lifetime hitting statistics would undoubtedly be even more impressive. He almost certainly would have reached the coveted 3,000 hit mark (he got to 2,654) and the 600-home run plateau.

A first ballot Hall of Famer in 1966, Williams studied hitting the way some physicists study atoms. Rarely a day went by when Williams didn't ponder the mysteries of hitting a baseball, even after he retired. He even wrote about it, most notably in his excellent book, *The Science of Hitting*.

As great a hitter as Williams was, he opened his book with: "Hitting a baseball—I've said it a thousand times—is the single most difficult thing to do in sport." Published in 1971, *The Science of Hitting* offers all kinds of insights Williams gained from years of thought and experience. For instance, he advised against leaving a bat lying in the dirt, where it might soak up moisture, making it heavier. Williams was a big proponent of using a lighter bat when many other players swore that a heavier one produced better results.

Williams' fascination with hitting began as a youth in San Diego and soon turned into an obsession. That he had extraordinary eyesight, monk-like discipline, an unceasing desire to be the best, and a determination to know everything possible about hitting made Williams who he was. *The Science of Hitting* contains all his ideas and theories about hitting a baseball. If you're a serious ballplayer, read it and study it and apply it. If you're a serious fan, read it to increase your understanding of one of the essential elements of baseball.

The Science of Hitting by Ted Williams remains in print and available from most bookstores and online booksellers. Also recommended: Williams' baseball memoir, *My Turn at Bat: My Story of My Life* (Fireside, 1969). Leigh Montville's *Ted Williams: The Biography of an American Hero* (Anchor, 2005), and a visit to the Ted Williams Museum located at Tropicana Field in St. Petersburg, Florida.

144 SEE THE BLUE JAYS PLAY AT THE ROGERS CENTRE

Major League Baseball offers no ballpark experience quite like catching a game at the Rogers Centre, home of the Toronto Blue Jays. For starters, it's the only MLB ballpark located in Canada. Approaching it, you may feel like you're not just in another country, but on a science fiction movie set; Toronto's largest and most famous landmark, the CN Tower, looms over the Rogers Centre like something out of *War of the Worlds*. Inside, you'll note the distances on the outfield fences measured in both feet and meters and that many of the club's fans cheer the Jays on in French.

Known as the SkyDome when it opened in 1989, it was renamed when the Canadian company, Rogers Communications, bought the Blue Jays in 2004. Back in its day, the SkyDome was a baseball architectural marvel. The first stadium in the majors with a retractable roof, it enabled games to be played during Canada's often cold and wet weather. Unlike the newer retractable roof parks (like Miller Park and Safeco Field), the SkyDome/Rogers Centre was, and still is, a multi-use sports and entertainment facility; the Blue Jays share the structure with the Toronto Argonauts of the Canadian Football League, and the NFL's Buffalo Bills even occasionally play there.

So it's not surprising that the concrete structure lacks any semblance of traditional baseball architecture. A bit bland and colorless, the Rogers Centre recalls an era when multiuse stadiums were all too common in major league cities. The metallic painted fiberglass sculptures called "The Audience" by Michael Snow, add some life to the external walls,

Rogers Centre: home of the Toronto Blue Jays.

but they are too cartoonish to suggest much about real baseball fans.

The Roger Centre sits up to 50,000 fans in Blue Jay blue seats set at a steep angle to its synthetic field. Above the outfield sits another unique Rogers Centre characteristic: windows of 70 rooms of the Renaissance Toronto Hotel; guests can watch a Blue Jays game while lolling around in their pajamas in their room.

Despite its unique features, the Rogers Centre is not on par with the average contemporary major league ballpark, and the Blue Jays aren't planning on replacing it anytime soon. Fortunately, Toronto is a wonderful city, so the time and money you spend to go a ballgame in the Rogers Centre and check off another entry in your *Baseball Fan's Bucket List* won't be a total letdown.

> For information on tours of Rogers Centre and tickets to Toronto Blue Jays games, go to *www.torontobluejays.com.*

145 SEE A SHORT-SEASON A LEAGUE GAME

The minor league baseball configuration can be confusing. The easiest parts are the upper levels of the system: Single-A, Double-A, and Triple-A. Most players move up and through each level before achieving their objective: playing in the majors. However, before a player even gets to Single-A, he probably has to spend a couple years climbing the pro ladder from its lower rungs: the Rookie Leagues, followed by the Rookie Advanced Leagues, and then the Short-Season A Leagues.

Short-Season ball is just that, an abridged baseball season that runs from June through early September across a 76-game schedule, not including the playoffs. The Short-Season classification was created so that the college players who dominate the league's rosters could complete their collegiate careers and still experience a summer of professional baseball in the Short-Season A's New York-Penn League or Northwest League. As a *Bucket List* fan, you need to experience Short-Season A to say that you've seen a game on every level of minor league play.

The New York-Penn League was established in 1939 and originally called the Pennsylvania-Ontario-New York League, or PONY League. It is currently made up of three divisions, consisting of teams from Maryland, Pennsylvania, Ohio, New York, Massachusetts and Vermont. The Northwest League, which began operations in 1955, emerged from the old Western International League and includes two divisions and eight clubs from the U.S. states of Washington, Idaho and Oregon, plus British Columbia in Canada.

The quality of play in the Short-Season A isn't exceptional and though many of the players are being paid to play baseball for the first time, they aren't being paid much. But most of them love the game and know that excelling in Short-Season A is critical to fulfilling their dream of one day playing in the major leagues. So they play hard and with passion. In an age when many professional athletes are accused of being jaded and lackadaisical, a Short-Season A game can help reconnect you with what still makes the game of baseball so great.

> Short-Season A games take place every year from June through early September in the Mid-Atlantic, Northeastern and Northwestern regions of the United States, and in British Columbia, Canada. You can find complete schedules for both the New York-Penn and Northwest Leagues at *www.minorleaguebaseball.com.*

146 SEE THE MARLINS PLAY AT LAND SHARK STADIUM

Miami's Land Shark Stadium is fine for football. It's already hosted five Super Bowls and dozens of home games for the NFL's Miami Dolphins and University of Miami football Hurricanes, as well as numerous Orange Bowls. But as a place to play baseball, let's just say there's a reason why attendance for Marlins' home games has been among the worst in Major League Baseball since the team's inception in 1993, despite their winning two world championships.

Like most multi-use stadiums, Land Shark offers little or no baseball atmosphere. Tens of thousands of it seats remain empty for most every game, creating a depressing panorama that saps the excitement generated on the field. But those few fans who do show up for Marlins' home games are loud and passionate, screaming at the umpires and visiting team in both English and Spanish. Most of them occupy seats behind home plate and on the first- and third-base lines, while entire outfield seating sections remain closed for baseball games.

Land Shark Stadium underwent a $250 million renovation in 2007. But it remained clear that the Marlins needed a place of their own. In 2012, the Marlins are slated to move to a brand new ballpark in the Little Havana section of Miami. The new location will hopefully inspire more members of Miami's large Latin population, traditionally big fans of baseball, to attend more Marlins home games.

The only reason why attending a game at Land Shark Stadium is a *Baseball Fan's Bucket List* entry is to complete the quest to visit all the major league ballparks in your lifetime. Though you could wait and substitute catching a game at Land Shark Stadium with catching a game at the new Marlins ballpark.

The new Marlins home will hold less than half of Land Shark's 75,000 seats, making it the smallest and most intimate of all the recently built major league parks. Its retractable roof will shield players and fans from the area's fast-moving summer thunderstorms that have delayed so many Marlins' games at Land Shark. The roof will also act as a giant shade from the sun for the rare Marlins' day games. What Marlins officials plan to do to protect fans and players from South Florida's stifling humidity is unknown.

> For more information about the Marlins' new ballpark and tickets to Marlins' game, visit the team's website at *www.marlins.com*.

147 ATTEND THE CARIBBEAN SERIES

Held each February at the end of Winter Leagues and just before the start of spring training, the Caribbean Series, or *Serie del Caribe*, stakes intense national pride and annual bragging rights for the region's Spanish-speaking, baseball-loving fans and players, whose passions often boil over. In 2009, for instance, a particularly bad call by one umpire nearly caused an on-field riot when a player charged the ump, threatening to kill him.

The Caribbean Series began in the 1940s for national teams from members of the Baseball Confederation of the Caribbean (Cuba, Panama, Puerto Rico, and Venezuela). It provided formal closure to the annual Caribbean baseball season and attracted scouts from major league teams who often invited the event's best players to their teams' spring training. But after the 1960 Series, Cuba's communist dictator Fidel Castro cancelled professional baseball in Cuba, a frequent Series winner and host. The Caribbean Series fell apart.

The event got revived in 1970 and has taken place every year since, except for 1981. Participants now include Mexico, the Dominican Republic, Puerto Rico and Venezuela, who take turns hosting the event. The series runs over the course of a week, with each team playing the other three teams twice. Doubleheaders are the rule.

Instead of official national all-star squads, the Caribbean Series now involves teams that won their national championship that season, with their rosters enhanced with top players from other clubs in their countries. Creating teams this way enables each country in the series to field an established team as its core and supplement pitching staffs and other key positions with other top players to make up for star players lost to the World Baseball Classic (played around the same time every four years) or MLB spring training (pitchers and catchers report in February, a month before the traditional start of spring training).

Taking place in the dead of winter, the Caribbean Series gives U.S. fans the opportunity to escape to where the weather is a lot more pleasant and watch baseball for a week. It provides a good excuse for a nice vacation while knocking off another *Bucket List* item.

> The Caribbean Series takes place every February in Mexico, Venezuela, Puerto Rico or the Dominican Republic. For schedules, locations and other information, check the website of Major League Baseball at *www.mlb.com.*

148 FIX UP A BASEBALL FIELD ⚾⚾⚾⚾

If you've played baseball and have been a fan of it for most of your life, then, chances are, the game has been good to you. So making sure that the joy of baseball gets passed to future generations is not just your responsibility, it's an honor. Fixing up a baseball field not only allows you to give a little back to the game that has given you so much, it enables youngsters to learn and enjoy the game on a nice field, helping make them baseball lovers who will one day give back to the game themselves.

The inner cities offer a wealth of opportunities for baseball field renovation. Neglect, lack of space and a lack of interest have all lead to many urban fields deteriorating. Contact the community relations department of the nearest city's major league or minor league baseball club and inquire about programs to renovate neglected baseball fields (or to create new ones).

If your area's pro clubs don't sponsor official field renovation programs, check the Parks and Recreation department in your hometown, or the local Little League organization. Chances are, they will know where and how you can help. Often, the fathers of Little League players get together before the season starts to get a field or fields ready for play. Offer your assistance. Your efforts will be appreciated.

If no such programs exist, then start one. Go to your local park and check out the baseball diamonds there. If they need work, organize neighbors to get it done. If the field is on public property, you'll need to get permission to work on it. Don't do anything without clearing your baseball diamond renovation plans with the proper people. If they turn down your good intentions, then put pressure on your local city council members to do something about the less-than-acceptable condition of the local baseball field.

In the end, it really doesn't matter how the job gets done, or by whom. Helping youngsters gain a safe and attractive place to play baseball is what this *Bucket List* entry is all about.

> For contact information for all Major League Baseball clubs, go to *www.mlb.com*. You can find out how to get in touch with your area Little League through your local government or by visiting *www.littleleague.org*. Check your area phone book for information on contacting your local Parks and Rec department.

149 VISIT THE GRAVESITE OF ALEXANDER CARTWRIGHT, JR.

While visiting the gravesites of some baseball legends can get a bit dreary, traveling to the final resting place of one, often overlooked, early baseball giant offers an excuse for a trip to beautiful Hawaii.

Alexander Cartwright, Jr. set many of baseball's primary rules and standards, helping distinguish it from rounders and cricket, two English games from which baseball evolved. He formalized many baseball rules (including that 90 feet should be the distance between bases and that nine innings should comprise a full game) while watching the Knickerbockers and the Excelsiors from Brooklyn, and other New York base ball clubs play at the Elysian Fields in Hoboken, New Jersey. Cartwright then helped spread baseball across the country when he headed to California to chase the gold rush of 1848 and convinced early West Coast players to adopt his rules. He then introduced the game to Hawaii, where he organized games and tournaments involving natives, missionaries and military personnel on the islands, leading to baseball's introduction throughout the South Pacific.

The Cartwright family burial plot is located in Oahu Cemetery (formerly Nuuanu Valley Cemetery) in the Nuuanu Valley. It's not a large cemetery, so it's quite easy to find the Cartwright's pink granite monument on the small road

1918 Alexander Cartwright Grave Site.

leading to the cemetery's chapel. You'll know you've come to it because of two things: the baseballs, caps, pennants, and other assorted baseball items left at the base of the monument; and the bronze plaque that sits just off the road, adjacent to the step that leads onto the family's final resting place. Not unlike the kind of bronze plaque you'll find at the National Baseball Hall of Fame and Museum in Cooperstown, it outlines Cartwright's importance to baseball, stating, among other things, that he was a member of the Hall of Fame's Class of 1938, and that without his efforts, baseball might have been a long time coming to Hawaii and the rest of the Pacific.

For directions to the graveyard of Alexander Cartwright, Jr., check its website at *www.oahucemetery.org*. The final resting place of numerous prominent people, including mythologist Joseph Campbell, Oahu Cemetery is often called Hawaii's most historic graveyard. When visiting Cartwright's grave, don't forget to honor the tradition of leaving some baseball item behind as a tribute to one of the game's early champions.

SEE THE RAYS PLAY AT TROPICANA FIELD

The Minnesota Twins' 2010 departure from the Metrodome left the Tampa Bay Rays as the only major league team still playing its home games in a domed stadium—Tropicana Field. A regular open-air ballpark isn't practical in an area where summer means oppressive heat and humidity, along with frequent thunderstorms from the Gulf of Mexico. But lacking a retractable roof, the Trop traps the Rays inside, even on the nicest spring and early fall days.

Located not in Tampa, but in nearby St. Petersburg, which owns the stadium, Tropicana Field is one of the least inviting places to watch baseball in the major leagues. FieldTurf, the artificial grass successor to AstroTurf, covers its field, except for the natural dirt spread over the majority of its infield and base paths. The ballpark has 44,000 seats, and behind the right-center field wall, there's the 10,000 gallon Rays Tank that contains live cownose rays, the kind you'll find prowling the sandy bottom of the nearby Gulf. For young fans, there is also an interactive area with video games, simulated broadcast booths, and a New York-style stickball alley, not to mention batting cages and a place to test young pitching arms. None of this, of course, makes the ballgame experience at Tropicana Field any better. It merely saps the interest of young Rays' fans and forces parents to babysit kids instead of watching the game with them.

The east end of the ballpark's main rotunda, which resembles the Brooklyn Dodgers' old Ebbets Field rotunda, provides a more endearing distraction, especially for all the retired New Yorkers in the St. Petersburg area. You need to also check out the best thing about Tropicana Field: the terrific Ted Williams Museum and Hitters Hall of Fame. Plan to spend an hour in the museum if you want to read and see everything on display. The Hitters Hall of Fame includes tributes to such great hitters as Babe Ruth, Joe DiMaggio, Willie Mays, Hank Aaron, and Mickey Mantle, to name just a few.

You can't help noticing (no matter how hard you might try) the four infamous Tropicana Field catwalks, located above the field. Part of the dome's support structure, they are considered fair territory, and batted balls do occasionally hit them, enlivening a pretty drab major league ballpark experience.

> For information on tours of Tropicana Field and tickets to Rays' games, check the team's website at *www.devilrays.com*.

READ THE BOOK, *THE UNIVERSAL BASEBALL ASSOCIATION, INC., J. HENRY WAUGH, PROP.* ✦✦✦✦

It has an unusual title, but the theme of this stellar baseball novel strikes a familiar chord: how obsessive fans who engage an imaginary baseball world can get caught up in their fantasies at the expense of their real lives. Such is the case with Henry Waugh, a lonely, middle-aged accountant who creates a game called the Universal Baseball Association. Waugh is the owner of the league and all its teams; he fulfills the roles of all the teams' managers and players; he is the league's broadcaster and the fan who sits in the imaginary grandstand. He is the supreme ruler of the Universal Baseball Association, as well as all of its constituents.

While Waugh could have devised a world in which he controlled virtually everything, he leaves fate to the roll of the dice in his Universal Baseball Association. And that's where he runs into trouble. A young pitcher in his league, Damon Rutherford, throws a perfect game. Waugh grows increasingly fascinated with Rutherford. But then the unthinkable occurs; while at bat, Rutherford is beaned by another pitcher, and dies. Waugh is devastated and his anguish takes over the Universal Baseball Association and his real-life world. It becomes more and more difficult for him to separate reality from his fantasy baseball world.

Author Robert Coover clearly had a lot more on his mind than baseball when he wrote *The Universal Baseball Association, Inc., J. Henry Waugh, Prop.* Coover tackles such heady topics as the role of a supreme being in a world gone astray, and what happens when an orderly society hits a big bump and goes off the road. Highly entertaining, Coover's novel is also quite disturbing. We come to realize that there is a little bit of its pathetic main character in most of us. Helping readers recognize how they manage their our own inner "Waugh" makes *The Universal Baseball Association* an important work, in baseball literature and beyond.

Published in 1971, Coover's novel reflected the growing desire for escape and fantasy in American culture. With the widespread popularity of fantasy baseball leagues these days and escapism in general, *The Universal Baseball Association* retains its relevance and entertainment value. Coover's dark comic masterpiece still says a lot about the real world—and the fantasy worlds—that we live in.

> Robert Coover's novel *The Universal Baseball Association, Inc., J. Henry Waugh, Prop.* (Plume, 1971) remains in print and is available from most bookstores and online booksellers.

152 WATCH THE MOVIE, *COBB*

Cobb is no ordinary baseball movie. It's not for kids or adults offended by bad language, reckless living, and racism. The film offers no warm-hearted moments or feel-good scenes, and not a whole lot of people playing baseball, either. Because while Ty Cobb was maybe the greatest baseball player of all time, he was definitely the meanest, angriest, and vilest, both on- and off-the-field.

The film depicts Cobb in the final year of life, at age 72, when he decides to set the record "straight" before he dies by penning his life story with writer Al Stump. Stump really did write Cobb's bio, and it's a fascinating read. But the story about Stump writing Cobb's story is interesting enough to make *Cobb* the movie a more worthy *Bucket List* item.

Written and directed by Ron Shelton (*Bull Durham*), the film stars Tommy Lee Jones, who brilliantly portrays the sheer vulgarity, unchecked hatred, and general nastiness that raged in Cobb. According to the film, the murder of his father and the infidelity of his mother when he was a boy never stopped haunting Cobb, even at age 72. Despite all this, Cobb was one great ballplayer (see *Bucket List* item #100), as well as a vicious one who sent 12 players to the hospital over the course of a single season. He played with a passion that tore through his soul and made each game a personal war that belied his sweet nickname, "Georgia Peach."

The film shows Cobb wallowing in his past glories, mostly in drunken rages and drug-induced euphoria, while insisting Stump write a whitewashed version of his life. But Stump aims for something truer: the story of a broken man who has finally succumbed to all his non-baseball failures. And that's just what this movie delivers.

What you ultimately think of *Cobb* will be based, in part, on how you feel Ty Cobb should be judged: for his baseball brilliance or for his appalling character? The two are fields apart.

> *Cobb* is available from most video stores or online movie retailers. Many of the film's baseball scenes were shot in Birmingham, Alabama's historic Rickwood Field (see *Bucket List* item #20). Keep an eye out for a cameo by Roger Clemens as a rival pitcher.

153 VISIT THE CANADIAN BASEBALL HALL OF FAME AND MUSEUM

Located in St. Marys, Ontario, a couple of hours outside Toronto, the Canadian Baseball Hall of Fame and Museum honors amateur and professional players, executives, managers, coaches, and teams from Canada who have significantly contributed to Canadian baseball.

Although Canada boasts a proud baseball heritage, baseball isn't the country's national pastime. That honor belongs to hockey. (If you need proof, visit the Hockey Hall of Fame and Museum in Toronto, one of the best sports museums in North America.) Still, the Canadian Baseball Hall of Fame has inducted some eighty members since its 1983 inception. You'll know at least a few of the names: major league managers Sparky Anderson and Tommy Lasorda, general manager Pat Gillick, and players Gary Carter, Joe Carter, Andre Dawson, Ferguson Jenkins, Tony Fernandez, Cito Gaston and Dave Stieb.

The Canadian Baseball Hall of Fame is located in a cozy, century-old building that provides limited room for expansive exhibits. But you'll be able to check out displays on Canada's major league teams, the Toronto Blue Jays and the now-defunct Montreal Expos, as well as other exhibits, including one on Jackie Robinson's time playing minor league ball in Montreal before being called up to the Brooklyn Dodgers in 1947. The museum also offers exhibits on the Vancouver Asahi (a team of interred Japanese-Canadians who played minor league ball during World War II) and the various Canadian ballparks, including Exhibition Stadium, Olympic Stadium, Jarry Park, and the SkyDome/Rogers Centre.

The most intriguing exhibit deals with the very origins of baseball. According to a *Sporting News* article that ran in 1886, the first baseball game took place in a pasture in Beachville, Ontario in 1838, a full eight years before the game at Elysian Fields in Hoboken, New Jersey that is generally considered the first true baseball game (see *Bucket List* item #162). The game played in Beachville didn't exactly resemble baseball as we'd come to know it. But the museum provides just enough evidence to make you wonder.

> For more information about the Canadian Baseball Hall of Fame and Museum, including hours of operation, admission fees, and directions, call (519) 284-2838 or check out its website at *www.baseballhalloffame.ca.*

154 | SEE A ROOKIE LEAGUE GAME

Rookie League games can drag a bit, their quality hindered by the mostly raw players who make up the leagues. But the *Baseball Fan's Bucket List* includes watching games from each of the four other minor league classifications—Triple-A, Double-A, Class A, and Short Season A. So you might as well add Rookie ball to the list and complete the minor league experience.

Good young baseball players hoping to make the big leagues have to start their pro careers somewhere after high school or college, and for most of them, Rookie League baseball is that place. The Rookie classification includes two levels: Rookie and Rookie-Advanced. Like Short Season A, both begin play in June and end in early September. Teams play a 60-game regular season, followed by a brief championship series to crown league winners.

The Rookie Leagues consist of the Arizona League (not to be confused with the Arizona Fall League—see *Bucket List* item #137) and the Gulf Coast League in the U.S., plus two foreign affiliates—the Dominican Summer League and a Venezuelan Summer League. The Dominican and Venezuelan Leagues were created after major league teams realized that Latin America was overflowing with raw baseball talent. These leagues enable MLB clubs to see young Latin players in action without investing much money in them. But players who excel in these leagues and further refine their baseball fundamentals at any of their local baseball academies can win the opportunity to travel north to play in the U.S. minor league system.

If a player is successful in Rookie ball, then the next stop is usually a Rookie-Advanced league. (Rookie-Advanced also contains recently drafted players who skipped the first level of Rookie League ball.) There are two Rookie-Advanced Leagues: the Appalachian League and the Pioneer Baseball League. Appalachian League clubs reside in towns and small cities in the East, while the Pioneer Baseball League serves as Minor League Baseball's western front for Rookie-Advanced ball.

Most Rookie and Rookie-Advanced games are free; some don't even have concession stands. This is baseball, minus any frills, and although the quality of play is a long way from the major leagues, these leagues boast an enjoyable purity of play and purpose.

For a full list of Rookie League and Rookie Advanced teams, go to www.minorleaguebaseball.com.

155 SEE THE A'S PLAY AT THE OAKLAND COLISEUM

The Oakland-Alameda Coliseum, known as the Oakland Coliseum, or, if you're an Oakland A's fan, simply, "the Coliseum," is one of the least interesting and most unsightly of all major league parks. How bad is the Oakland Coliseum? Consider this: nearly every other major league park offers fans the opportunity to tour its facilities. The Coliseum doesn't even bother, because as one front office person wondered: "Who'd want to tour the Coliseum?"

The Coliseum is located east of downtown Oakland. The best way to get there is by taking BART (Bay Area Rapid Transit). But you have to walk across a pedestrian bridge that spans a badly polluted stream littered with urban debris and prowled by stray dogs. Made of concrete with no distinguishing architectural marks, the Coliseum's exterior looks drab and soulless. If the A's didn't fly the few banners that celebrate its greatest players, you might mistake the Coliseum for a large, abandoned warehouse.

The interior is just as bad. Almost half of the Coliseum's 60,000 seats are covered and cordoned off, leaving it with one of the smallest capacities in Major League Baseball. Sitting along first or third base in most any other ballpark means you've got a good seat. But the Coliseum's bowl design puts a lot of ground between fans along the baselines and the action on the field. Bring your binoculars to the Oakland Coliseum to help you see across the majors' largest foul territory. Concession stands sell, at best, average ballpark fare, and the overall attitude of ushers and other ballpark personnel is hardly fan-friendly.

Still, the Coliseum warrants a visit to fulfill the *Bucket List* requirement of seeing a game in every MLB ballpark. And it's hosted a lot of baseball history since welcoming the A's after their 1968 move from Kansas City. The A's won three consecutive world championships from 1972 to 1974, and another one in 1989, and have provided plenty of entertainment and controversy over the decades with players like Reggie Jackson, José Canseco and Rickey Henderson, plus manager Billy Martin and eccentric owner Charley Finley.

An air of gloom hangs over the Oakland Coliseum even when the sun is shining and the A's are winning. Message to Major League Baseball's front office: the Oakland A's need a new place to call home, and quick.

> For Oakland A's ticket information, check the team's website at *www.oaklandathletics.com.*

156 VISIT GEORGE M. STEINBRENNER FIELD

You don't need to be a Yankees' fan to appreciate George M. Steinbrenner Field, formerly known as Legends Field. Located in Tampa, near Raymond James Stadium where the NFL's Tampa Bay Buccaneers play, it serves as the Yankees' spring training complex. But Steinbrenner Field is no ordinary preseason facility. A replica of the old Yankee Stadium, its playing field features the same odd dimensions as the House That Ruth Built and boasts an elegance and a sense of greatness that no other Major League Baseball spring training complex comes close to matching.

It's not surprising that the Yankees play spring training games in what amounts to a full-blown stadium, complete with luxury suites; premium box seats; a large store that not only sells Yankees merchandise, but also Yankees memorabilia; something called the Yankees Pavilion Party Area, suitable for special events and private entertainment; and grounds that resemble a golf course. After all, the team has always been known for its class, along with its over-the-top spending. The club owns the greatest success and tradition and all-time roster in baseball history, and Steinbrenner Field serves as another proud testament to those facts.

Start your visit to Steinbrenner Field at Monument Park, which sits just outside the stadium and honors the many players who have donned pinstripes and achieved baseball greatness. Each player celebrated at Monument Park has his retired number and a bronze plaque that summarizes his career accomplishments. The players are: Billy Martin, Babe Ruth, Lou Gehrig, Joe DiMaggio, Mickey Mantle, Yogi Berra, Bill Dickey, Roger Maris, Phil Rizzuto, Thurman Munson, Whitey Ford, Don Mattingly, Elston Howard, Casey Stengel, Reggie Jackson, and Ron Guidry. There's plenty room for others, too. Sometime in the future, expect the likes of Derek Jeter, Alex Rodriquez, and Mariano Rivera to join this exclusive club.

With more than 10,000 seats, Steinbrenner Field is the largest spring training site in the Grapefruit League. But it often sells out, so don't count on a walk-up ticket purchase the day of the game.

After the Yankees depart Steinbrenner Field for New York at the end of spring training, the stadium becomes the home of the Tampa Yankees of the Florida State League. When attention turns to the Bronx, the site takes on a more relaxed feel. For non–Yankees fans, it might be the best time to catch a game at Steinbrenner Field.

> For more information about George M. Steinbrenner Field, visit *www.steinbrennerfield.com*.

157 ATTEND A NEGRO LEAGUES DAY CELEBRATION AND GAME

It took awhile, but Major League Baseball and other baseball entities finally gave the old Negro Leagues the tributes they deserve through displays at the National Baseball Hall of Fame and Museum (see *Bucket List* item #2), the Negro Leagues Baseball Museum (see *Bucket List* item #11), and Pittsburgh's PNC Park (see *Bucket List* item #30), plus events like Jackie Robinson Day (see *Bucket List* item #82) and the Civil Rights Game (see *Bucket List* item #135).

Then there's Negro Leagues Day, a less heralded, but equally interesting celebration during the Major League Baseball season. There is no official day for it, and not all teams celebrate it annually. But a number of teams, especially those located in cities that once had a strong Negro League presence, include a Negro Leagues Day on their schedules.

The best place to catch a Negro Leagues Day game is Kansas City. The home of the Negro Leagues Baseball Museum also served as home for the Kansas City Monarchs, arguably the greatest of all the Negro Leagues teams. And the Kansas City Royals stage special events and programs to celebrate the history of black baseball and the players still around to tell its stories.

A typical Negro Leagues Day (or Salute to the Negro Leagues as the day is also sometimes called) might consist of the Royals and their major league opponent donning the uniforms of old Negro Leagues teams. Negro League veterans are honored with plaques and participate in autograph signings and fan "meet-and-greets." One of the Royals' corporate sponsors often steps up with free Negro Leagues caps or t-shirts. The ceremonial first pitch (see *Bucket List* item #139) is usually thrown by a prominent Negro Leagues player.

Some minor league teams celebrate their own version of Negro Leagues Day. By far the best one to attend is the one hosted by Alabama's Birmingham Barons at Rickwood Field (see *Bucket List* item #20). The city's minor league team wears the uniforms of the Birmingham Black Barons. The old uniforms coupled with all the black baseball history infusing Rickwood make for a perfect setting to salute the legacy of the Negro Leagues baseball.

> For more information on Negro Leagues Day, visit the websites of individual major league and minor league teams, links to which can be found at *www.mlb.com*.

158 VISIT THE SPORTS MUSEUM OF LOS ANGELES

You can visit a number of local sports museums around the country, most of them small and uninteresting to the serious baseball fan because they contain so few significant baseball objects. They also try to do too much. Covering baseball, football, basketball, hockey and other sports all under one roof makes it difficult to tell interesting, in-depth stories about any of them.

The Sports Museum of Los Angeles is a notable exception. Open by appointment only, this obscure museum contains an astounding number of impressive baseball artifacts, many of them as good as anything you'll find at the National Baseball Hall of Fame and Museum in Cooperstown. Gary Cypres, the museum's collector, founder and curator, has spent more than twenty years amassing artifacts pertinent to the story of baseball, not to mention numerous other sports. But his baseball collection is superior. The Brooklyn-born Cypres holds a special affinity for the Dodgers and has secured an Ebbets Field turnstile, instruments played by the Dodgers' Brooklyn band, bats, uniforms, balls, caps and other memorabilia that tells the story of one of baseball's most storied franchises.

But there's so much more. Take the museum's Joe DiMaggio material. The Sports Museum of Los Angeles displays one of the balls that the Yankee Clipper smacked to extend his incredible 56-game hitting streak in 1941, along with the one Cleveland Indians' infielder Ken Keltner caught to end what many regard as sport's most impressive and untouchable individual run of success. There's also plenty of Babe Ruth memorabilia on display, plus beautiful models of many of baseball's classic parks, reams of rare baseball cards, vintage equipment, and dozens of baseball movie posters.

The Sports Museum of Los Angeles has no curatorial or education staff, and the exhibit design is pedestrian. A visitor gets precious little historical context to help him appreciate the artifacts' pertinence to the bigger baseball story. But the artifacts themselves are so good, that a visit to the museum is a must. Plan to spend at least an hour perusing the baseball exhibits, more if Cypres is on hand to tell you stories behind his favorite objects. You could spend the better part of day at the Los Angeles Sports Museum if you plan to check out the artifacts from other sports on display, and it would be a day well spent.

> For more information, visit the Sports Museum of Los Angeles website (*www.sportsmuseumla.com*) or call (888) 540-8223.

159 VISIT BOWMAN FIELD

Like Rickwood Field in Birmingham, Alabama and Bosse Field in Evansville, Indiana, Bowman Field in Williamsport, Pennsylvania is a classic ballpark that deserves a visit. Williamsport hosts the annual Little League World Series (see *Bucket List* item #91). But they also serve as home to the Williamsport Crosscutters, currently a Philadelphia Phillies farm team in the New York-Penn League.

Bowman Field has hosted baseball games since 1926, making it one of the oldest minor league ballparks still in existence. Named after local businessman, J. Walton Bowman in 1929, the ballpark's earliest occupant was the minor league Williamsport Grays. Over the years, Bowman lost and gained several minor league franchises and much of Bowman's original structure has been replaced. Yet, despite all the changes, Bowman's old-style ballpark charm remains, accented by its city park setting and the rural Pennsylvania landscape that surrounds it.

The first thing that catches your eye at Bowman is its unique architecture. Highlights include: a triangle-shaped main entrance; a small tower-like structure next to the ticket windows; its brick walls; its exposed steel trusses under the grandstand roof; and Fenway-style foul poles. Bowman seats approximately 4,000, and when it's filled to capacity, the park is one of the prettiest sights in minor league baseball.

Aside from its long history and picturesque look, Bowman Field is famous as the site of one of minor league baseball history's quirkiest moments. In a game in 1987, Williamsport Bills catcher Dave Bresnahan called time out with a runner on third and got another catcher's mitt from the dugout. Bresnahan had hidden a potato shaved to resemble a baseball in the new mitt. After returning to his place behind home plate and receiving the next pitch, Bresnahan rose as if trying to catch the runner off third and fired the potato into the outfield. The baserunner raced home, where Bresnahan tagged him out with the real ball.

Temporary chaos—and lots of laughter—ensued. The ump ruled the runner safe and the league president ruled Bresnahan ineligible for future play. But the fans thought the "Great Potato Incident" innovative and fun and later convinced the Williamsport Bills to retire Bresnahan's #59.

> For more information about Bowman Field and for tickets to Williamsport Crosscutters games, check the team's website at *www.crosscutters.com*.

160 CATCH A MEXICAN LEAGUE GAME

Though it's one of three Triple-A leagues sanctioned by Major League Baseball, the Mexican League stands atop the baseball world south of the border. Its fans and players take the games seriously. Few countries or cultures embrace the game of baseball with such passion.

In the late 1930s, Mexican baseball entrepreneur Jorge Pasquel had visions of the Mexican League becoming an equal to the MLB's American and National Leagues. Pasquel lured players mostly from the Negro Leagues and a few from the majors to come to increase the league's quality of play. But Pasquel's efforts collapsed, along with the league, which was brought back to life in 1953 as a Triple-A league. The Mexican League is the only Triple-A League whose teams lack direct affiliations with specific Major League Baseball clubs. It fields 16 teams and starts its season in late March and ends in late July.

Seeing a baseball game in Mexico can be an interesting experience. But it can also be time-consuming and costly. Your best bet is to pick a team that plays out of a major Mexican city with a large airport, ground transportation, and good hotels. Mexico City is a wise choice. Most Mexican League games get about four thousand fans, about the same number you'll find at Triple-A games in the U.S. The Monterrey Sultans, however, average above 12,000. Still, tickets to most Mexican League games are not hard to come by, so buying a ticket the day of the game should not be a problem.

Safety should be a concern when traveling in Mexico. Every now and then, American baseball fans have become victims of pickpockets, or worse, muggers. So, when you go, keep a low profile and don't go to the game alone, especially if you don't speak Spanish. It's best to attend with a local; not only will he explain Mexican baseball customs, you're also likely to be hassled less and enjoy the game more.

You can find more information on the Mexican League by going to *www.minorleaguebaseball.com*, clicking on "Leagues" and scrolling down to "Mexican League." The league's website is in Spanish, so if you're unfamiliar with the language, ask a friend who knows Spanish to translate for you. It's wise to use a travel agent to help with your Mexican baseball journey. The agent should be able to track down ticket information and hopefully suggest a suitable hotel.

161 READ *ELYSIAN FIELDS QUARTERLY* ✷✷

The Elysian Fields Quarterly is baseball's quirkiest journal. It asks regular readers to appreciate baseball poetry and amateur fiction, plus oddball humor and unique opinion pieces. Rarely contributed to by the game's best writers, *The Elysian Fields Quarterly* gives regular fans a literary platform from which to sound off and show off, to think out loud and share ideas about baseball topics that would never see the light of day in *Sports Illustrated* or *Baseball America*. According to its editors, "anything having to do with baseball is fair game."

Published out of St. Paul, Minnesota, *Elysian Fields Quarterly* began life as *The Minneapolis Review of Baseball* in the early 1990s. It's always had a zany quality to it, which is what continues to make it an appealing and unique read. If you're a baseball fan who would like to write about the game and still keep your day job, submitting an article to *Elysian Fields Quarterly* is your best bet to get published. That doesn't mean that anyone who submits an article will automatically get a by-line. But you stand a far better chance of getting your article published in *Elysian Fields Quarterly* than more scholarly journals.

Although you can find *Elysian Fields Quarterly* on some newsstands or in the magazine section of the large bookstore chains like Borders or Barnes & Noble, it's best to get it via mail. An annual subscription costs less than $25 and includes four issues.

As *The Baseball Fan's Bucket List* was going to press, *The Elysian Fields Quarterly* temporarily suspended publication. But don't worry: it's not the first time the journal has taken a break. While we await its rebirth, you can find old copies of it to read in better libraries, or else purchase them online by going to the *Quarterly's* website, *www.efqreview.com*.

> For more information about *The Elysian Fields Quarterly*, call (888) 5-ELYSIA, go its website (www.efqreview.com) or write the journal at P.O. Box 14385, Saint Paul, MN 55114-0385.

162 VISIT ELYSIAN FIELDS

Baseball lends itself to myth and legend more readily than perhaps any other sport. That's part of its charm and enduring allure. So you have to grab onto concrete evidence of baseball history wherever you can find it, especially when dealing with the "origins" of the game. While they didn't host the first baseball game anymore than Cooperstown did, Hoboken and Elysian Fields still own a piece of early baseball history, and an important one at that.

On June 19, 1846, the Knickerbocker club (generally regarded as the first organized baseball team) played another team known as the New York Club (or New York Nine) in what is generally regarded as the first recorded baseball game (or match) in Hoboken on Elysian Fields. The rules they played by were set on paper by a New York bank clerk, Alexander Cartwright, one of the fathers of baseball (see *Bucket List* item #149). For the record, the Knickerbockers lost, 23 to 1, proving that even back then, home field advantage had its limitations.

So a visit to the place where the grasses of Elysian Fields once grew and bent as batted baseballs rolled over them is mandatory for all true baseball fans. It is located in the middle of downtown Hoboken, which is now packed with people, apartment houses, restaurants, and stores. There are only two indications that baseball history was actually made in Hoboken. One is the outline of a baseball diamond that approximates where the 1846 game got played. The other is a plaque, located at the intersection of 11th Street and Washington Avenue, that reads: "On June 19, 1846, the first match game of baseball was played here on the Elysian Fields between the Knickerbockers and the New Yorks. It is generally conceded that until this time, the game was not seriously regarded."

Hoboken hasn't capitalized on its place in baseball history and mythology the way Cooperstown has. There is no museum, but to stand on the site of the Elysian Fields, the place where the earliest baseball history was made, and to ponder what that June day in 1846 must have been like, will have to suffice. It is, in many ways, an apt way to appreciate the vague origins and enduring mysteries of the game of baseball.

> For more information about how to locate the site of Elysian Fields, contact the Cultural Affairs office of Hoboken, New Jersey at (201) 420-2207.

THE CHECKLIST

☐ 1. TAKE A BASEBALL ROAD TRIP

NOTES:

___/___/___

☐ 2. VISIT THE NATIONAL BASEBALL HALL OF FAME AND MUSEUM

NOTES:

___/___/___

☐ 3. GO TO OPENING DAY

NOTES:

___/___/___

☐ 4. ATTEND A WORLD SERIES GAME

NOTES:

___/___/___

☐ 5. SEE THE CUBS PLAY AT WRIGLEY FIELD

NOTES:

___/___/___

☒ 6. WATCH THE KEN BURNS DOCUMENTARY, *BASEBALL*

NOTES: *HAVE THE DVD Set.* ☒
4/1/07

☒ 7. SEE THE RED SOX PLAY AT FENWAY PARK

NOTES: *ME & Kellie –*
8/3/92

☐ 8. EXPERIENCE A HALL OF FAME INDUCTION WEEKEND IN COOPERSTOWN

NOTES:

___/___/___

☒ 9. PLAY FANTASY BASEBALL IN A ROTISSERIE LEAGUE

NOTES: *STARTED The L.T.S.*
FANTASY BASEBALL League 4/1/92

☒ 10. GO TO A MAJOR LEAGUE BASEBALL ALL-STAR GAME

NOTES: *In PHX This Year 2011 –*
DId Not Attend. 7/_/11

☐ 11. VISIT THE NEGRO LEAGUES BASEBALL MUSEUM

NOTES:

___/___/___

☒ 12. LEARN TO KEEP SCORE

NOTES: *Learn A Long Time Ago.*
GReAt for Math ✓ ___/___/___

☒ 13. SEE SOME GRAPEFRUIT LEAGUE SPRING TRAINING GAMES

NOTES: *TRy EvRRy SPRing – PHX*
___/___/___

☒ 14. WATCH THE MOVIE, *BULL DURHAM*

NOTES: *HAVE DVD IN B.B.Library*
4/30/88

☒ 15. SEE SOME CACTUS LEAGUE SPRING TRAINING GAMES

NOTES: *HAVE For YeARS – GIANTS –*
A's-MARiNeRs-ANgels – 2/20/81

☒ 16. TAKE A KID TO HIS OR HER FIRST MAJOR LEAGUE BASEBALL GAME

NOTES: *PATRiCk-KiRsTeN FATHeRS DAY*
ReDS-DBACkS 6/_/_

☒ 17. READ THE BOOK, *BALL FOUR*

NOTES: *GREAT BOOK – HAve 1st.Ed.* ✓
HAVE 1ST. EDiTioN ___/___/___

☐ 18. ATTEND A MAJOR LEAGUE BASEBALL FANTASY CAMP

NOTES:

___/___/___

☒ 19. WATCH THE MOVIE, *THE NATURAL*

NOTES: *HAVE DVD + SoundTrack*
OWN IN Library __/__/84

☐ 20. VISIT RICKWOOD FIELD

NOTES:

___/___/___

☒ 21. WATCH THE MOVIE, *FIELD OF DREAMS*

NOTES: *DVD + SoundTrack*
Go THE DISTANce. __/__/89

☒ 22. SEE THE DODGERS PLAY AT DODGER STADIUM

NOTES: *V.S. Phillies*
___/___/83

23. READ THE BOOK, *THE BOYS OF SUMMER* ☒

NOTES: All-Time Great - In My B.B.
Collection 1st Edition __/__/72

24. OWN A BASEBALL GLOVE ☒

NOTES: Since About Age 10 ☆☆☆
☆ __/__/__

25. SEE THE YANKEES PLAY THE RED SOX ☐

NOTES:
__/__/__

26. GO TO THE COLLEGE WORLD SERIES ☐

NOTES: ☆
__/__/__

27. WATCH THE MOVIE, *A LEAGUE OF THEIR OWN* ☒

NOTES: With Kellie In Maryland-
Baltimore ☆☆☆☆☆ 8/10/92

28. SEE THE ORIOLES PLAY AT ORIOLE PARK AT CAMDEN YARDS ☒

NOTES: Visit BallPark- No Game
8/1/92

29. READ THE BOOK, *MONEYBALL* ☒

NOTES: Good Read
In Library ✓ __/__/__

30. SEE THE PIRATES PLAY AT PNC PARK ☐

NOTES:
__/__/__

31. WATCH THE DOCUMENTARY, *VIVA BASEBALL* ☒

NOTES: DVD - In My Library
__/__/__

32. WATCH THE MOVIE, *EIGHT MEN OUT* ☒

NOTES: DVD Baseball Collection
✓ Own ✓ __/__/88

33. SEE THE CARDINALS PLAY THE CUBS ☐

NOTES:
__/__/__

34. TOUR THE LOUISVILLE SLUGGER MUSEUM AND FACTORY ☐

NOTES:
__/__/__

35. SEE THE GIANTS PLAY AT AT&T PARK ☐

NOTES: At old CandleStick Park
The Stick - __/__/86

36. ATTEND THE WORLD BASEBALL CLASSIC ☐

NOTES:
__/__/__

37. READ THE BOOK, *BASEBALL: A LITERARY ANTHOLOGY* ☒

NOTES: B.B. Library - GREAT BOOK!
1st. Edition ✓ 4/1/02

38. SEE A TRIPLE-A PACIFIC COAST LEAGUE GAME ☒

NOTES: The old PHX Giants -
PHX Municipal Stadium 7/1/74

39. WATCH THE MOVIE, *THE ROOKIE* ☒

NOTES: In DVD B.B. Library
Own ✓ __/__/__

40. SEE A TRIPLE-A INTERNATIONAL LEAGUE GAME ☐

NOTES:
__/__/__

41. SEE THE INDIANS PLAY AT PROGRESSIVE FIELD ☐

NOTES:
__/__/__

42. COACH A SEASON OF LITTLE LEAGUE BASEBALL ☒

NOTES: 28 Years And Counting
Prescott Little League 3/1/82

43. WATCH THE MOVIE, *FOR LOVE OF THE GAME* ☒

NOTES: DVD B.B. Library
✓ __/__/__

44. OWN A PIECE OF VINTAGE BASEBALL CLOTHING ☒

NOTES: Classic Hats In Collection.
☆ __/__/__

45. VISIT THE LEGENDS OF THE GAME MUSEUM ☐

NOTES:
__/__/__

46. SEE THE MARINERS PLAY AT SAFECO FIELD ☐

NOTES:
__/__/__

[X] 47. LEARN TO FIGURE IMPORTANT BASEBALL STATISTICS

NOTES: EARLY IN MY CAREER ✱
      IX   _/_/_

[X] 48. BECOME A MEMBER OF SABR

NOTES: Since 1996 - SABR Member
                        1/30/96

☐ 49. VISIT THE CINCINNATI REDS HALL OF FAME AND MUSEUM

NOTES: FREE Pete!
HOF: Pete Rose #14   _/_/_

☐ 50. GO TO THE MIDNIGHT SUN BASEBALL CLASSIC

NOTES:
                        _/_/_

[X] 51. PLAY IN AN ADULT BASEBALL LEAGUE

NOTES: PHX - SUMMER 1981
                        _/_/_

☐ 52. ATTEND A FAN FEST

NOTES:
                        _/_/_

[X] 53. MAINTAIN A BASEBALL CARD COLLECTION

NOTES: Still Going - late 60's -
                        4/1/70

[X] 54. WATCH THE MOVIE, 61*

NOTES: DVD BASEBALL Library
       ✓   _/_/_

☐ 55. SEE THE PADRES PLAY AT PETCO PARK

NOTES: old JACK Murphy PARK - 8
V.S. ALt. BRAVES   _/_/82

☐ 56. ATTEND A THEATRICAL PRODUCTION OF DAMN YANKEES

NOTES:
                        _/_/_

☐ 57. ATTEND THE HALL OF FAME CLASSIC WEEKEND IN COOPERSTOWN

NOTES:
                        _/_/_

☐ 58. SEE AN INTERLEAGUE GAME

NOTES:
                        _/_/_

☐ 59. SEE THE DODGERS PLAY THE GIANTS

NOTES:
                        _/_/_

☐ 60. READ THE WRITINGS OF A. BARTLETT GIAMATTI

NOTES:
                        _/_/_

☐ 61. VISIT THE YOGI BERRA MUSEUM AND LEARNING CENTER

NOTES:
                        _/_/_

☐ 62. WATCH THE MOVIE, SOUL OF THE GAME

NOTES:
                        _/_/_

☐ 63. SEE THE ROCKIES PLAY AT COORS FIELD

NOTES:
                        _/_/_

☐ 64. ATTEND THE TRIPLE-A ALL-STAR GAME

NOTES:
                        _/_/_

☐ 65. SEE THE METS PLAY AT CITI FIELD

NOTES:
                        _/_/_

[X] 66. SUBSCRIBE TO AND READ BASEBALL AMERICA

NOTES: Been Reading Since 1980
1981 -   4/1/81

☐ 67. SEE THE YANKEES PLAY AT YANKEE STADIUM

NOTES:
                        _/_/_

☐ 68. CATCH A CAPE COD LEAGUE GAME

NOTES:
                        _/_/_

[X] 69. CREATE A BASEBALL REFERENCE LIBRARY

NOTES: Since 1980 - 1500 And
       Counting -   _/_/81

☐ 70. VISIT GREEN-WOOD CEMETERY

NOTES:
                        _/_/_

☐ 71. VISIT THE BABE RUTH BIRTHPLACE AND MUSEUM

NOTES:

___/___/___

☒ 72. OWN AN AUTOGRAPHED BASEBALL COLLECTION

NOTES: *Started In 1982* ✗

HAVE MANY!

___/___/___

☒ 73. WATCH THE MOVIE, *MAJOR LEAGUE*

NOTES: *In BASEBALL DVD Library*
✓

___/___/___

☐ 74. WATCH THE DOCUMENTARY, *THE LIFE AND TIMES OF HANK GREENBERG*

NOTES:

___/___/___

☐ 75. SEE THE BREWERS PLAY AT MILLER PARK

NOTES:

___/___/___

☒ 76. WATCH THE MOVIE, *THE PRIDE OF THE YANKEES*

NOTES: *In BASEBALL DVD Library*
✓
___/___/___

☐ 77. VISIT THE *FIELD OF DREAMS* MOVIE SITE

NOTES:

___/___/___

☐ 78. ATTEND A THEATRICAL PRODUCTION OF *BLEACHER BUMS*

NOTES:

___/___/___

☒ 79. READ THE BOOK, *VEECK AS IN WRECK*

NOTES: *In BASEBALL Library*
✗
___/___/___

☐ 80. SEE THE PHILLIES PLAY AT CITIZENS BANK PARK

NOTES:

___/___/___

☒ 81. READ THE BOOK, *A FALSE SPRING*

NOTES: *In B.B. Library —*

___/___/___

☐ 82. ATTEND JACKIE ROBINSON DAY

NOTES:

___/___/___

☒ 83. OWN A COPY OF *THE NEW BILL JAMES HISTORICAL BASEBALL ABSTRACT*

NOTES: *In B.B. Library*

___/___/___

☒ 84. OWN A CLASSIC BASEBALL PHOTOGRAPH

NOTES: *FENWAY PARK - THE BEST!*
A Signed 1954 W.S. The CATCH - W.M.

☐ 85. SEE THE ANGELS PLAY AT ANGEL STADIUM

NOTES:

___/___/___

☒ 86. LEARN THE STORY BEHIND "TAKE ME OUT TO THE BALL GAME"

NOTES: ✓

☒ 87. READ THE BOOK, *THE GLORY OF THEIR TIMES*

NOTES: *In B.B. Library - A Classic!*
Ritter ✓ ___/___/___

☐ 88. LISTEN TO *THE GREAT AMERICAN BASEBALL BOX*

NOTES:

___/___/___

☒ 89. START A BASEBALL BOBBLEHEAD COLLECTION

NOTES: *HAVE MANY! LOTS & LOTS!*
Bobble - Bobble - ___/___/___

☐ 90. SEE THE CARDINALS PLAY AT BUSCH STADIUM

NOTES:

___/___/___

☒ 91. ATTEND THE LITTLE LEAGUE WORLD SERIES

NOTES: *ONE DAY!*

___/___/___

☐ 92. SEE THE RANGERS PLAY AT RANGERS BALLPARK

NOTES:

___/___/___

☐ 93. VISIT DEDEAUX FIELD AND THE USC BASEBALL HALL OF FAME

NOTES:

___/___/___

☒ 94. READ THE BOOK, *YOU KNOW ME AL*

NOTES: *In B.B. Library*

___/___/___

❋❋❋❋

⊠ 95. WATCH THE MOVIE, *BANG THE DRUM SLOWLY*

NOTES: *My All-Time Favorite BB Movie ~ DVD + BOOK —/—/—*

☐ 96. ATTEND THE COOPERSTOWN SYMPOSIUM ON BASEBALL AND AMERICAN CULTURE

NOTES:

—/—/—

☐ 97. VISIT THE BOB FELLER MUSEUM

NOTES:

—/—/—

☐ 98. SEE AN INDEPENDENT LEAGUE GAME

NOTES:

—/—/—

⊠ 99. READ THE BOOK, *ONLY THE BALL WAS WHITE*

NOTES: *In B.B. Library ~ Read ✓ 1st. Edition.* —/—/—

☐ 100. VISIT THE TY COBB MUSUEM

NOTES:

—/—/—

⊠ 101. UMPIRE A BASEBALL GAME ✓

NOTES: *Never Again!*

—/—/—

☐ 102. JOIN THE BASEBALL RELIQUARY

NOTES:

—/—/—

⊠ 103. WATCH THE ABBOTT & COSTELLO SKIT, "WHO'S ON FIRST?"

NOTES: *DVD + CD ✓ Great Fun.*

—/—/—

☐ 104. SEE A DOUBLE-A GAME

NOTES:

—/—/—

⊠ 105. SEE THE ROYALS PLAY AT KAUFFMAN STADIUM *2 Games ~ Orioles ~*

NOTES: *Yankees ~* 5/—/85

⊠ 106. OWN A PIECE OF BASEBALL ART

NOTES: *Many Various Items ✓* 4/1/80

⊠ 107. READ THE BOOK, *BASEBALL: A HISTORY OF AMERICA'S FAVORITE GAME*

NOTES: *In My Baseball Library.*

—/—/—

☐ 108. SEE A DURHAM BULLS GAME

NOTES:

—/—/—

☐ 109. SEE THE TWINS PLAY AT TARGET FIELD

NOTES:

—/—/—

⊠ 110. LISTEN TO LOU GEHRIG'S FAMOUS FAREWELL SPEECH

NOTES: *In Book And Audio Library ✓* ❋ —/—/✓

☐ 111. SEE THE TIGERS PLAY AT COMERICA PARK

NOTES:

—/—/—

⊠ 112. HIT IN THE BATTING CAGES ✓

NOTES: *Here's the Pitch...........*

—/—/—

⊠ 113. GO TO AN OLD TIMERS' DAY

NOTES: *1969 ~ Cubs V.S. Mets PHX Municipal Park ~* 2/—/81

⊠ 114. WATCH THE MOVIE, *SUGAR*

NOTES: *In DVD Library ✓*

—/—/—

☐ 115. VISIT THE IVAN ALLEN, JR. BRAVES MUSEUM AND HALL OF FAME

NOTES:

—/—/—

☐ 116. SEE THE WHITE SOX PLAY AT U.S. CELLULAR FIELD

NOTES:

—/—/—

⊠ 117. PLAY APBA *O.K. ✓* ✓

NOTES: *Have Game In Collection ✓*

—/—/—

☐ 118. SEE THE REDS PLAY AT GREAT AMERICAN BALL PARK

NOTES:

—/—/—

☐ 119. PLAY IN A VINTAGE BASE BALL LEAGUE

NOTES:

___/___/___

☐ 120. SEE THE BRAVES PLAY AT TURNER FIELD

NOTES:

___/___/___

☒ 121. OWN A BASEBALL ANTIQUE

NOTES: *HAVE MANY IN MY* Baseball Collection* ___/___/___

☒ 122. READ THE BOOK, *SHOELESS JOE*

NOTES: MY All-Time Favorite * *Book AND DVD * Cards Too!

☐ 123. SHOP FOR BASEBALL MEMORABILIA IN COOPERSTOWN

NOTES:

___/___/___

☒ 124. READ THE BOOK, *THE SUMMER GAME*

NOTES: In B.B. Library A long Time Ago, ___/___/___

☒ 125. PLAY STRAT-O-MATIC BASEBALL ✗✗✗✗✗

THE BEST) NOTES: A Veteran Player - Started Playing In the 1970's 4/1/70

☐ 126. SEE THE NATIONALS PLAY AT NATIONALS PARK

NOTES:

___/___/___

☒ 127. OWN A COPY OF *THE BARRY HALPER COLLECTION OF BASEBALL MEMORABILIA*

✓ NOTES: In MY B.B. Library - A Collectors DREAM! ___/___/___

☐ 128. HOST A MINOR LEAGUE BALL PLAYER

NOTES:

___/___/___

☒ 129. SEE THE DIAMONDBACKS PLAY AT CHASE FIELD

NOTES: MANY Times ✗✗✗✗ ___/___/___

☒ 130. TAKE IN A LOCAL MUSEUM BASEBALL EXHIBIT

NOTES: Anytime I CAN ✗✗✗✗ ___/___/___

☒ 131. READ THE BOOK, *THE TEAMMATES*

NOTES: In my B.B. Library * ___/___/___

☒ 132. DELVE INTO SOME BASEBALL SCHOLARSHIP

NOTES: HAVE MANY IN Collection* ___/___/___

☒ 133. SEE A SINGLE-A GAME

NOTES: Frederick Keys - Orioles ME & Kellie Baby - 8/___/92

☒ 134. WATCH THE MOVIE, *FEVER PITCH*

NOTES: In DVD Baseball Library - Fuck the Yankees! ___/___/___

☐ 135. ATTEND THE ANNUAL CIVIL RIGHTS GAME

NOTES:

___/___/___

☐ 136. SEE THE ASTROS PLAY AT MINUTE MAID PARK

NOTES:

___/___/___

☐ 137. CATCH AN ARIZONA FALL LEAGUE GAME

NOTES:

___/___/___

☒ 138. WATCH THE MOVIE, *THE SANDLOT*

NOTES: In B.B. DVD Collection * Smalls Your Killing Me! ___/___/___

☒ 139. THROW OUT THE FIRST PITCH

NOTES: 2008 LL Dist 10 Tournament - PRE9OH 7/___/08

☐ 140. EAT AT A FAMOUS BALLPLAYER'S RESTAURANT

NOTES:

___/___/___

☐ 141. VISIT THE BARNSTABLE BAT COMPANY

NOTES:

___/___/___

☐ 142. TAKE A BASEBALL TOUR OF JAPAN

NOTES: No WAY! ___/___/___

☒ 143. READ THE BOOK, *THE SCIENCE OF HITTING*

NOTES: In Baseball Library - Teddy Ball Game. __/__/__

☐ 144. SEE THE BLUE JAYS PLAY AT THE ROGERS CENTRE

NOTES: __/__/__

☐ 145. SEE A SHORT-SEASON A LEAGUE GAME

NOTES: __/__/__

☐ 146. SEE THE MARLINS PLAY AT LAND SHARK STADIUM

NOTES: __/__/__

☐ 147. ATTEND THE CARIBBEAN SERIES

NOTES: __/__/__

☒ 148. FIX UP A BASEBALL FIELD

NOTES: Every Season - PLL __/__/__

☐ 149. VISIT THE GRAVESITE OF ALEXANDER CARTWRIGHT, JR.

NOTES: __/__/__

☐ 150. SEE THE RAYS PLAY AT TROPICANA FIELD

NOTES: __/__/__

☒ 151. READ *THE UNIVERSAL BASEBALL ASSOCIATION, INC., J. HENRY WAUGH, PROP.*

NOTES: In Baseball Library ★ Neat Book ★★★★ __/__/__

☒ 152. WATCH THE MOVIE, *COBB*

NOTES: Own DVD - In Library. __/__/__

☐ 153. VISIT THE CANADIAN BASEBALL HALL OF FAME AND MUSEUM

NOTES: __/__/__

☐ 154. SEE A ROOKIE LEAGUE GAME

NOTES: __/__/__

☐ 155. SEE THE A'S PLAY AT THE OAKLAND COLISEUM

NOTES: __/__/__

☐ 156. VISIT GEORGE M. STEINBRENNER FIELD

NOTES: __/__/__

☐ 157. ATTEND A NEGRO LEAGUES DAY CELEBRATION AND GAME

NOTES: __/__/__

☐ 158. VISIT THE SPORTS MUSEUM OF LOS ANGELES

NOTES: __/__/__

☐ 159. VISIT BOWMAN FIELD

NOTES: __/__/__

☐ 160. CATCH A MEXICAN LEAGUE GAME

NOTES: __/__/__

☒ 161. READ *ELYSIAN FIELDS QUARTERLY*

NOTES: HAVE Already! ★ ✓ __/__/__

N 162. VISIT ELYSIAN FIELDS

NOTES: __/__/__

DEDICATION
To Oregon State Baseball...

Boo!

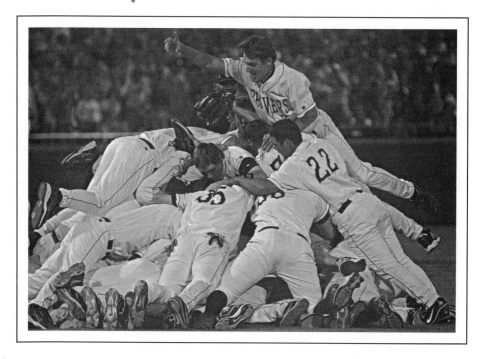

ACKNOWLEDGEMENTS

We wish to offer our heartfelt thanks to the following: Jim Anderson, David Brewer, Steve Densa, Bob DiBiasio, Bob DeCarolis, Jim Gates, Jeff Giblin, Tom Gitter, Steve Havick, James Hernandez, Bob Horn, Brad Horn, Nate Janoso, Anne Jewell, John Keenan, Bob Kendrick, Sarah Lake, Becky Lansing, Nick Lilja, Dawne Massey, Nancy Mazmanian, Nicholas Min, Mick McDonald, Craig Muder, Brett Picciolo, Candy Ross, Ryne Reynoso, Jake Santelli, Jaron Santelli, Bob and Cindy Senkar, Jill Seib, Mark Shapiro, Bob Shulock, Ken Spindler, Eric Stock, Peter Strong, Joe Tully, Francisco Vargas, Mike Vassallo, Steve Whisnant, and Marc Whycraff.

A special thanks goes to our editor at Running Press, Greg Jones, who believed in the book from day one and whose friendship and advice we most appreciate; to art director Josh McDonnell for his vision and baseball acumen; and for Mike Regan, whose editing contributions and sage advice proved invaluable down the stretch. Finally, much love and appreciation go out to my "soul" sister, Syd Whalley, for all of her support and for use of her dining room table during all the months of writing and research; and to my wife (and Jenna's mom) Cindy Kraft for her love and endless help whenever we needed it.